ABITUR-TRAINING ENGLISCH

Rainer Jacob

Themenwortschatz

Aufgaben und Lösungen

STARK

Bildnachweis

S. 12: © Zeh Fernando 2001
S. 26: © ullstein/ddp
S. 29: © ullstein/Reuters
S. 44: © prokino/Cinetext
S. 64: Stark Verlag GmbH & Co. KG
S. 71: © Cinetext
S. 90: Rod Stewart, George Harrison: © Cinetext/Allstar; Charlie Watts: © Cinetext/Max Kohr
S. 92: Stark Verlag GmbH & Co. KG
S. 102: © Cinetext/Allstar
S. 105: © ullstein/AP
S. 125: Lyndon B. Johnson: Foto von Hanns Hubmann, © bpk Berlin; Ronald Reagan: © Cinetext/Allstar
S. 126: Bill Clinton, George W. Bush: © Cinetext/Allstar
S. 140: © ullstein/ullstein bild
S. 154: © Cinetext

ISBN: 3-89449-153-1

© 1993 by Stark Verlagsgesellschaft mbH & Co. KG
D-85318 Freising · Postfach 1852 · Tel. (08161)1790
v 05-02
Nachdruck verboten!

Inhalt

Vorwort

Environment 1
1 Word field 1
2 Idioms and phrases 7
3 Practice 8

World affairs 19
1 Word field 19
2 Idioms and phrases 23
3 Practice 25

Consumer / Health 37
1 Word field 39
2 Practice 41

Work 51
1 Word field 51
2 Practice 56

Science and technology 65
1 Word field 65
2 Practice 69

Crime, law and drugs 79
1 Word field 79
2 Idioms and phrases 83
3 Practice 84

Politics in Great Britain 97
1 Word field 97
2 Practice 101

Politics in the US 113

1 Word field 113
2 Idioms and phrases 118
3 Practice 119

Immigration 131

1 Word field 131
2 Idioms and phrases 137
3 Practice 138

Civil rights 149

1 Word field 149
2 Idioms and phrases 152
3 Practice 153

Key 163

Wordfamilies 193

Autor: Rainer Jacob

Vorwort

Liebe Schülerin, lieber Schüler,

mit dem vorliegenden Band „Abitur-Training Englisch: Wortschatz" wird Ihnen ein Trainingsbuch an die Hand gegeben, mit dem Sie sich gezielt auf Ihre Klausuren und Ihre Abiturprüfung vorbereiten können: In diesem Buch finden Sie eine umfassende Sammlung der **für das Abitur relevanten Vokabeln und Idiome** der letzten Jahre.

- Im **umfangreichen Übungsteil** wird der Wortschatz zu zehn Themenbereichen des Oberstufenlehrplans in übersichtlicher Form präsentiert und auf vielfältige Weise eingeübt.

- Grundlage für die Vokabelarbeit sind **aktuelle Texte**, die ebenso für weitere Bearbeitungsformen *(discussion, comment, summary, translation)* verwendet werden können. Da Wortschatzarbeit nicht immer einfach ist, sorgen auch unterhaltende Übungen und Rätsel für die nötige Auflockerung.

- Selbstverständlich finden Sie zu allen Aufgaben **Lösungen**, damit Sie Ihren Lernerfolg selbstständig überprüfen können.

- Darüber hinaus enthält dieses Buch einen **umfassenden, systematischen Anhang**. Darin werden die einzelnen Stichwörter im Satzzusammenhang dargestellt und um *synonyms* und *opposites* erweitert. Andere Wortformen aus der jeweiligen Wortfamilie *(noun, verb, adjective* und *adverb)* ergänzen die Einträge.

Ich wünsche Ihnen viel Erfolg für Ihre Klausuren und Ihre Abiturprüfung.

Rainer Jacob

Environment

1 Word field

abundant	reichlich
acid rain	saurer Regen
(to) advance	Fortschritte machen; Fortschritt
aerosol can	Spraydose
ailing	kränkelnd, dahinsiechend
alkaline	alkalisch, basisch
appliance	(Haushalts-) Gerät
balance	Gleichgewicht
biodegradable	biologisch abbaubar
biodiversity	Artenvielfalt
biosphere	Biosphäre, Lebensraum
birth rate	Geburtenrate
(to) bleach	bleichen
carbon	Kohlenstoff
carbon monoxide	Kohlenmonoxyd
centigrade	Celsius
chain of life	Lebenskette
chimney	Schornstein, Kamin
chlorofluorocarbon (CFC)	Fluorchlorkohlenwasserstoff (FCKW)
climate	Klima
climatologist	Klimaforscher
coastal waters	Küstengewässer
combustion	Verbrennung
composition	Zusammensetzung
concern	Anliegen, Sorge

2 Environment

conclusive	schlüssig, überzeugend, endgültig
conservation	Erhaltung, Bewahrung
(to) contaminate	verseuchen
contamination	Verseuchung
creature	Geschöpf
delicate	empfindlich
dense	dicht
depletion	Verringerung, Schwund
detergent	Reinigungsmittel
(to) devastate	vernichten, verwüsten
(to) diminish	sich verringern, abnehmen
disastrous	katastrophal, verheerend
(to) discharge	(Abwasser) einleiten, ablassen
disease	Krankheit
(to) disintegrate	zerfallen, sich auflösen
disposable bottle	Einwegflasche
disposal	Beseitigung
(to) disrupt	stören, zum Erliegen bringen
domestic	häuslich, Haushalt-
drought	Dürre
dump	Müllhalde
dumping ground	Müllhalde, -kippe
ecology	Ökologie
emission	Ausstoß, Emission
endangered	gefährdet
energy conservation	Energieeinsparung
energy consumption	Energieverbrauch
environment	Umwelt
environmental studies	Umweltforschung
environmentalist	Umweltschützer

Environment 3

environmentally aware	umweltbewusst
equilibrium	Gleichgewicht
(to) erode	etw. auswaschen
erosion	Erosion, Abtragung, zerstörende Wirkung von Wasser und Wind
evidence	Beweis
exhaust	Auspuff (von Autos)
exhaust fumes	Auspuffgase, Abgase
(to) expose	bloßlegen, sich etw. aussetzen
fallout	(radioaktiver) Niederschlag
fertile	fruchtbar
fumes	Dämpfe
garbage	Abfall, Müll
global warming	Erwärmung der Erde
(to) graze	grasen, weiden
greenhouse effect	Treibhauseffekt
harmful	schädlich
hazard	Gefahr
hostile	feindlich
hydrocarbon	Kohlenwasserstoff
hygiene	Hygiene
impact	Auswirkung, Einfluss
imperilled	gefährdet
indicator	Anzeiger, Anzeichen
indispensable	unentbehrlich, unerlässlich
inedible	ungenießbar
infant mortality	Kindersterblichkeit
interference	Störung
(to) inundate	überschwemmen
(to) irradiate	verstrahlen
(to) irrigate	bewässern
junk	Müll, Abfall

Handwritten notes:
move e. sensitive

floodplain
— Überschwemmungs-
gebiet

bereits? already!

4 Environment

layer	Schicht
lead [e]	Blei
litter	Müll, Abfall
(to) load	belasten; Last
measurement	Messung, Messwert, Maßstab
(to) menace	bedrohen; Bedrohung
natural gas	Erdgas
negligible	unwesentlich, unbedeutend
nuclear power plant	Atomkraftwerk
nuclear waste	Atommüll
nutrient	Nährstoff
oil spill	Ölteppich
overpopulation	Überbevölkerung
ozone layer	Ozonschicht
packaging	Verpackung
peril	Gefahr
poisonous	giftig
pollutant	Schadstoff
(to) pollute	verschmutzen
polluting	umweltschädlich
pollution	Verschmutzung
power station	Kraftwerk *power plant*
precipitation	Niederschlag
prediction	Vorhersage
preservation	Erhaltung
(to) presume	vermuten
(to) protect	schützen
(to) purify	reinigen
quality of life	Lebensqualität
radiation	Strahlung
rain forests	Regenwälder
(to) ravage	verwüsten

(to) recur	wieder passieren, sich wiederholen
(to) recycle	wieder verwerten
recycling	Wiederverwertung
refrigerant	Kühlmittel
(to) reinforce	verstärken, bestätigen
renewable	erneuerbar
repercussion	Auswirkung
reprocessing plant	Wiederaufbereitungsanlage
resources	Mittel, Schätze, Ressourcen
(to) restore	wiederherstellen
(to) retreat	zurückziehen, den Rückzug antreten
return bottle	Mehrwegflasche
(to) reveal	zum Vorschein bringen, aufdecken
(to) reverse	etw. umkehren
(to) revert	zu etw. zurückkehren
salubrious	gesund; vornehm
severe	schwer, schlimm
sewage	Abwasser
sewage plant	Kläranlage
skin cancer	Hautkrebs
soil	Boden
soil erosion	Bodenerosion
solar system	Sonnensystem
species	Gattung
(to) spill	verschütten
strife	Streit, Auseinandersetzung
(to) substitute	ersetzen; Ersatz(stoff)
(to) suffocate	ersticken
sulphur	Schwefel
sulphur dioxide	Schwefeldioxid
supply	Vorrat
surface	Oberfläche

6 / Environment

survival	Überleben
threat	Bedrohung
(to) threaten	(be)drohen
throw-away	Wegwerf-
tide	Gezeiten
timber	Bau-, Nutzholz
topsoil	Mutterboden
toxic waste	Giftmüll
ultraviolet rays	UV-Strahlen
uninhabitable	unbewohnbar
unleaded [e]	bleifrei
unprecedented	noch nie da gewesen
unpredictable	unvorhersehbar
untreated	unbehandelt
(to) urbanise	verstädtern
urbanization	Verstädterung
vapour	Dampf
variety	Vielfalt, Mannigfaltigkeit; Sorte
vengeance	Rache
vicious	gemein, boshaft
vigorous	energisch
(to) waste	vergeuden; Abfall
waste disposal	Müllbeseitigung
waste heat	Abwärme
waste management	Müllbeseitigung
waste water	Abwasser
widespread	weit verbreitet

Environment 7

2 Idioms and phrases

to contract (a disease)	When the boy was 10, he contracted a rare disease.	sich zuziehen, erkranken an
to upset the delicate balance	In many places of the world the delicate balance between flora and fauna has been upset.	das empfindliche Gleichgewicht zerstören
to set in motion	The United Nations Conference on Environment and Development has set a stricter legislation in motion.	in Gang setzen
to strike a bargain	At the conference bargains were struck between the rich and the poor countries.	ein Geschäft machen
to put into force	The success of the summit depends on how well the resolutions are put into force.	in Kraft setzen
to be scheduled for	A major conference on population is scheduled for next year.	geplant sein für
to be charged	Farmers are charged less for their water supply than domestic consumers.	zahlen müssen
to phase out	Developing countries have more time to phase out CFC production.	stufenweise aus dem Verkehr ziehen
to miss out on	Friends of the Earth are warning that Britain risks missing out on a European market for renewable energy.	sich entgehen lassen
to be set to do	The government is set to raise the tax on petrol.	wohl tun werden
to be resisted by	Plans of the government to compel electricity companies to buy expensive atomic energy were strongly resisted by the European Commission.	auf Widerstand seitens … stoßen
to be subject to	Years after the Chernobyl accident hundreds of British farms were still subject to strict anti-radiation rules.	unterliegen
to lift a ban	The Ministry of Agriculture lifted the ban on the import of beef from France.	ein Verbot aufheben

8 / Environment

3 Practice

Exercise 1 **What we are doing to our environment**

Complete the text with words from this list:

agriculture	desert	heating	reduction
Amazon	detergents	increase	released
attempts	droughts	levels	sewage
attention	expands	poisoning	temperature
burning	global	predicted	yields

Many rivers and the sea have long been polluted by untreated _sewage_ [1]
to which we now add chemicals used in farming, industrial wastes and domestic _detergents_ [2]. It is madness to improve our crop _yields_ [3] by
using chemicals to repel insects and pests, if by doing so we destroy all the fish
in rivers and the sea. People have already died of mercury poisoning from
eating fish caught off the coast of Japan, and it is _released_ [4] that more
might die from food _poisoning_ [5].
The so-called "greenhouse effect" is an issue that has gained more _attention_ [6]
since farmers experienced an enormous drought in the American cornbelt.
The Earth is _heating_ [7] up, because the balanced exchanges of carbon
dioxide between plants and animals, the sky, the sea and earth have been upset
by the _burning_ [8] of fossil fuels. In the next 50 years the mean
temperature [9] of the globe could rise between one or four degrees centigrade.
The first effect of this temperature _increase_ [10] would be to alter the
world's climate and weather patterns. Water _expands_ [11] with heat. Most
authorities now think that the world should prepare for a metre rise in sea
_____ [12] some time in the course of the next century. _____ [13]
could become more frequent, so could storms. _____ [14] and the forests
could be disastrously hit. In addition to this: As the rain forests of the
_____ [15] and the Congo basins are levelled and burned, yet more
greenhouse gases are _____ [16]. More soil is eroded, more land turns
to _____ [17].
Numerous international _____ [18] have been undertaken to avert a
catastrophic change in the world's climate. However, these negotiations on
how to cut the pollution that causes _____ [19] warming often failed.
Strongest opposition to a stricter clean-up policy came from the US, which
rejected treaties because the American administration argued that _____ [20]
of greenhouse gas emissions should be linked to economic growth.

Environment / 9

Exercise 2   The vital importance of our oceans

Translate into English or German respectively.

Seen from outer space the Earth looks different from all
the other planets in our solar system. Our globe has been
referred to as the "Blue Planet" because of the 300
million cubic miles of water which cover 70 per cent of
the Earth's _____[1] (Oberfläche). This fact, and
the Earth's average temperature of 13 °C, makes it suit-
able for life. The oceans' *currents* (_____)[2]
drive and *moderate* (_____)[3] weather and
climate and provide us with food. The coastal seas play
the most important role in the chain of life. The majority
of marine species spend at least part of their lives in the waters over the continental shelves, which are the world's richest fishing grounds. As the oceans
are so _____[4] (riesig) man has become _____[5] (gewohnt)
to thinking that they are *indestructible* (_____)[6] and can absorb
everything.

We have used the oceans as dumping grounds to get rid of our toxic waste in a
cheap way. Industrialized and *wasteful* (_____)[7] fishing methods have
depleted (_____)[8] once bountiful fish populations and _____[9]
(gefährdet) the oceans' capacity for *sustaining* (_____)[10] life. Every year
millions of tons of fish, hundreds of thousands of whales, dolphins, seals, sea
lions and sea birds, and countless numbers of other ocean animals are caught,
killed, and *discarded* (_____)[11]. Efforts are now being made to help
endangered fish by limiting the amount to be caught each year and creating
laws to protect the fish's _____[12] (Lebensraum).

Our oceans are also an important economic factor. Millions of people earn
their _____[13] (Lebensunterhalt) in the shipping industry handling
goods at the *ports* (_____)[14], working in the cruise branch or attending
to hundreds of millions of people who flock to the coasts to spend their
holidays there. In fact, tourism and recreation *constitute* (_____)[15]
some of the fastest-growing business sectors – enriching economies and
supporting jobs in communities virtually everywhere along the coasts. The
oceans' *plight* (_____)[16] has gone undetected for too long. It is time
to realize that _____[17] (auszubeuten) every advantage granted by
nature cannot go on for ever.

10 / Environment

Exercise 3   Global warming

In the following text some words are incomplete. Only a couple of letters are given. Try to complete with words that would fit the context.

The most compre_____[1] study of climatic history has reve_____[2] that the earth is warmer now than it has been at any time in the past 2,000 years. The newly published fin_____[3] are a blow to sceptics who main_____[4] that global warming is part of the natural climatic cycle. It confirms the wor_____[5] fears of environmental scientists that the climate change is a conse_____[6] of human industrial activity. One of the authors of the research, said: "You can't explain this rap_____[7] warming in the late 20th century in any other way. It's a resp_____[8] to a build-up of green_____[9] gases in the atmosphere."

The study reinforces recent concl_____[10] published by the UN's inter-governmental panel on climate change (IPCC). Scien_____[11] on the panel looked at tempe_____[12] data from up to 1,000 years ago and found that the late 20th century was the warmest period on record.

To find out whe_____[13] the planet was warmer in the past, the scientist looked at tree trunks, which keep a record of the local climate: the rings sprea_____[14] out from the centre grow to different thicknesses according to the climate a tree grows in. The scientists looked at sections taken from trees that had lived for hundreds and even thousands of years from different regions and used them to piece together a picture of the plan_____[15] climatic history.

Climato_____[16] have welcomed the new study as the most conclusive evid_____[17] to date that the increase in temperature is a result of human activity.

"The importance of the finding is that it shows there's something going on in the climate system that's cert_____[18] unusual in the context of the last 2,000 years, and it's lik_____[19] that greenhouse gases are playing the major role," said Prof Chris Folland of the Met Office's Hadley Centre. "If you look at the natural ups and downs in temperature, you'll find nothing remo_____[20] like what we're seeing now."

Environment 11

Exercise 4 How can we save our atmosphere?

Complete the text with words from this list:

aerosol	emissions	nuclear	reduced
atmosphere	fertilizers	ozone	renewable
cancer	intensify	quantity	shield
chemical-free	livestock	raising	substitutes
decreasing	network	rays	threat
efficiennt	nitrate	recommendation	

The _____[1] layer, which protects living things from the sun's harmful
ultraviolet _____[2], has been further depleted in many areas of the
globe. The weakened ozone _____[3] lets in more ultraviolet light, a
cause of skin _____[4]. What must be done?

First of all, carbon dioxide _____[5] into the atmosphere – the burning of
fossil fuels – should be _____[6] by 20 per cent by using improved
technologies to get more energy out of the same _____[7] of coal or oil
– thus burning less. We could also try other ways of _____[8] energy: the
so-called _____[9] techniques, as well as increased use of _____[10]
power.

But this is only part of the solution. Some of the _____[11] comes from
the steady rise in other gases, such as the nitrous oxides from agricultural
_____[12] run-off and the chloro-fluorocarbons. They are 10,000 times
more _____[13] than carbon dioxide at trapping heat as well.

So we should encourage farmers to return to _____[14] farming. Well-
managed alternative farms use less synthetic chemical _____[15], pesti-
cides and antibiotics without necessarily _____[16] crop yields and the
productivity of _____[17].

In addition, industry should find safe _____[18] for the chlorofluoro-
carbons, which have been widely used as refrigerants, solvents and propellants
in _____[19] cans. These dangerous chemicals should be phased out
soon.

Another important _____[20] of scientists is that the world should
_____[21] meteorological and oceanographic research in an effort to
complete the picture of the complex _____[22] of links between the
rocks, the water, the _____[23] and all living things.

12 Environment

Exercise 5 Too many people

In the following text some words are jumbled. To give you some help the first letter of the word in question is given. Try to complete with words that would fit the context.

The strain on the global environment (d-s r v e i e) _____¹ mainly from the growth of the industrial (e-s o o i c m n e) _____², but also from that of the world's population. It threatens the (s-r a i u l v v) _____³ and development of future generations. Demographers observe a dramatic change taking place: for the first time in history more people will live in cities than in (r-l r a u) _____⁴ areas. The world's urban population will continue to rise, whereas the rural population is expected to (d-e c i n e l) _____⁵. This means that today's mega-cities will become even more overpopulated than they are at (p-e t e n r s) _____⁶ already. Tokyo will remain the largest city with 36 million people, (f-e o l w d l o) _____⁷ by two Indian mega-cities – New Delhi, with 21 million and Mumbai (Bombay), with 23 million people. Especially Mumbai, which was the headquarters of the British (E-s t a) _____⁸ India Company until 1858, has experienced a population boom as a result of immigration, rural migration, and an increasing (b-r e a h i t r t) _____⁹. Its famous 'Gateway to India' was the first sight many colonists had of India. Next in line is Mexico City, with 20.6 million inhabitants. The city suffers from overcrowding and high levels of (p-i n u l o l t o) _____¹⁰, and is vulnerable to earthquakes. Sao Paulo, with 20 million, rounds up the world's five most populous cities.

Environment 13

Many countries, in (p-u a r i c l t r a) _____[11] in the Third World, are concerned about the (r-d p i a) _____[12] population growth and are addressing the (i-s e s u) _____[13] of teenage pregnancy. Take Colombia for example. About 45 million people live in the South American (r-b i p l u e c) _____[14] today, one-third of whom are under 15 years old. In 2000 an estimated 400,000 young women between the ages of 15 and 19 were (p-e n n r g t a) _____[15] or already had children. Colombia expects a 13 million increase in population by 2015. There is a growing (t-d e r n) _____[16] toward teen pregnancy especially among young women living in rural areas, with low (l-v l e e s) _____[17] of education. The government's campaign includes the distribution of educational brochures on how to (p-e e t r n v) _____[18] pregnancy and how to use condoms. In addition, the ministry wants different sectors of society, including families, schools, and the teenagers themselves, to (i-c e s r e n a) _____[19] dialogue about sexual education and ways to prevent early pregnancies and, consequently, (a-o o t s r i b n) _____[20].

Exercise 6   Synonyms

Find synonyms for the words in italics.

1. Recent *advances* in science and technology have made   _____
    it possible for man to influence his environment.

2. Household *appliances* relieve housewives from *dull*   _____
    work.   _____

3. The earth's biosphere is in a state of *delicate balance.*   _____

4. Fossil fuel *combustion* is responsible for the earth's   _____
    warming.

5. Perhaps we could do without one or the other
    detergent.   _____

6. We cannot *refuse* to cure *disease* in order to limit   _____
    world population.   _____

7. Any drink sold in a *disposable* bottle should cost   _____
    twice as much as the same drink offered in a
    returnable bottle.

8. *Waste disposal* will cost us more and more.   _____

14 / Environment

9. *Dumps* overflow with cans, bottles and cartons.   _____

10. We have thrown into the *seas* of the world millions   _____
    of tons of *garbage*.   _____

11. In many cases scientists disagree about the medical
    hazards of chemical substances.   _____

12. We have ignored the warnings of *poisonous* air too   _____
    long.

13. Fluorocarbons are extremely *polluting* chemical agents   _____
    which destroy the ozone layer.

14. Oxygen helps *purify* our water.   _____

15. Algae bloom will *ravage* fishing grounds and   _____
    swimming areas.

16. Many rivers and lakes have long been polluted by
    untreated *sewage*.   _____

17. Another *threat* to the seas of the world is beginning to   _____
    get more attention: algae bloom.

Exercise 7   **Word families**

Supply the missing forms.

noun (abstract)	noun (concrete)	verb	adjective
presidency	president	preside	presidential
environment	_____	---	_____
_____	---	erode	_____
_____	_____	_____	polluting, polluted
_____	_____	survive	_____
nutrition	_____	---	_____
_____	---	_____	nourishing
_____	---	waste	_____
---	_____	inhabit	_____
_____	scientist	---	_____
_____	---	_____	pure

Environment 15

Exercise 8 Matching words and their definitions

Match the words from list 1 with their appropriate definitions in list 2.
Please note: There are more words than definitions!

A   wood that can be used for building and making things

B   (of substances) which decompose naturally without any special scientific treatment

C   substance used in households to remove dirt

D   supply land or crops with water

E   part of the earth's surface and atmosphere which is inhabited by living things

F   gases expelled from a car or engine

G   lack of rain

H   form of oxygen with a pleasant smell

I   place where rubbish may be unloaded and left

J   substance which provides nourishment

K   practice of cleanliness to prevent diseases

L   state of being balanced

M   substance that replaces something else – hopefully less dangerous

N   very small particles of a radioactive substance that can cause illness or death

(1)   biodegradable
(2)   biosphere
(3)   coastal waters
(4)   detergent
(5)   drought
(6)   dump
(7)   ecology
(8)   equilibrium
(9)   exhaust fumes
(10) hygiene
(11) irrigate
(12) nutrient
(13) ozone
(14) pollutant
(15) radiation
(16) refrigerant
(17) species
(18) substitute
(19) timber
(20) ultraviolet rays
(21) waste heat

A	B	C	D	E	F	G	H	I	J	K	L	M	N

Exercise 9 Crossword puzzle

Try to sovle the crossword puzzle.

Across
1   verschmutzen (7)
7   verstädtern (8)
9   (be)drohen (8)
10 zum Vorschein bringen (6)
14 verseuchen (11)

Down
1   schützen (7)
2   Blei (4)
3   unbehandelt (9)
4   Müll (4)
5   Boden (4)

16 Environment

15 (Bau-)Holz (6)
19 zerfallen (12)
22 Schwefel (7)
23 (radioaktiver) Niederschlag (7)
25 unvorhersehbar (13)
28 Gattung (7)
29 Gezeiten (4)
30 Schicht (5)
32 Mittel (9)
33 Verschmutzung (9)
34 Küste (5)
35 Klima (7)
36 Ökologie (7)
37 Erdgas (7,3)

6 Verpackung (9)
8 schwer (6)
11 Fortschritte machen (7)
12 katastrophal (10)
13 Rache (9)
16 Sterblichkeit (9)
17 verschütten (5)
18 Beseitigung (8)
20 Kühlmittel (11)
21 Gleichgewicht (11)
24 stören (7)
26 Strahlung (9)
27 Biosphäre (9)
31 kränkelnd (6)

Environment 17

exercise 10   Word square

Try to spot these words:

1. unpredictable, 2. uninhabitable, 3. biodegradable, 4. biodiversity,
5. contaminate, 6. composition, 7. widespread, 8. conclusive, 9. combustion,
10. centigrade, 11. untreated, 12. depletion, 13. biosphere, 14. vigorous,
15. survival, 16. delicate, 17. creature, 18. abundant, 19. vicious, 20. variety,
21. surface, 22. sulphur, 23. fertile, 24. concern, 25. climate, 26. chimney,
27. balance, 28. advance, 29. vapour, 30. threat, 31. supply, 32. carbon,
33. bleach, 34. ailing, 35. waste, 36. dense, 37. coast, 38. birth, 39. tide,
40. rate

D	E	N	S	E	U	N	I	N	H	A	B	I	T	A	B	L	E	V
Q	E	C	N	A	V	D	A	E	R	P	S	E	D	I	W	V	K	A
B	U	N	T	R	E	A	T	E	D	Y	U	T	I	D	E	I	C	R
I	C	Y	S	U	R	V	I	V	A	L	N	A	Q	J	D	C	O	I
O	M	B	C	R	E	A	T	U	R	E	P	R	F	Z	D	I	M	E
D	C	L	T	C	A	I	V	I	G	O	R	O	U	S	D	O	B	T
E	O	E	S	E	S	U	R	F	A	C	E	O	X	E	N	U	U	Y
G	M	A	A	N	K	T	B	C	W	B	D	G	L	V	R	S	S	S
R	P	C	O	T	R	H	I	S	O	Z	I	N	U	I	N	T	U	
A	O	H	C	I	M	R	O	K	S	N	C	O	Q	I	O	E	I	L
D	S	I	B	G	K	E	D	O	V	A	T	P	S	I	L	O	O	P
A	I	M	A	R	A	A	I	L	T	N	A	A	T	P	F	I	N	H
B	T	N	L	A	B	T	V	E	Q	V	B	E	M	M	H	R	A	U
L	I	E	A	D	U	F	E	R	T	I	L	E	X	I	J	E	H	R
E	O	Y	N	E	N	B	R	H	D	P	E	N	F	P	N	J	R	W
M	N	E	C	R	D	I	S	T	E	S	U	P	P	L	Y	A	P	E
U	E	V	E	F	A	R	I	D	C	L	I	M	A	T	E	Y	T	B
C	A	R	B	O	N	T	T	E	V	I	S	U	L	C	N	O	C	E
E	T	S	A	W	T	H	Y	C	O	N	C	E	R	N	B	U	J	M

18 Environment

Exercise 11 **Word grid**

Find the words.

1. existing or available in large quantities, 2. to suffer, to be in poor health, 3. (of a substance or object) capable of being decomposed by bacteria or other living organism and thereby avoiding pollution, 4. to move forwards, to make progress 5. the regions of the surface and atmosphere of the earth or another planet occupied by living organisms, 6. putting an end to debate or question, 7. equilibrium, 8. the start of life as a physically separate being, 9. seashore, 10. the Celsius scale of temperature, 11. speed, frequency, 12. a vertical channel or pipe on the roof of a building which conducts smoke and combustion gases up into air.

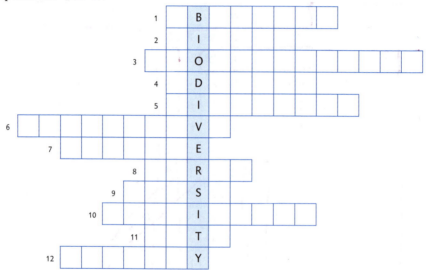

World affairs

1 Word field

abuse	Missbrauch
adequate	ausreichend
(to) advocate	etwas unterstützen
(to) anticipate	etwas erwarten, mit etwas rechnen
appalling	entsetzlich, erschreckend
apparently	anscheinend probably - wahrs.
arsenal	Waffenarsenal
assassination	Attentat
(to) assess	beurteilen, einschätzen, bewerten
assistance	Hilfe
attrition	Zermürbung
average	Durchschnitt
balance	Gleichgewicht
bargain	(gutes) Geschäft, vorteilhafter Kauf
blast	Explosion
bomb bay	Bombenschacht
bonded labour	Zwangsarbeit
calorie intake	Kalorieneinnahme, -zufuhr
commodity	(Handels-) Ware, Gebrauchsartikel
comparison	Vergleich
(to) confound	verwirren, verblüffen
congested	überfüllt, übervölkert
considerably	beträchtlich, erheblich
(to) constitute	etwas ausmachen
crops	Feldfrüchte, Saat, Gesamternte
currency	Währung

20 / World affairs

dairy produce	Milch- und Molkereiprodukte
decent	anständig
decisive	entscheidend
deficiency	Mangel
desert	Wüste
desperate	verzweifelt
(to) deteriorate	sich verschlechtern
devastation	Verwüstung
devoted	ausgerichtet auf, gewidmet
diet	Kost, Nahrung
disarmament	Abrüstung
disgust	Abscheu
disparity	Ungleichheit, Verschiedenheit
(to) dispossess	enteignen, zur Räumung zwingen
(to) disrupt	stören
donation	(Geld-) Spende
downtown	Innenstadt, Geschäftsviertel
drought	Dürre
earnings	Verdienst
enduring	dauerhaft, beständig
energy consumption	Energieverbrauch
enforcement	Durchsetzung (eines Rechts oder Gesetzes)
(to) engulf	überfluten, verschlingen
essential	lebensnotwendig, wesentlich
family planning	Familienplanung
(to) feed	füttern, ernähren, versorgen
fierce	heftig, scharf, grimmig
fission	(Kern-) Spaltung
(to) forebode	Schlimmes ahnen
(to) groan	ächzen

gross national product	Bruttosozialprodukt
guide-line	Richtlinie, Richtschnur
harvest	Ernte(zeit)
hazardous	gefährlich
(to) hoard	horten, hamstern
illiteracy	Analphabetentum
imbalance	Ungleichgewicht
imminent	bevorstehend
impact	Auswirkung, Einfluss
impartial	unparteiisch
(to) include	umfassen, einschließen, beinhalten
income	Einkommen
income per head	Pro-Kopf-Einkommen
indicator	Anzeiger, (Leistungs-) Messer
industrialized nations	Industrieländer
infant mortality	Kindersterblichkeit
intensity	Stärke
leading edge	Speerspitze
life expectancy	Lebenserwartung
literacy	Lese- und Schreibfähigkeit
(to) loom	sich bedrohlich abzeichnen
loom	Webstuhl
lure	(Ver-)Lockung
malnutrition	Unterernährung, schlechte Ernährung
medical care	medizinische Betreuung, Versorgung
migrant	Zuwanderer
mortality rate	Sterberate
nightmare	Alptraum
nutritious	nahrhaft
observance	Einhaltung

open-sewer	offener Abwasserkanal
(to) outstrip	überholen, hinter sich lassen
parched	verdörrt, versengt
peasant	Kleinbauer
pitiful	bemitleidenswert
plight	Not(lage)
population growth	Bevölkerungswachstum
poverty	Armut
(to) predict	etwas vorhersagen
predominantly	überwiegend
(to) prevail	(vor)herrschen, bestehen
productive effort	Produktionsanstrengung, -leistung
(to) propel	vorantreiben
prosperity	Wohlstand
purchasing power	Kaufkraft
(to) rank	ordnen, einreihen, klassifizieren
reference (to)	Bezug (auf)
(to) relieve	jdm. (in einer Notsituation) helfen
(to) rely (on)	sich verlassen (auf)
resolve	Entschlossenheit
resources	Reichtümer eines Landes, Bodenschätze
root	Wurzel
rural	ländlich
(to) safeguard	jdn./etwas vor etwas schützen
scale	Maßstab
scarce	knapp, spärlich
secure	sicher
sentiment	Stimmung, Meinung
sewage	Abwasser
shantytown	Baracken-, Hüttenstadt
(to) shatter	zerspringen, zerbrechen
sombre	düster, trübe

World affairs 23

starchy	stärkehaltig
starvation	Hunger
subsidy	Subvention
subsistence	Lebensunterhalt, Auskommen
(to) supplement	ergänzen
(to) sustain	stützen, tragen
trafficking	Handel
underfed	unterernährt
undernourished	unterernährt
unmet need	ungedeckter Bedarf
urgency	Dringlichkeit
(to) vaporize	verdampfen
vicinity	unmittelbare Umgebung
vicious circle	Teufelskreis
violation	Verletzung (eines Rechts)
vulnerable	verwundbar, verletzlich
warfare	Kriegführung
weapon	Waffe
widespread	weit verbreitet

2 Idioms and phrases

politics	The fight against poverty and injustice must become a key issue in world politics.	Staatskunst, Politik
policy	The fight against excessive inflation in the western world was fought with "monetarist" policies and a sharp rise in world interest rates.	Verfahrensweise, Taktik, Politik
to lend money	The bankers were eager to lend the money to Third World countries.	jdm. Geld ausleihen
to borrow money	Developing countries have to pay low interest rates when they borrow money from foreign banks.	jdm. Geld leihen

to earn (bear) interest	The oil producers put their dollars into the banks of the rich countries where they expected the money to earn interest.	Zinsen tragen
to meet one's debt	The government of the developing country announced that it could not meet its debts.	seine Schulden begleichen
to bear the brunt	It is a reality today that children all over the world are bearing the brunt of the crisis of poverty, famine and war.	die Hauptlast tragen
to pose a threat	But it is known that the threat posed by disease and malnutrition can be defeated.	eine Bedrohung darstellen
to bear children	Women in the Third World often bear more than ten children.	zur Welt bringen, gebären
to widen the gap	Now an economic and technological colonialism is widening the gap between rich and poor.	die Kluft verbreitern
to make short shrift of	The World Bank's report makes short shrift of the notion that economic development can solve the population problem.	kurzen Prozess machen mit
to resort to force	There is a great likelihood that people will resort to force if their basic needs are neglected.	zu gewaltsamen Mitteln greifen
to seek refuge	Through the ages people have been forced to leave their country and seek refuge, especially from political and religious persecution.	Zuflucht suchen
to step up pressure	The US government is stepping up pressure on the conflicting parties to negotiate a peace settlement.	den Druck verstärken

World affairs 25

3 Practice

Exercise 1 A world of disparities

Complete the text with words from this list.

common	industrial	place	relieve
development	literacy	plight	responsibility
disparity	malnutrition	poverty	rose
donation	market	primarily	subsidies
experienced	obligations	property	subsistence

Developing countries (_____¹ in Africa, Asia, and Latin America) differ greatly from one another geographically. What they have in _common_², however, is a low standard of living, _poverty_³, a poor distribution of wealth, low levels of _property_⁴, and high rates of population growth. During the 20th century the world's population _rose_⁵ rapidly, but the major increase took _place_⁶ in less developed countries. Today five out of six people in the world live in developing countries and in 30 years, it will be seven out of eight.

As those nations have little or no _industrial_⁷ base, the primary mode of _____⁸ is farming. Peasants work their small pieces of land, hardly producing enough food for their own families. In recent years some countries, especially in Asia and Latin America, have _experienced_⁹ rapid economic development, which has resulted in a widening of the gap within the group of the less developed countries. To reduce this imbalance and _relieve_¹⁰ the poorer countries from their _disparity_¹¹ more development aid is needed. The European Union and the United States have increased foreign aid programmes, but _subsistence_¹² levels are still too low. The industrialised countries spend five times as much on agricultural _subsidies_¹³ and ten times as much on defence as on development assistance. This reduces the chances of people in the Third World of escaping from _malnutrition_¹⁴, hunger and disease. In addition, the developed countries need to open their markets to give less developing countries a fairer chance on the world _market_¹⁵.

On the other hand, the poor countries themselves have to fulfil their _responsibility_¹⁶ of the bargain and see that the donations are used efficiently. They have to accept the primary _donation_¹⁷ for their own development. Arrangements must be made to prevent foreign aid from being hoarded by a privileged few. Political, legal and economic reforms must be introduced which will guarantee that benefits flow through to people in poverty and that the rights of individuals, and the _____ [18] rights of foreign investors, are protected.

As it stands now, our world is in a state of imbalance and a growing _____ [19] of people, resources, and the environment is predicted. To rebalance our world means to give everyone the chance of a secure life – with the right of expression and the right to _____ [20].

Exercise 2 **The plight of working children**

In the following text some words are jumbled. To give you some help the first letter of the word in question is given. Try to complete with words that would fit the context.

It is a reality today that children all over the world are particularly vulnerable to the crises of poverty, (f-n m e a i) _____ [1] and war. Whenever a war or a natural catastrophe such as a flood or poor (h-t r e a v s) _____ [2] ravages a country, it is the children who have to bear most of the (b-u t r n) _____ [3]. In order to survive poor, unemployed parents (b-o r w o r) _____ [4] money from an employer and in return hand a son or daughter over to him. The family receives an (a-n v e a c d) _____ [5] payment for which the boy or girl then has to work. In most cases the child cannot work off the (d-b e t) _____⁶, nor can the family raise enough money to buy the child back. This form of child labour is a new form of (s-a e y r v l) _____⁷ – wholly different from the form which existed in the south of the United States more than two centuries ago. The term 'slavery' is rarely used anymore; instead, it is usually referred to as 'bonded labour' or 'human trafficking.'

It is (e-m t t d e a i s) _____⁸ that of the 246 million child labourers in the world, 8.4 million are bonded or forced labourers. In rural areas most children work in agriculture. In El Salvador they (h-e t r s v a) _____⁹ sugar cane using machetes to cut cane for up to nine hours a day in the hot sun. Injuries to their hands and legs are common and medical (c-r a e) _____¹⁰ is often not available. Other children work long hours as domestics; in (t-a e d r) _____¹¹ and services, in manufacturing and construction – often in dangerous and unhealthy conditions. Working at rug looms weaving (c-e r s t a p) _____¹² has left children disabled with eye damage and (l-n g u) _____¹³ disease. Children making silk thread in India dip their hands into boiling water that (b-r s n u) _____¹⁴ and blisters them.

The worst forms of child labour – 'bonded labour', hazardous work or prostitution – constitute a violation of basic (h-m n a u) _____¹⁵ rights and must therefore be stopped. In some cases, it is true, a child's work can be (h-f l l p u e) _____¹⁶ to him or her and to the family; working and earning can be a positive (e-e r c p i e x e n) _____¹⁷ in a child's growing up. What we must not (t-t l r e o e a) _____¹⁸ any longer, however, is children being used as an expendable commodity. Laws must be (p-e s s d a) _____¹⁹ to prevent children from losing their childhood, education, and opportunities by being entrapped in bonded (l-u b a o r) _____²⁰.

Exercise 3   **The day that changed the world: Hiroshima**

Complete the text with words from this list.

altitude	devastations	height	populated
arms	disarmament	horrifying	proliferation
arsenals	engaged	limitation	target
course	fission	mushroom	vicinity
deteriorated	glance	negotiations	warfare

August 6, 1945 was the day that changed the _____[1] of history and the nature of _____[2]. On that day, at exactly fifteen minutes past eight in the morning, the first atomic bomb was dropped on a _____[3] area. At 8:15 a.m., a B29 bomber, which the pilot had nicknamed after his mother "Enola Gay", approached the first choice _____[4], the Japanese city of Hiroshima, in clear weather. The plane's bomb bay sprang open and dropped the bomb, dubbed "Little Boy", from an _____[5] of 31,600 feet. It exploded 1,900 feet above the city and only missed its target, the Aioi Bridge, by approximately 800 feet. The crew saw the enormous _____[6] cloud developing, a bubbling mass of purple-grey smoke, with a red core burning inside, looking like lava or molasses. The cloud is estimated to have reached a _____[7] of 40,000 feet. On the ground the explosion vaporized everything in the immediate _____[8], completely burned about 4.4 square miles of the city, killing between 70,000 and 80,000 people. Another 70,000 were wounded.

The appearance of people who had survived the blast was _____[9]. Their skin was blackened by burns, their hair was burned, and at a _____[10] you couldn't tell whether you were looking at them from the front or back. Their skin – not only on their hands, but on their faces and bodies too – hung down. Many of them died walking along the road.

The atomic bombs on Hiroshima and later Nagasaki (9. 8. 1945) brought about the end to the Second World War in the Pacific. Despite the horrors and _____[11] in Japan, militaries in East and West looked upon the atom bomb as a "useful strategic weapon" and, consequently, created massive nuclear weapon _____[12]. When relations between the United States and the Soviet Union _____[13], the possibility of an atomic war, which would end all life on earth, became more imminent. During the period of the Cold War both nations were _____[14] in a nuclear arms race. They developed thermonuclear bombs which had many times the power of _____[15] bombs. In protest against the constant atomic threat campaigns for nuclear _____[16] were launched in many countries, pressing on the United States and the Soviet Union to reduce their arsenals and prevent the _____[17] of nuclear weapons technology. Only in the late 1980s, after a near-disastrous accident at the nuclear power station at Three Mile Island (1979 in the US) and the melt-down of the atomic reactor at Chernobyl (1986 in the Ukraine), did the two superpowers take up _____[18] on a _____[19] of nuclear arms production. They eventually agreed on a reduction of their nuclear forces and the strategic _____[20].

World affairs / 29

Exercise 4   The day that changed the world: 9/11

Translate into English or German respectively.

On Tuesday, September 11, 2001, 19 men armed with knives, box-cutters, mace and pepper spray carried out an _____ (Angriff)[1] on the United States, the most powerful nation in the world and turned the international _____ (Ordnung)[2] upside down. Within less than twenty minutes two *hijacked* (_____)[3] passenger jets crashed into the twin towers of the World Trade Centre in New York. Huge jet fuel fireballs erupted upon *impact* (_____)[4], setting the buildings afire. Eventually what no one could anticipate happened: both towers _____ (stürzten ein, brachen zusammen)[5] in ten seconds, claiming the lives of 2,973 people altogether, among them many police officers and fire-fighters, called "First Responders."

In his first *address* (_____)[6] after the event to the shocked nation the American President Bush said that "thousands of lives were suddenly ended by *evil* (_____)[7]" and asked for prayers for the families and friends of the _____ (Opfer)[8]. "These acts shattered steel, but they cannot dent the steel of American *resolve* (_____)[9]," he added. In later statements he told the nation to be prepared for a long and difficult struggle against a *determined* (_____)[10] enemy who sees his actions as a war of attrition. The terrorist attacks, which were politically as well as religiously motivated, have affected people's opinions on a number of _____ (Streitfragen)[11] and influenced public life in general.

To begin with, ordinary _____ (Staatsbürger)[12] and politicians have become more *concerned* (_____)[13] about international threats. Since September 11th, the US intelligence and law enforcement agencies have been reformed. To make America more secure the government created a special department: the *Department* (_____)[14] of Homeland Security. Several Terrorist Threat units were established to prevent, disrupt, and

30 / World affairs

respond to terrorist attacks. All over the world, more people than ever believe that the world has become a more dangerous place and *consequently* (_____)[15] support stricter security _____ (Maß-nahmen)[16] to safeguard against terrorist attacks. As a result extensive checks and controls at airports have been introduced and travellers have to allow more time to check in to avoid _____ (Verspätungen)[17] or missing a flight. On the other hand, 9/11 has had an *enduring* (_____)[18] impact on how Americans feel about their own country. The United States has always been a highly patriotic country, but since the attacks on the WTC, which shocked the nation more than the attack on Pearl Harbor or the Kennedy _____ (Ermordung)[19], there has been a significant increase in the intensity of that patriotic *sentiment* (_____)[20].

Exercise 5   Amnesty: fighting for human rights

In the following text some words are incomplete. Only a couple of letters are given. Try to complete with words that would fit the context.

Amnesty International is an organisation which protests against the unfair or cruel trea____[1] of political prisoners and campaigns for the observance of fundamental human rights. Advocating non-violence, and politically impa____[2], it opposes the use of torture and the death pe____[3]. Based in the UK, and funded entirely by private donat____[4], AI encourages the individuals to participate in activities and especially young people who might not be interested in politics generally. One of the many volun____[5] who invested their time helping Amnesty was Joanne Kathleen Rowling, the famous authoress of the Harry-Potter book series. As a post-gra____[6], she worked at Amnesty International in London doing res____[7] into human rights abu____[8] in French-speaking African countries.

Amnesty International was fo____[9] in London by lawyer Peter Benenson, who had represented political pris____[10] in South Africa, Hungary, and Spain. In 1961 Benenson wrote an article for The Observer news____[11] about human rights violations. It began with these words: 'Open your newspaper any day of the week and you will find a report from somewhere in the world of someone being imprisoned, tor____[12] or executed because his opi____[13] or religion are unacceptable to his government… The newspaper reader feels a sickening sense of impotence. Yet if these feelings of disgust could be united into common action, something effe____[14] could be done.' The article app____[15] to

World affairs 31

many readers who joined Benenson in "common action" to establish an international agency "in defence of freedom of opinion and religion."
Until today people are inspired to join Amnesty because they feel frust____[16] in
the face of institutionalised state violence, thinking that they are not doing
enough constructive and useful things against the injus____[17] in our world
today. As members of Amnesty they can become directly involved in the
organization's work. Suppo____[18] are encouraged to write letters of protest to
foreign governments. This form of direct lobbying has become the "unique
selling point" for the charity, distingui____[19] it from other organisations and
making work at Amnesty attractive for younger people in particular. Today, the
human rights organisation has about two million members and offices in more
than 40 countries. AI's long-serving cha____[20] was Irish statesman Seán
MacBride, whose service was recognized by the Norwegian Nobel Committee
when it awarded him the Nobel prize for peace in 1974. The organization itself
received the Nobel peace prize in 1977.

Exercise 6   Synonyms

Find synonyms for the words in italics.

1. The commonest way to *assess* a country's degree of   _____
   development is by reference to its Gross National
   Product (GNP).

2. We often *rank* countries according to their GNP per   _____
   head of population.

3. Most problems of the developing countries arise from
   two *roots*: too little food and unemployment.   _____

4. An *apparently* satisfactory calorie intake hides a   _____
   widespread *deficiency* of essential vitamins.   _____

5. Developing countries differ *considerably* from one   _____
   another.

6. We must enable the poor people in the LDC's to
   provide a *decent* standard of living for their families.   _____

7. *Decisive* victories over a lot of illnesses have been   _____
   won.

8. Poor people spend a high proportion of their *earnings*   _____
   on food.

32 / World affairs

9. Today in all of the developing countries a *fierce* struggle for survival is taking place. _____

10. Mexico City, Sao Paolo and Shanghai are among the largest, most *congested* cities on earth. _____

11. Development policies should *include* national population programmes. _____

12. It is our duty to abolish the *prevailing* misery among the poorest people in the world. _____

13. There are more mouths to *feed* as people are healthier and live longer. _____

14. In the poor countries diets are *predominantly* starchy. _____

Exercise 7   Opposites

Find opposites for the words in italics.

1. Resources are *squandered* without consideration of their renewal. _____

2. After the official *disappearance* of the Soviet Union Americans are reassessing their view of the former enemy and of America as well. _____

3. Amnesty's central function was to campaign against unjust *imprisonment* on the grounds of individual belief. _____

4. Amnesty has always fought against the *violation* of human rights. _____

5. Amnesty's *income* comes from membership and donations. _____

6. Many people feel *frustrated* in the face of institutionalised state violence. _____

7. Of *paramount* importance is the need to build up more confidence and to curb the mounting spiral of sophisticated and expensive weaponry. _____

8. The messages which the agent passed on to head-quarters were *incomprehensible* to outsiders. _____

World affairs / 33

9. A large number of *civilians* were killed in an air raid on _____
a giant bunker in Baghdad.

10. Amnesty has never been *reluctant* to criticize governments that otherwise enjoy popular support. _____

Exercise 8   Matching words and their definitions

*Match the words from list 1 with their appropriate definitions in list 2. Please
note: There are more words than definitions!*

A   injury from a knife or bullet for example

B   to damage sth. so badly that it cannot be used again

C   beat someone in a game or battle

D   a process in which countries agree to reduce the
number of weapons they have

E   to give up a thing for some noble reason

F   anger that makes you ready to attack other people

G   to go into another's country as an act of war

H   to take and hold possession of (a city, a country)

I   one who seeks shelter from danger, e. g. in a foreign
land

J   person who serves as a soldier of his choice

K   chief place of business; place where the
commanding officer is

L   heavy motor-car with guns in it

M   weapon that moves long distances through the air
and explodes

N   a man who has done something very brave

O   someone who works secretly to find out things

P   group of people fighting for a world without war

(1)   aggression
(2)   casualties
(3)   defeat
(4)   defence
(5)   destroy
(6)   detente
(7)   disarmament
(8)   headquarters
(9)   hero
(10) invade
(11) martial law
(12) missile
(13) occupy
(14) peace
      movement
(15) refugee
(16) sacrifice
(17) spy
(18) supplies
(19) tank
(20) volunteer
(21) wound

A	B	C	D	E	F	G	H	I	J	K	L	M	N	O	P

34 / World affairs

Exercise 9   Word families

Supply the missing forms.

noun (abstract)	noun (concrete)	verb	adjective
presidency	president	preside	presidential
_____	_____	_____	deterrent
_____	_____	operate	_____
_____	_____	_____	allied
armament	---	_____	_____
---	volunteer	_____	_____
protection	_____	_____	_____
_____	---	grieve	_____
explosion	---	_____	_____
_____	---	endure	_____
_____	_____	object	_____
_____	navigator	_____	_____
invasion	_____	_____	---
_____	---	_____	deceitful
_____	---	defy	_____
_____	---	_____	courageous
conspiracy	_____	_____	_____
_____	conqueror	_____	---
_____	_____	_____	captive
blood	---	_____	_____

Exercise 10   Word square

Try to spot these words:

1. malnutrition, 2. resolution, 3. tolerance, 4. terrorism , 5. volunteer,
6. armistice, 7. deterrent, 8. conscript, 9. literacy, 10. alliance, 11. conquest,
12. nuclear, 13. warfare, 14. detente, 15. warfare, 16. hijack, 17. occupy,
18. threat, 19. draft, 20. ally,

World affairs 35

M	E	R	T	T	P	T	F	A	R	D	U	N	N	W	E
V	F	Y	B	O	B	U	J	M	D	D	O	O	T	A	L
E	B	S	N	L	O	F	M	T	T	I	I	A	P	R	I
E	K	X	T	E	C	Q	S	A	T	T	R	L	I	F	T
C	L	KI	H	R	Z	U	S	U	I	K	A	L	R	A	E
I	T	H	J	A	L	Y	L	R	D	Q	E	I	C	R	R
T	J	C	E	N	C	O	T	L	Y	O	L	A	S	E	A
S	M	Z	F	C	S	U	C	M	J	K	C	N	N	H	C
I	N	D	N	E	N	O	S	Z	O	X	U	C	O	R	Y
M	L	S	R	L	N	I	B	T	S	M	N	E	C	E	D
R	F	I	A	Q	R	D	E	T	E	R	R	E	N	T	E
A	U	M	U	O	B	O	C	C	U	P	Y	N	T	U	T
I	Z	E	R	E	E	T	N	U	L	O	V	U	R	X	E
W	S	R	K	D	H	I	J	A	C	K	A	L	L	Y	N
T	E	Y	U	T	H	R	E	A	T	S	K	A	E	E	T
T	W	A	R	F	A	R	E	N	K	C	H	Q	W	M	E

Exercise 11 Crossword puzzle

Try to solve the crossword puzzle.

Across

2 Ungleichheit (9)
4 Gleichgewicht (7)
6 ordnen (4)
7 Attentat (14)
10 Explosion (5)
13 Mangel (10)
14 Unterernährung (12)
15 Missbrauch (5)
16 Wüste (6)
19 überwiegend (13)
22 Ernte(zeit) (7)
24 entscheidend (8)
26 Milch- und Molkereiprodukte (12)
28 Armut (7)
30 (Ver-)Lockung (4)
31 knapp (6)
34 anständig (6)
36 Maßstab (5)

Down

1 Waffe (6)
2 Abrüstung (11)
3 stützen (7)
4 Zwangsarbeit (12)
5 dauerhaft (8)
8 Anzeiger (8)
9 Pro-Kopf-Einkommen (13)
11 Stimmung (9)
12 bemitleidenswert (7)
17 weit verbreitet (10)
18 füttern (4)
20 beurteilen (6)
21 s. verlassen (auf) (4)
23 unmittelbare Umgebung (8)
25 Feldfrüchte (25)
27 verzweifelt (9)
29 Abwasser (6)
30 Lese- und Schreibfähigkeit (8)

World affairs

38 Waffenarsenal (7)
39 ausreichend (8)
40 Analphabetentum (10)

32 Entschlossenheit (7)
33 ländlich (5)
35 überfluten (6)
37 Kost (4)

Consumer/Health

1 Word field

accusation	Beschuldigung
(to) acknowledge	(Empfang) bestätigen, anerkennen
adequate	ausreichend, genügend
adolescent	Jugendliche(r)
advance	Fortschritt; Vorrücken
advantageous	vorteilhaft
advertisement	(kurz: ad) Anzeige
advertising	Werbung
advice column	Ratgeberspalte
after-sales service	Kundendienst
alert	wachsam
(to) argue	streiten; erörtern, argumentieren
assumption	Annahme
at random	blindlings
bar code	Strichcode
benefit	Nutzen
bewildering	verwirrend
blatant	lärmend, krass
branded goods	Markenartikel
campaign	Aktion, Feldzug, Werbekampagne
carbohydrate	Kohle[n]hydrat
cereal	Getreide
clumsy	plump
commercial	Werbespot
commodities	Waren
commodity trade	Warenhandel

38 / Consumer/Health

(to) compel	zwingen
competitive	konkurrenzfähig
competitor	Konkurrent
(to) comprise	bestehen aus
(to) conceal	verbergen
concealed advertising	Schleichwerbung
(to) conceive	planen, ausdenken
(to) confine	begrenzen, beschränken
(to) consolidate	festigen; zusammenlegen
consumer goods	Konsumgüter, Verbrauchsgüter
consumer guidance	Verbraucherberatung
consumer protection	Verbraucherschutz
content(s)	Inhalt
convenience food	Fertiggericht
conviction	Überzeugung
(to) cope	zurechtkommen
coverage	Berichterstattung
(to) crease	knittern, zerknittern
customer-oriented	kundennah
(to) deceive	betrügen, täuschen
dentistry	Zahnmedizin
(to) depreciate	(Wert) mindern, abschreiben
diet	Nahrung, Kost
discernible	erkennbar, unterscheidbar
discerning	kritisch, scharfsichtig
(to) dismantle	zerlegen, demontieren
distress	Schmerz, Leid, Kummer, Sorge
distributor	Verteiler, Händler
(to) emerge	entstehen, hervorgehen
ensuing illness	Folgekrankheit

Consumer/Health 39

(to) evaluate	abschätzen, bewerten, beurteilen
executive	leitender Angestellter
expenses	Unkosten, Spesen
facilities	Einrichtungen, Anlagen
fee	Gebühr, Honorar
(to) flatter	schmeicheln
(to) gather	sammeln
glance	Blick
goods on stock	Warenbestand
(to) ignite	anzünden, entzünden
imbalance	Ungleichgewicht
(to) impose	durchsetzen
inaccurate	ungenau, unrichtig
intention	Absicht
intrusion	Störung
(to) inundate	überschwemmen
irritation	Gereiztheit, Ärger
lawsuit	Klage
leaflet	Prospekt, Flugblatt
loyalty	Treue
manufactured goods	Fertigwaren
(to) mention	erwähnen
merchandise	Handelsware
(to) mislead	irreführen, verleiten
moderation	Mäßigung, Maß
non-profit	gemeinwirtschaftlich
nutritionist	Ernährungswissenschaftler
obese	fett
obesity	Fettleibigkeit
package	Packung
performance	Leistung; Vorstellung

40 / Consumer/Health

precedent	vergleichbarer Fall, Präzedenzfall
preference	Vorliebe, Vorzug
prescription	Rezept
privacy	Privatsphäre
(to) promote	(Verkauf durch Werbung) steigern, fördern
(to) prosecute	(auch strafrechtlich) verfolgen
prosperity	Wohlstand, Gedeihen
pulse	Hülsenfrucht
purchase	Kauf, Ankauf
pursuit	Streben
quality failure	Qualitätsmangel
quality protection	Qualitätssicherung
quality requirement	Qualitätsanforderung
range	Kollektion, Sortiment
recession	Konjunkturrückgang
retailer	Einzelhändler
seal	Siegel
service department	Kundendienst
(to) shrink	zusammenschrumpfen, einlaufen
standard	Niveau, Stand, Norm
starchy	stärkehaltig
stock, storehouse	Warenlager
(to) store	speichern
striking	auffallend, eindrucksvoll
subscriber	Abonnent
subtle	fein, feinsinnig
successive	aufeinander folgend
(to) suspect	verdächtigen
suspicion	Verdacht
tag	Schild
transgression	Vergehen, Übertretung
undaunted	unerschrocken

Consumer/Health 41

unrivalled	konkurrenzlos
varicose veins	Krampfadern
vast	ungeheuer groß
wasteful	verschwenderisch

2 Practice

Exercise 1 "Big Brother" in our supermarkets

In the following text some words are jumbled. To give you some help the first letter of the word in question is given. Try to complete with words that would fit the context.

One day you won't have to write your own shopping list – your favourite supermarket will do it for you, because the management is informed in (d-i t a e l) _____[1] about your buying (h-t b s a i) _____[2]. Tesco, Sainsbury and Safeway know what you buy, how much you buy each time and when and at what time of day you do your shopping. How do they know? All big stores have (p-e i o r d v d) _____[3] their customers with so-called loyalty cards or shopper club cards. With the help of such a card, companies (c-l e t o l c) _____[4] a vast amount of data about their customers.

To spare the labour of putting a price tag on every (i-e m t) _____[5] supermarkets introduced the system of "bar coding". Merchandise is packaged with identifying bar codes which are (s-d a n n c e) _____[6] into a computerized register which reads the code and "rings up" the item at a price which is pre-programmed into the system. So when the price of an item changes the shop keeper need not (r-p e a e c l) _____[7] all price tags on the packets in the shop, he simply (a-t a p d s) _____[8] the price in his computer system. The bar code also keeps a (r-r c d e o) _____[9] for the shop managers. At a glance they know how many items they have sold and how many are (l-f e t) _____[10] in their stores – and also what has been taken but not been paid for, i. e. (s-o e t l n) _____[11]! They see which article sells well and which doesn't.

After the introduction of bar codes for merchandise bar codes for the customers came into being. The (l-y l y o a t) _____[12] cards store all sorts of information about the customer. Supermarket managers claim that customers profit from loyalty cards. The detailed information about a customer's buying habits allows the stores to (t-r e t g a) _____¹³ shoppers better with specific offers. They know what the shopper prefers and therefore can serve him more accurately.

Critics of the system (m-t i i n a n a) _____¹⁴ that "Big Brother" has entered the shops. In George Orwell's pessimistic novel "1984" Big Brother represents absolute control in a (t-a t l r t a o i n a i) _____¹⁵ state. Like Big Brother the shops gather private data without the customer's knowledge of what sort of information is being (s-e o r t d) _____¹⁶. Many critics regard this as an intrusion on the customer's privacy. Another reason why privacy campaigners find the cards alarming is their suspicion that retailers might turn their knowledge into (p-o i f r t) _____¹⁷, since they know the person they want to sell something to. They might inundate households with individualised ads and other selling (m-s a e s e g s) _____¹⁸ based on the information about your buying habits, thus adding to the already enormous (f-d o o l) _____¹⁹ of brochures, leaflets in your post box at your front door and (j-n u k) _____²⁰ mail in your email post-box in your computer.

Exercise 2   **Glass against plastic**

In the following text some words are incomplete. Only one or a couple of letters are given. Try to complete with words that would fit the context.

Over the last two dec____¹ our consumer habits have mov____² in a distinctly un-green dire____³. Look at the drinks packages. The superm____⁴ style of retailing does not enco____⁵ the use of reusable containers. Supermarkets want drinks in containers which do not break if dro____⁶, which are light and which stack eas____⁷. The two signif____⁸ changes in drinks packaging – increasing popula____⁹ of cans and substit____¹⁰ of plastics for glass for bottles – is merely a respo____¹¹ to consumer preference.

From the manufac____¹² point of view, it is clear that the pattern of demand has chan____¹³; but the crucial question is whether this demand comes from shoppers or from shopk____¹⁴. Research indicates that shoppers show a prefer____¹⁵ for glass over plastic on ten important points:

- it keeps its cont____¹⁶ well,
- it doesn't affect tas____¹⁷,
- it is resealable,
- it opens easily,
- it has a quality im____¹⁸,
- it is conve____¹⁹ to store,

Consumer/Health 43

- it gives good visibility,
- it can be recy_____ [20],
- it can be us_____ [21] at the table,
- and it can be reused.

Plastic scores on only two points – durabi_____ [22] and lightness.

Yet out_____ [23] of glass containers for soft drinks has fallen and there has been an incr_____ [24] in the use of plastic bot_____ [25]. The change from glass to plastic is not un-green: the change from retur_____ [26] to one-trip bottle is.

There is an important diffe_____ [27] between reusability and recyclability. More large supermarkets are putting bottle banks outs_____ [28] their stores. But this encourages only the energy-consuming recycling of raw mate_____ [29] rather than the reuse of the bottle. It is estim_____ [30] that making one milk bottle – the star of reusable packaging – uses as much energy as filling, delive_____ [31], collecting and was_____ [32] it for ten subsequent journeys. Apply the same economics to other bottles, and the total energy saving could be spectac_____ [33].

Exercise 3   **Teenage obesity**

Translate into English or German respectively.

Almost forty per cent of American children and _____ [1] (Jugendliche, Heranwachsende) are carrying too much fat and two out of every three adults are overweight or *obese* _____ [2]. Who is to blame: the fast-food corporations or the _____ [3] (Kunden)? Two teenage girls – one weighed 135 kilos – took the fast food chain McDonald's to court, *arguing* _____ [4] that McDonald's was responsible for their obesity because it did not provide the necessary information about the health risks *associated* _____ [5] with its meals. The _____ [6] (Klage) was eventually dismissed because the judge said that the girls themselves were responsible for their _____ [7] (Gewicht). Common sense should have told them that eating many fatty meals was not good for them. The case made the headlines because it clearly showed the popularity of *convenience foods* _____ [8] on the one side and, on the other, the necessity to educate children about the nutritional facts and contents of fast food. A healthy _____ [9] (Kost, Nahrung) in childhood plays an essential role in growth and development, current well-being, educational _____ [10] (Leistung) and avoidance of chronic disease throughout life.

Nutritionists _____ [11] agree that childhood obesity has multiple causes: it most likely results from an interaction of nutritional, psychological, familial, and physiological factors. The main reason for overweight, however, is the _____ [12] (Ungleichgewicht) between energy input (calories obtained from food) and energy output (calories expended in the basal metabolic rate and physical activity). In other words, an unhealthy diet together with little _____ [13] (Bewegung) causes overweight and *ensuing illnesses* _____ [14]. An American documentary filmmaker carried out a test on himself, rigorously eating a diet of McDonald's fast food, three times a day for a whole month. Gaining 11 kilos in weight, he _____ [15] (anschaulich, lebhaft) illustrated the negative effects of this one-sided diet on his physical and mental health.

A healthy dietary intake should comprise _____ [16] (Kohle[n]hydrat[e]), fats, proteins, minerals and vitamins – all in moderation. You should eat a certain amount of bread, cereals and other *starchy* _____ [17] foods, plus meat, fish or pulses, fruits and vegetables, and low amounts of fat, sugar or salty foods. Any one-sided diet causes more _____ [18] (Schaden) than good. Nutritional experts encourage people to eat at least five portions of fresh fruit and vegetables a day, because this ensures an *adequate* _____ [19] supply of micronutrients like vitamins. Evidence is growing about other _____ [20] (Nutzen, Vorteile) of fruit and vegetable too – they can help prevent heart disease, some types of cancer, the most common form of diabetes and obesity.

Consumer/Health ✒ 45

Exercise 4   School meals: Pupils' health at risk

Complete the text with words from this list:

authorities	diabetes	introduced	provided
bags	diet	lunches	recent
catering	evidence	lunchtime	recruits
choice	fizzy	making	sales
compelled	habits	nutritional	vegetable
damaging	healthy	offer	wholemeal

Schoolchildren eat more chips in their school _____[1] than any other food, despite increasing _____[2] that a high fat diet is _____[3] to health. Chips account for almost a quarter of the _____[4] in the cash cafeterias in Britain's schools. Canned _____[5] drinks, pizzas and biscuits are also high on the list.

Secondary schools which allow children out at _____[6] find themselves competing with the local fish and chip shop and feel _____[7] to offer chips, burgers and fizzy drinks to attract children into the canteen.

School meals, _____[8] at the time of the Boer War because the army was so appalled by the health of its _____[9], have been falling in popularity in _____[10] years. No fewer than half of all pupils eat a school meal at lunchtime.

The cafeteria service at schools is usually _____[11] by a private _____[12] firm. The choice of meals is limited and teenagers often choose foods which are not _____[13] at all: chips, puddings, confectionery and _____[14] of crisps.

Opinions differ about whether a more healthy _____[15] would be popular. Nevertheless, some education _____[16] have made a serious effort to provide a healthier _____[17] in their schools and ensure that the children in their care do not develop the kind of long-term problems, such as obesity, _____[18] and heart disease, that can result from poor eating _____[19].

In some canteens the kitchen staff use only _____[20] oil (unsaturated fat) in cooking, _____[21] flour in baking, and skimmed-milk in dessert-_____[22]. Salad bars are available in some schools and a choice of fresh fruit is always on _____[23]. So pupils are eating a substantial and varied meal with a high _____[24] value.

46 / Consumer/Health

Exercise 5 The British National Health Service (NHS)

Complete the text with words from this list:

afford	cover	emerge	prescriptions
bearable	coverage	examinations	preventive
cabinet	demand	geriatric	succeeded
cancer	discouraged	patient	taxation
care	dismantle	precedent	transplants

At the beginning, the National Health Service was financed entirely out of _____ [1] and there were no charges of any kind to the _____ [2]. This ideal state of affairs did not survive very long, and surprisingly it was the Labour Party which started to give up the principle of free health _____ [3]. Small charges for dentistry and glasses were introduced after a savage political battle which drove Aneurin Bevan, the creator of the NHS, out of the _____ [4]. Bevan argued that any charges, however small, would create a _____ [5] for the introduction of other fees. He was right. Charges for _____ [6] have been increased regularly by successive governments. There are now charges for eye tests and dental _____ [7]. Opponents of the new charges say poor people will be _____ [8] from having important tests. Only the most short-sighted government would impose charges for tests which are an essential part of _____ [9] medicine and could save the NHS money in the long run.

The trouble with the NHS is that although it copes well with emergencies and serious illness like _____ [10], it is not much use if you have a distressing but non-emergency condition like varicose veins. Waiting lists for non-emergency ops are already extremely long.

Part of the problem is the ever increasing _____ [11] for health services. Expensive operations like _____ [12] used to be quite rare. They are now increasing rapidly and so are the lists of people wanting them. New diseases _____ [13] like Aids, which cost a fortune in prevention and care, never mind the cost of looking for a cure. Even more frightening is the growing number of old people who need special _____ [14] care. Thanks to the progress of medicine we live longer, but can the National Health Service make our old age _____ [15]?

We should oppose any plans to _____ [16] the NHS and create an American-style private health service in its place. In the USA one in every four people has no medical _____ [17] and private insurance costs thousands of dollars a year. Today, the NHS is the largest employer in the UK.

Consumer/Health 47

Exercise 6 Synonyms

Find synonyms for the words in italics.

1. You shouldn't *depreciate* the information offered in shopping advice columns.

2. High quality products are easily *discernible* as they bear a quality mark stamped on them.

3. An important *distributor* will always try to sell his own brand of goods.

4. The chairman started to *evaluate* the financial situation of the company.

5. The description on the label of these jeans is *inaccurate*.

6. The *intention* of the writer of this article is to give real objective information.

7. I am convinced of your *loyalty* to the company.

8. You have to sign here and *acknowledge* receipt of the consignment.

9. Economic growth is *advantageous*.

10. His suggestions are based on the *assumption* that the new product will sell better on the market.

11. Many readers *benefit* from the information supplied in shopping advice columns.

12. Housewives today are confronted with a *bewildering* variety of articles offered in the shops.

13. A large number of *commodities* bear a guarantee or trade mark.

14. No manufacturer is *compelled* to give a guarantee mark.

15. We must try to be better than our foreign *competitor*.

16. It's very hard to *conceive* a better marketing policy for our new product.

17. It never pays to *deceive* the consumer with bright and colourful packages.

18. "We are now entering a period of *prosperity* for all!"

48 / Consumer/Health

19. The little corner shop sells only a limited *range* of foodstuffs.

_____

20. During a *recession* the economy of a country is less successful.

_____

21. As an immediate *response* the firm reduced the price of its product by 20 per cent.

_____

22. The most *striking* feature of our new model is its low petrol consumption.

_____

23. Any *transgression* of the British Retail Trade Standards will be prosecuted.

_____

24. The *vast* majority of our customers are satisfied with our products.

_____

Exercise 7   Word families

Supply the missing forms.

noun (abstract)	noun (concrete)	verb	adjective
presidency	president	preside	presidential
advantage	---	---	_____
_____	---	benefit	_____
_____	---	_____	compulsory
_____	consumer	_____	_____
_____	_____	create	_____
difference	---	_____	_____
_____	economist	_____	_____
_____	_____	employ	---
influence	---	_____	_____
_____	---	respond	_____
_____	_____	---	scientific
_____	---	specialize	_____
_____	successor	_____	_____

Consumer/Health 49

exercise 8   Matching words and their definitions

Match the words from list 1 with their appropriate definitions in list 2. Please note: There are more words than definitions!

A temporary decline in economic activity or prosperity

B advertising or other activity intended to increase the sales of a product

C required, expected or accepted level of quality

D person who pays to receive a copy of a newspaper regularly

E person who buys something from a tradesman, shop etc.

F agent who supplies goods to shops in a certain area

G amount paid for professional advice or service, e. g. to private teachers, doctors, etc.

H money spent in doing a specific job, or for a specific purpose

I condition or circumstance that gives one superiority or success (esp. when competing with others)

J box, etc. in which things are packed

K person or firm that makes goods on a large scale using machinery

L advertisement on TV or radio

(1) advantage
(2) commercial
(3) commodity
(4) competitor
(5) customer
(6) distributor
(7) expenses
(8) fee
(9) manufacturer
(10) package
(11) promotion
(12) recession
(13) standard
(14) stock
(15) subscriber
(16) variety
(17) waste

A	B	C	D	E	F	G	H	I	J	K	L

50 / Consumer/Health

Exercise 9   Crossword puzzle

Try to solve the crossword puzzle.

Across
1   telling people about products to buy
4   headline of all police notices
11 to examine
13 opp. of "yes"
14 buyer
15 after midday
16 we don't have your shoe size in …
18 the good English pronunciation: received
    ronunciation
19 to take part in a play
21 United States in Spanish = abbreviation
22 fingers on your hand, and … on your feet
    (singular)
23 Has this cardigan a wool …?
24 to pass sugar or flour through a sieve
25 to have a pain
26 dangerous explosives
27 give up one's work because of age
29 special version of a car (of the VW Golf e. g.)
30 clash between police and demonstrators
31 very small (skirt, computer etc.)

32 Chinese leader (long dead)
33 companies must not … their customers
34 he buys and uses products
35 Adam and … (his beloved one)

Down
1   a tiny animal; first name "Adam"
2   opp. of out
3   not making any profit
5   to judge, to try and find out
6   easily seen
7   money paid for professional advice or service
8   prices just as low as your rival's
9   a special kind of chocolate: fruit and …
10 consumer … is more necessary than ever
12 I've broken my hand, so I can't do any letter …
    for a couple of weeks
16 regular monthly payment to employees
17 Helen is a regular … in Tesco's
20 to warn for danger
28 period of time

Work

1 Word field

account	Konto; Bericht
(to) take into account	berücksichtigen
(to) acquire	erwerben
(to) advertise	ankündigen, inserieren
alienation	Entfremdung
(to) alleviate	Mängel beheben, lindern
appalling	entsetzlich, erschreckend
(to) apply (for)	sich bewerben (um)
apprentice	Auszubildender, Lehrling
apprenticeship	Lehre, Lehrzeit
(to) assemble	montieren
assembly line	Fließband
(to) assess	einschätzen
(to) attach	beilegen; befestigen
(to) avert	abwenden
awareness	Bewusstsein
bankrupt	bankrott
bargain	vorteilhafter Kauf, Gelegenheit
(to) bargain	verhandeln
blackleg	Streikbrecher
blueprint	Blaupause, Modell
board of directors	Verwaltungsrat
breadwinner	Ernährer
(to) broaden	verbreitern, breiter werden
by trade	von Beruf

52 Work

(to) call a strike	Streik ausrufen
career	berufliche Laufbahn, Karriere
careers officer	Berufsberater
chore	Routinearbeit
collective bargaining	Tarifverhandlungen
commerce	Handel
commitment	Engagement
company	Firma
concurrent	gleichzeitig
conveyor belt	Fließband
(to) cope	zurechtkommen
counterpart	Gegenüber
cradle	Wiege
craft	Handwerk, Gewerbe
craftsman	Handwerker
(to) crush	zerquetschen
customer	Kunde
(to) deduct	abziehen
delivery	Lieferung, Zustellung
(to) deprive	jdm. etwas entziehen
(to) dismiss	entlassen
dispute	Streit
disruption	Unterbrechung
diversion	Ablenkung, Unterhaltung
divorce	Scheidung
embedded	verankert, verwurzelt
(to) employ	beschäftigen
employee	Arbeitnehmer
employer	Arbeitgeber
equal opportunities	Chancengleichheit
exploitation	Ausbeutung

extent	Größe, Ausmaß
(to) fire	entlassen, rausschmeißen
foreman	Vorarbeiter
foundation	Stiftung
free enterprise	freie Marktwirtschaft
gender	Geschlecht
(to) hire	einstellen
immaturity	Unreife
implication	Verwicklung, Auswirkung
incentive	Anreiz
industrial action	Arbeitskampf
insufficient	ungenügend, zu wenig
interview	Vorstellungsgespräch
job centre	Arbeitsamt
job creating measure	Arbeitsbeschaffungsmaßnahme
job creation	Arbeitsbeschaffung
job hunter, job seeker	Arbeitsuchender
job market	Arbeitsmarkt
labour costs	Arbeitskosten
labour exchange	Arbeitsamt
lay-off	vorübergehende Entlassung
literacy	Lese- und Schreibfähigkeit
livelihood	Lebensunterhalt
lock-out	Aussperrung
manpower	Arbeitskräfte [Plural]
manufactured goods	Fertigwaren
(to) moonlight	schwarzarbeiten, einen Nebenjob haben
negotiation	Verhandlung, Unterhandlung
notice	Kündigung
numeracy	Rechnen

occupation	Beruf
occupational disease	Berufskrankheit
(to be) on the dole	stempeln gehen
(to) originate	entstehen, seinen Anfang nehmen
outlet	Ausgang, Ausdrucksmöglichkeit; Verkaufsstelle
output	Produktion, Ausstoß
(to) perceive	wahrnehmen
personnel	Belegschaft
picket	Streikposten
place of work	Arbeitsplatz
plant	Anlage, Fabrik
position	Stellung, Posten
poverty	Armut
pre-requisite	Grundvoraussetzung
primary	primär, Haupt-
principal	hauptsächlich
principle	Grundprinzip, Leitsatz
profession	(höherer) Beruf
(to) promote	befördern
prospect	Aussicht
(to) pursue	verfolgen
(to) qualify	befähigen
raise [AE]	Lohn-, Gehaltserhöhung
(to) rate	einschätzen
(to) restore	wiederherstellen
(to) retire	sich zur Ruhe setzen
rise	Lohn-, Gehaltserhöhung
(to) sack	entlassen
salary	Gehalt
shift	Schicht, Arbeitsschicht, Verlagerung
shop-steward	gewerkschaftl. Vertrauensmann

short-time working	Kurzarbeit
skill	Fertigkeit
skilled worker	Facharbeiter
staff	Belegschaft, Personal
staff manager	Personalchef
strike	Streik
strike vote	Urabstimmung
striking	bemerkenswert, auffallend
(to) supplement	ergänzen
supply and demand	Angebot and Nachfrage
surge	Anstieg
trade	Handel
trade union	Gewerkschaft
trade unionist	Gewerkschafter
trainee	Praktikant
unemployed	arbeitslos
unemployment assistance	Arbeitslosenhilfe
unemployment benefit	Arbeitslosengeld
unemployment funds	Arbeitslosengeld
union dues	Gewerkschaftsbeiträge
vacancy	freie Stelle
vocational guidance	Berufsberatung
vocational training	Berufsausbildung
wage(s)	Lohn, Arbeitslohn
white-collar worker	Büroangestellter
wildcat strike	wilder Streik
without notice	fristlos

56 / Work

2 Practice

Exercise 1 Upheaval in the labour lovement

Translate into English or German respectively.

The trade union movement originated in Great Britain in the 19th century. Workers began to organise to *avert* (_____)[1] the social evils which accompanied the otherwise profitable industrial revolution. Mechanization was a doubled-sided weapon. On the one hand it *contributed* (_____)[2] to the economic growth of the industry because production methods were more effective. On the other hand, however, it made life worse for _____[3] (die Hilfsarbeiter). Thousands lost their jobs to machines and were thrown into poverty. As there were *virtually* (_____)[4] no social welfare programmes for the unemployed, the sick, the injured, and the elderly, these _____[5] (benachteiligten) people could only try to find help at private charitable organisations. The situation for the working classes improved when the trade unions began to represent their interests *bargaining* (_____)[6] with the employers about pay, hours of work, employment and insurance. Strike – also called "industrial action" – became their strongest and most hurting weapon. The unions *eventually* (_____)[7] became so powerful that in 1974 they even brought down a Conservative government led by Prime Minister Edward Heath.

The Conservatives never forgave the unions for this sacrilege and started their _____[8] (Feldzug) against unionism. They blamed the system of organised labour for the economic problems of the country, the symptoms of which became known worldwide as the 'British _____[9] (Krankheit)': industrial disruption by numerous strikes, wage inflation, *backwardness* (_____)[10] in production and management and low investment rates. In the 1980s, the Tory government of Margaret Thatcher took on the unions and passed a number of anti-union laws which eventually *crushed* (_____)[11] their influence. As a consequence, union membership fell from more than half of the _____[12] (Arbeiterschaft) in 1979 to less than a third in 1995. Today the Trades Union Congress (TUC) – the central organisation of unions in Britain – *claims* (_____)[13] to represent about 7 million workers. The number of firms recognising unions fell sharply from about two-thirds to less than half. More important, the _____[14] (Beziehung) between employers and those unions that continued to be recognised changed radically. *By and large* (_____)[15]

the unions became more co-operative and began to regard strikes as a last rather than first *resort* (_____)[16].

Like the British parliament, "the cradle of democracy", British trade unionism has served as a blueprint for other countries to establish associations supporting the interests of the working classes. Its principles and practices have become firmly *embedded* (_____)[17] in the economic systems of all non-communist industrial countries. _____[18] (Die Tarifverhandlung) has become the principal means of settling _____[19] (Auseinandersetzungen) about wages and working conditions. Trade unions in the USA, however, have always been different from their British counterparts in as much as U.S. labour unions and their members do not *pursue* (_____)[20] political aims; they have generally supported the capitalist economic order.

Exercise 2   When one job is not enough

In the following text some words are incomplete. Only a couple of letters are given. Try to complete with words that would fit the context.

We talk of moonlighting when somebody works in a second job, usually during hours after the primary job is comp_____[1]. In recent years the number of women who hold more than one job has incr_____[2], whereas the figures for men have changed little in decades. Economists and government officials say that the reasons for the moonlighting surge among women are to be found in social and eco_____[3] shifts. The last two decades have brought a record number of div_____[4] and families maintained by single women, many of whom take two jobs as it is the only way to stay above the po_____[5] line. Single mothers who do not receive any money from the child's father simply have to moonlight to make ends meet. There is also the group of the "working poor"; i. e. people in low paid jobs who work around the clock but whose income from the primary job is insuff_____[6] to pay the bills. They moonlight to earn enough to live dec_____[7].

However, in recent years another trend can be obs_____[8]. While people once moonlighted to simply support themselves, today there are those who take on extra work because their life_____[9] is higher than the primary job allows them to afford. They want to live in a ple_____[10] neighbourhood where rents are high or they want their children to attend better schools which charge fees. These people have become accus_____[11] to a degree of luxury in their lives which they would not like to give up, living well b_____[12] their means. Theoretically they could live on the income they earn in their primary job, but they have become used to spending more on holidays, vac_____[13] homes or perhaps buying new cars.

For others moonlighting is some sort of personal outlet or personal expre_____[14]. They are not looking for extra cash. They see the moonlighting job as a pleasurable dive_____[15]. This explains why many people seek out opportu_____[16] that are very different from their primary employ_____[17]. Take a musician for example who holds a nine-to-five job to earn his living. After his routine office day, he comes alive at night performing in a band.

Today, thanks to the Internet, people can have a moonlighting job any time, even concurrent with a primary job to suppl_____[18] their income. They can work from home using their computer, which makes a second job easier. At any rate, most experts advise people to be realistic about ear_____[19] and always take into account the amount of time involved before taking up a moonlighting position. If the extra job does not leave enough time to rest and regen_____[20] oneself, moonlighting becomes an unbearable chore.

Exercise 3   A safer place of work

In the following text some words are jumbled. To give you some help the first letter of the word in question is given. Try to complete with words that would fit the context.

William is fourteen and works in a (c-t n o o t) _____[1] mill in the Midlands. If you asked him how many hours he works each day, he probably couldn't tell (e-l x c y a t) _____[2]. He usually works from 5 in the morning to 7 at night, but there are times when the factory owner, Mr Bullfinch, keeps him working for as long as he wants him to. There are no (c-s l k o c) _____[3] in the mill, anyway. If William is late for work, he is punished, takes a beating, and has money (d-u e t c d d e) _____[4] from his pay which comes to 2 shillings 3 pence (about 12p). It is very hot in the machine room, much hotter than outside. William does not leave the factory during the day because the (c-o a t t s r n) _____[5] in temperature would make him ill. His friend James was injured last week. His job was to dive in and out of the machinery (p-i n k p g i c) _____[6] up bits of stray cotton. Unfortunately he became entangled in the machinery and lost his left arm. Not only has he suffered this bad (i-y u n j r) _____[7], he has also been sacked from his job, and Mr Bullfinch does not pay for James' medication. A catastrophe for his family as James was the only (b-r e n a w d r e n i) _____[8].

This is what working conditions were like in the early 19th century – until the Factory Acts designed to improve the working conditions of employees, especially women and children, were passed. Michael Thomas Sadler was among the (p-n e s i e o r) _____ [9] of these laws. He had become concerned about the condition of working children when he worked for his brother's company importing Irish linen. Sadler introduced a bill into Parliament that (p-s r d o e o p) _____ [10] limiting the working hours of all persons under the age of 18 to ten hours a day. At first Parliament was unwilling to pass Sadler's bill, but eventually agreed to a parliamentary (e-u n r i q y) _____ [11] into child labour, chaired by Michael Sadler. The committee interviewed 48 people who had worked in textile factories as children. They discovered that it was quite common for children to be working over 12 hours a day in what by today's standards are the most appalling and brutal (c-o d t o s n i i n) _____ [12]. Sadler's fight for social reforms was supported by Anthony Ashley Cooper, 7th Earl of Shaftesbury, later Lord Ashley, who carried out a (s-v y u r e) _____ [13] of doctors and used their comments to persuade Members of Parliament that children could not work more than ten hours without damaging their health. Eventually, in 1847, Parliament passed regulations for factories and coal mines that alleviated the worst (e-i l a n x i o t p t o) _____ [14] of women and children. Shaftesbury also fought to improve working-class housing and was (c-h n m i a r a) _____ [15] for 39 years of the Ragged School Union, an organization that created schools for poor children.

Today there are strict regulations protecting the health and (s-y e a t f) _____ [16] of young people in the workplace. These regulations are based on the (p-l n r i c e i p) _____ [17] that young workers are particularly at risk in the workplace for a variety of reasons, such as their general lack of (e-x e i e n e p r c) _____ [18], their lack of awareness about occupational risks to their health and safety and their possible immaturity. Therefore employers are (r-d u e e q i r) _____ [19] to take these facts into account when they assess the risk of a certain work and (d-n e m e t i e r) _____ [20] whether or not a young person is prohibited from doing such work. The regulations also demand the employer to introduce control measures to reduce health and safety risks.

60 / Work

Exercise 4   Young people's life-skills

Complete the text with words from this list:

acquire	develop	implications	requisite
aesthetic	emerged	perceived	research
attach	essential	promote	stressed
commissioned	extent	prospects	sufficiently
commitment	gender	rated	varying

Young people rate work experience very highly because it helps them to develop the skills they see as _____[1] for all aspects of life, in particular communication and interpersonal skills. This is one of the key findings of _____[2] into young people's views on life-skills published by the Scottish Council for Research in Education. The study, _____[3] by the Lifelong Learning Foundation, looked at young people's views on key life-skills to find out which they consider important, how they believe they _____[4] these skills and how necessary they see them to their future lives.

More than 200 young people aged 16 to 21 from Scotland and the North of England took part. Despite _____[5] social backgrounds, levels of educational qualification, _____[6] of work experience and differences in age, strikingly common themes _____[7]. Young people saw communication and interpersonal skills as the most important for all aspects of life, a view which is shared by employers. Creative and _____[8] skills as well as physical skills were also regarded as important.

Young people understood the need to be _____[9] competent in numeracy and literacy to cope with changing employment possibilities. Otherwise they _____[10] work experience above schooling because they thought it provided more valuable opportunities to develop the life skills which are _____[11] as fundamental. They also saw computer skills as important but were quite confident that they could _____[12] these when necessary. One strong difference related to _____[13]: only young women said that the media, particularly TV and magazines, influenced the development of their personal skills.

Young people _____[14] the fact that life-skills on their own were insufficient, they also recognized the importance of such qualities as _____[15], motivation and patience, and of having pre-_____[16] knowledge to be successful in one's job.

Work 61

All in all, the findings highlight the importance young people _____[17] to work experience. This means that work experience should be developed systematically to _____[18] gains in young people's skills. There are _____[19] also for the long-term unemployed who are at a serious disadvantage. Being out of work they do not have the chance to develop certain life-skills, a fact which certainly limits their employment _____[20].

Exercise 5   Synonyms

Find synonyms for the words in italics.

1. A *blackleg* usually has to suffer a lot of insults from workers who are out on strike.   _____

2. *Commerce* between England and the USA has grown steadily.   _____   _____

3. Tom Birch stands at a *conveyor belt* all day.   _____

4. Mrs Hemming always does her shopping in Tesco's; she's been a regular *customer* for years.   _____

5. I cannot believe that they want to *dismiss* more than 500 people from their jobs!   _____

6. Every morning there is a long queue of job hunters outside the *job centre*.   _____

7. As the new product sold rather well, the firm decided to increase *manpower* in the production plant.   _____

8. More money is earned with the sale of *manufactured goods* than with the sale of primary products.   _____   _____

9. If *negotiations* fail the printers will go on strike and there won't be any newspapers tomorrow.   _____

10. There are rumours about a slight reduction of the *personnel* in the Hendon branch office.   _____

11. If the employers don't pay us more, there will be a *strike* soon.   _____

62 / Work

Exercise 6   Opposites

Find opposites for the words in italics.

1. Many of the *specific* effects of increasing automation are far from clear.   _____

2. The talk is forgotten the day after the unlucky ones have been *sacked*.   _____

3. The best training is done by employers who need to *hire* workers.   _____

4. Due to the benefits of automation in *heightening* efficiency firms will buy more and more machinery.   _____

5. The company got into a situation where it had to *dismiss* workers.   _____

6. The *defeats* at British Leyland have made some union leaders more determined.   _____

7. The *decline* of the economy is gathering speed.   _____

8. Female employment *increased* throughout the 20th century.   _____

9. The *affluent* workers are less concerned about social justice.   _____

10. *Continuing* unemployment is a big problem with serious consequences.   _____

11. The changes in technology *altered* the nature of market work.   _____

12. Some modifications of a "new" product are of slight *benefit* to the consumer.   _____

Exercise 7   Crossword puzzle

Try to solve the crossword puzzle.

Across
1 feeling of despair
8 someone who has more than one job is said to be … lighting
9 main artery through which blood leaves your heart
11 to tell people about a product in newspapers, on TV etc.

Down
2 opposite of hate
3 opposite of "out"
4 you've got two for better hearing
5 when you want to change your working place you have to give … first
6 German: song for one of the leading singers in an opera

Work ⁄ 63

14 meeting at which someone applying for a job is
   asked questions
16 boy's name: the lion
17 make
18 what everyone breathes
19 river in Italy (sorry!)
20 young person who learns a job
23 he saw how the accident happened
27 a "wall" that is built across a river to hold back
   the water
28 determined not to give up
30 terrorist organization in Northern Spain
31 give up one's work because of age
32 American for "tin"
34 talk between employers and trade unions

7 request to supply goods
8 workers
10 controversy
12 to hit an insect with your hand or an object
13 he is in charge of a group of workers
15 person learning a job
21 have you got any … what this is all about?
22 curiosity killed the …
24 German: act, deed
25 German: Happy Easter!
26 during the holidays good old Frieda likes to lie
   in the …
29 one of the two big trade union organizations in
   the USA
33 opposite of "yes"

		1	2	3	4	5	6		7	
	8			9						
10	11					12		13		
14		15				16				
	17				18					
19		20					21	22		
	23		24		25		26	27		
28			29							
	31					32		33		
	34									

Exercise 8   Word families

Supply the missing forms.

noun (abstract)	noun (concrete)	verb	adjective
presidency	president	preside	presidential
_____	_____	apply	_____
attendance	---	_____	_____
bankruptcy	---	---	_____
_____	_____	benefit	_____
_____	businessman businesswoman	_____	_____

64 / Work

competition			
_____	---	convey	---
_____	_____	_____	cooperative
_____	_____	employ	---
execution	_____	_____	_____
_____	industrialist	_____	_____
_____	_____	labour	_____
nation	---	_____	_____
_____	---	_____	vacant

Exercise 9   Matching words and their definitions

Match the words from list 1 with their appropriate definitions in list 2.
Please note: There are more words than definitions!

A occupation in which a particular skill or the use of the hands is needed

B regular fixed payment made to workers of higher rank

C a young person who works with someone in order to learn their skill

D meeting at which someone applying for a job is asked questions

E give up one's job because of age

F talks between employers and trade unions

G person who is in charge of a group of workers

H job that requires special training or a university education, e. g. law and medicine

I unfilled position or post

J not have enough money to pay one's debts

K raise somebody to a higher position or rank

L person controlling a business

(1) apprentice
(2) bankrupt
(3) blackleg
(4) craft
(5) foreman
(6) interview
(7) manager
(8) negotiations
(9) output
(10) picket
(11) profession
(12) promote
(13) raise
(14) retire
(15) salary
(16) shift
(17) skill
(18) vacancy

A	B	C	D	E	F	G	H	I	J	K	L

Science and technology

1 Word field

(to) abate	nachlassen
(to) abide	fortbestehen
(to) accelerate	beschleunigen
(to) access	zugreifen auf
accessible	erreichbar
account	Bericht; Konto
(to) accumulate	ansammeln
advanced	fortschrittlich
aircraft	Luftfahrzeug
(to) alert	alarmieren
angle	Winkel
(to) anticipate	etwas erwarten, mit etwas rechnen
artery	Arterie
(to) assess	einschätzen
barren	unfruchtbar, steril
beam	Lichtstrahl; ausstrahlen, senden
Bluetooth	drahtlose Übertragung
broadband	Breitband
calling card	Telefonkarte
cashless	bargeldlos
celestial	himmlisch, Himmels-
cellphone	Mobiltelefon, Handy
confidential	vertraulich
console	Schaltpult
constituent	Bestandteil
consumption	Verbrauch

66 / Science and technology

cord	Kabel; Netzteil
cost-effective	kostengünstig
debt	Schuld
dedicated connection	Standleitung
device	Gerät
(to) dial a number	eine Nummer wählen
dial-up setting	Einwähleinstellung
disastrous	katastrophal, verheerend
discord	Uneinigkeit
disk	Diskette
drawing-board	Zeichenbrett
(to) emit	abgeben
(to) exceed	überschreiten
excessive	übermäßig
extension	Verlängerung; Nebenanschluss (Telefon)
extensive	weit, ausgedehnt
extra-terrestrial	außerirdisch
forecast	Prognose, Vorhersage
gadgetry	Gerätschaften
gambler	Spieler
gear	Zeug; Zahnrad, Schaltung
handset	Hörer
host	Hauptrechner; Wirt, Gastgeber
hotspot	Hotspot (Sendebereich eines Wireless-LAN-Netzes)
imminent	bevorstehend
impairment	Schädigung
indispensable	unentbehrlich
insoluble	unlösbar, ausweglos

Science and technology 67

instant	Moment
inventive	erfinderisch, einfallsreich
itemized phone bill	Telefonrechnung mit Einzelverbindungsnachweis
IVF	(Abk.: in vitro fertilisation, wörtlich: Befruchtung im Reagenzglas) künstliche Befruchtung
jack	Stecker, Buchse; verbinden
jetliner	Düsenverkehrsflugzeug
letterhead paper	Firmenbriefpapier
limitation	Begrenzung
location-tracking	Standortverfolgung
marketing	Vermarktung
marrow	Knochenmark
mature	erwachsen, reif
messaging	Kommunikation per E-Mail, Mailing
mobile phone	Mobiltelefon, Handy
modification	Änderung
(to) modulate	anpassen
(to) monitor	beobachten, kontrollieren
neuro-	nerven-, Nerven-
option	Wahl
outside line	Amtsleitung
participant	Teilnehmer
(to) patch	etw. flicken
pelvis	Becken
plug	Stecker
post-mortem	Obduktion, Autopsie
power outlet	Steckdose
(to) predict	vorhersagen
prepaid	im Voraus bezahlt, bereits bezahlt
prevalent	vorherrschend
probe	Sonde
prolific	produktiv

68 / Science and technology

(to) purify	reinigen
radiation	Strahlung
reception	Empfang
(to) recharge a battery	einen Akku aufladen
rover	Sonde; Vagabund
runway	Piste, Startbahn
(to) safeguard	jdn./etw. vor etw. schützen
seaboard	Küste
skeleton	Skelett
SMS	(Abk.: Short Message Service) Kurznachricht
stem cell	Stammzelle
supersonic	Überschall-
take-off	Start
(to) tether	anbinden
(to) text	E-Mail schreiben und senden
tissue	Gewebe
(to) transform	verwandeln
transmission report	Übertragungsprotokoll
(to) transmit	übertragen, senden
(to) treat	behandeln
(to) trigger	etw. auslösen
tuner	Empfänger
tyre [BE]	Reifen (tire [AE])
ubiquitous	allgegenwärtig
unattainable	unerreichbar
uninhabitable	unbewohnbar
unique	einzigartig
unpredictable	unvorhersehbar
unsolicited	unerbeten
voltage	elektrische Spannung

Science and technology / 69

2 Practice

Exercise 1 Stem cells – We can rebuild you

Complete the text with words from this list:

arteries	limitations	purified	sufferers
attack	material	radiation	tissue
chromosome	matures	raises	transform
cloning	memory	repair	transplant
concerns	object	research	treatments
diseased	potential	sentence	

The possibility that a damaged or _____¹ organ could be repaired with tissue grown in the lab has increased with reports on the science of stem cells, the most talented cells in the body. Stem cell _____² is hailed as the start of a medical revolution that will lead to new _____³ for diabetes, Parkinson's, Alzheimer's, heart disease and cancer.

Every cell in an early embryo, one smaller than the full stop at the end of a _____⁴, is "totipotent", that is, can give rise to a fully developed organism. After two days, a totipotent stem cell divides, _____⁵ and gives rise to more restricted cells called "pluripotent" stem cells. Prof Fred Gage of the Salk Institute, La Jolla, found that multipotent cells can be grown from post-mortem brain _____⁶ after adding growth factors. The work _____⁷ hopes that such cells, like organs, could one day be taken from the dead – or living brain biopsies – and given to _____⁸ of Parkinson's disease.

In recent years, scientists have started to question long-held beliefs about the _____⁹ of adult stem cells. They can _____¹⁰ themselves into mature cells of other organs such as skeletal muscle, bone and brain. A bone marrow stem cell that can transform itself into almost any _____¹¹ type has been reported by American scientists. One researcher _____¹² bone marrow cells of male mice and took a single cell for transplant into female mice that had their bone marrow destroyed by _____¹³. Eleven months later, the team found male cells in the blood and bone marrow of the surviving female animals, using colour dyes that light up the Y (male)

70 ✦ Science and technology

_____[14]. The Cell study provides the strongest evidence yet that the adult body contains stem cells that are as flexible as embryonic stem cells. The potential of using cells for brain _____[15] has been demonstrated by other work, in which lab-grown human neural stem cells were successfully transplanted for the first time into old rats and significantly improved their _____[16]. Aged rats that had received transplants of the human stem cells, parent cells of nerves, were able to perform memory tasks as well as younger rats without memory impairments, according to the study at the University of Illinois, Chicago.

Doctors have also succeeded in patching up a patient's failing heart using stem cells taken from his bone marrow. Bone marrow stem cells were removed from a 46-year-old man's pelvis and injected into _____[17] near his heart. The cells should have developed into the constituents of blood. Instead, they migrated to areas damaged by a heart _____[18] and turned into healthy muscle cells which began to beat. The operation highlights the _____[19] for adult stem cells as a treatment for many problems. Even patients with the most seriously damaged hearts can be treated with their own stem cells instead of waiting and hoping on a _____[20]. The discovery that stem cell therapy could be more successful than all other previous treatments put together has triggered _____[21] that the development of successful treatments could lead to a level of demand that could be met only by the mass production of human embryos by IVF methods or _____[22]. Pro life campaigners _____[23] to plans to use stem cells taken from embryos as a source of tissue for transplant.

Exercise 2   Concorde: The dream of supersonic flight

Translate into English.

Commercial supersonic flight ended as a _____[1] (Albtraum) in July 2000 when an Air France Concorde _____[2] (abstürzte) outside Paris shortly after takeoff. During takeoff from runway 26 at Roissy Charles de Gaulle Airport, the front right tyre of the left landing gear was damaged and pieces of the tyre were thrown against the aircraft structure, causing a major fire under the left wing. The aeroplane was neither able to climb nor _____[3] (beschleunigen) and crashed onto a hotel nearby, killing all passengers and crew on board. Until that disastrous day, Concorde had been considered as one of the world's safest planes. Its only major scare was in 1979, when a bad landing blew out a plane's tyres. The plane was popular with _____⁴ (Prominenten), world-class athletes and the rich because of its speed, cutting down travelling time from London to New York to about 3 1/2 hours, less than half that of regular _____⁵ (Düsenflugzeugen).

In the sixties military aircraft had demonstrated that speeds, which were not so long before thought to be _____⁶ (unerreichbar), presented no insoluble problem. Why then should not the airliner of the seventies cruise at 1,300 miles per hour, and so _____⁷ (beträchtlich) reduce the travel time between major cities? This challenge to man's technical abilities and _____⁸ (erfinderischen, einfallsreichen) genius was taken up by the British and French Governments in an agreement, signed in November 1962, to _____⁹ (entwerfen, gestalten) and build jointly a supersonic passenger plane, which was given the (hopefully symbolic) name 'Concorde', a word which is common in both languages. The research and development costs, then _____¹⁰ (geschätzt) at between 150 and 170 million pounds and to be shared between the two partners, seemed a small price to pay for day return trips between Europe and the United States. Quite quickly a beautiful aircraft, a masterpiece of technological art, _____¹¹ (nahm Gestalt an) first in sketches and in models, then on the _____¹² (Zeichenbrett). The first Concorde prototype flew early in 1969 and went supersonic in October of that year. On January 21, 1976, British Airway's Concorde Alpha Alpha realised the first commercial flight, carrying passengers from London Heathrow to Bahrain. The plane went through Mach 2 (twice the _____¹³ (Schallgeschwindigkeit) over the Adriatic before landing in Bahrain after 3 hours and 37 minutes. Concorde was _____¹⁴ (verliehen, ausgezeichnet mit) the world speed record for a commercial flight at 1,826.379 km/hr covering the distance from Barbados to London in 3 hours and 42 minutes.

72 / Science and technology

From the beginning critics of Concorde questioned whether supersonic flight offered all the advantages it had been _____ [15] (vermutet, angenommen) to give. They pointed out the disadvantages, and even dangers, that were _____ [16] (untrennbar) from supersonic flight: the sonic boom, the take-off noise, higher fuel consumption, and pollution of the air. Could the side-effects, some known, some _____ [17] (nicht vorhersehbar), and the risk of long-term damage to the environment ever be acceptable? Concorde fans admitted that the plane was noisy, _____ [18] (verglichen mit) new airplanes, that it used more fuel and offered less luxury to passengers. However, they loved Concorde's elegant shape with its characteristic droop nose. Although flights were fully booked BA and Air France lost money just keeping Concorde in service for prestige reasons. In the end, the crash near Paris in 2000 did not only bring a single airliner down, it was also the beginning of the end of the whole project. Despite the fact that after _____ [19] (Änderungen) Concorde took off again, flights were finally stopped in August 2003 and today Concorde planes can only be seen on display in museums around the world. There is no _____ [20] (Nachfolger) in sight.

Exercise 3   **The wireless debt**

Translate into German.

The mobile phone has arrived and caused a wireless revolution, changing the way people communicate. In industrialised nations the technology is *virtually* (_____)[1] ubiquitous: on trains, buses, in cars and in the streets we *constantly* (_____)[2] see and hear people talking on the phone. In less developed countries the numbers of *users* (_____)[3] are increasing too. The secret of the success of the mobile phone lies in its simple *usefulness* (_____)[4]. If you want to phone your friends, family, or business colleagues you no longer need to look for a telephone *booth* (_____)[5], scrabble for small *change* (_____)[6] to feed the public phone – which might be out of order anyway. Keeping in touch with friends has never been easier and text messaging is short and simple. It is not surprising then that the practice of text messaging (SMS = Short Message Service) has *surpassed* (_____)[7] e-mail in popularity. Parents buy cell phones for their kids to increase safety and to keep their eye on them. They can stay in touch with each other more easily and the children can phone for help in case of an accident or in an *emergency* (_____)[8]. Mobiles phone signals can be used to trace the *whereabouts* (_____)[9] of those calling for help. The technology has become so advanced that people can use cellphones for almost anything. Customers make person-to-person *payments* (_____)[10], tourists take pictures, drivers pay for their parking spaces, and gamblers buy their lottery tickets, students answer questions about *coursework* (_____)[11] from home. Indeed, private individuals and business people have become so dependent on their mobiles that 7 out of 10 would *rather* (_____)[12] lose their wallet than their mobile phone.

In view of the advantages and *favourable* (_____)[13] usages the negative sides of this new technology must not be overlooked. *Educators* (_____)[14] claim that because of text messaging standards of *spelling* (_____)[15] and grammar have declined. Some scientists are worried about the safety of mobile phones. They suspect that mobile phone radiation may have a damaging biological effect on human brain cells. Young people love mobile phones, but as they normally do not have a constant income, many of them are running into debt – in particular because of *extensive* (_____)[16] text messaging. Consequently, mobile phone bills have become a challenging issue. About one in six young consumers seeking help from financial counsellors has problems with mobile phone debts. As one researcher put it: "We give health warnings on smoking, but we don't seem to give debt warnings, particularly for 18–24 year-olds using mobile phones. These people *accumulate* (_____)[17] charges without realising it." Therefore parents and educators have approached telecommunication companies and dealers to create *safeguards* (_____)[18] against debt. They demand to stop over-aggressive marketing of cellphones to young people. Companies should also provide standardised and easy to understand *contracts* (_____)[19] which inform young people about the terms, *obligations* (_____)[20], bills, and price changes so that the young users are able to make informed choices about providers. However, the best option to avoid mobile phone debt is a fixed limit on bills or using a prepaid card.

Exercise 4   **Is there life on other planets?**

In the following text some words are incomplete. Only a couple of letters are given. Try to complete with words that would fit the context.

Does alien life exist or are we alone in the uni_____? These are among the most fascinating questions in science and technology. Early speculations about extraterrestrial life included the belief that the Moon and even the Sun were inh_____². In the 19th century the French writer Jules Verne described a fantastic journey to the moon in his popular novel "From the Earth to the Moon" (1865). So did the English science fi_____³ writer H. G. Wells in "The First Men in the Moon" (1901). An American radio dramatisation of H. G. Wells's story "War of the Worlds" in 1938 sim_____⁴ a Martian invasion. The radio play was so realistic that it terrorized listeners and led to pa_____⁵ throughout the Eastern seaboard. What Verne and Wells had dreamed of has long become true: On July 20, 1969, the American space mission Apollo 11 landed the first hu_____⁶ on the moon, only to find that the planet was a barren uninha_____⁷ place. Other speculators concentrated on Mars as the home of "Little Green Men". In 1877 the Italian astronomer Giovanni Schiaparelli described a system of interconnecting channels on the planet. The American astronomer Percival Lowell believed these canals were dug by an adv_____⁸ civilisation to channel water from the frozen polar caps to the "deserts" near the equ_____⁹. However, pictures sent from the United States Mariner probes in 1969 showed many cra_____¹⁰, but nothing resembling manufactured channels or canals.

In 2004 the US space age_____¹¹ successfully landed the twin exploration rovers Spirit and Opportunity on Mars. The two dev_____¹² beamed back pictures of the surface of the Red Planet which made it clear that there can be no life resembling the 'Martians' of popular fictions. However, the geological expl_____¹³ carried out by the rovers proved that there was once water there, so simple life could have once existed. More recent disc_____¹⁴ of methane in the Martian atmosphere makes scientists believe that this could be a sign that some kind of life exists today on Mars.

The universe still holds many my_____¹⁵. Now and again radio telescopes pick up strange signals that modulate in a seemingly unnatural way, leading to the speculation that they may have been tran_____¹⁶ by an alien life form. Are we not alone? Sometimes the source of the signal was found to be an unknown astronomical object, such as a new star. In 1967 two British astrophysicists recorded strange beeping noises which they thought were em_____¹⁷ by some distant extra-terrestrial intelligence. In the end, however, it turned out that they had discovered the first pulsating radio stars – a special group of celestial objects which emit extremely regular pulses of radio waves.

The box-office success of films like E.T. – The Extra-Terrestrial, Blade Runner, the Alien sagas, the Star Wars series on TV, and the whole wave of fantasy films and video games about enc_____¹⁸ with alien life forms prove people's interest in UFOs, androids and alien creatures still exists. Most of us, including

Science and technology 75

the scientists, would be disappointed if all searches for alien life "out there" fai_____[19]. On the other hand, an unsuccessful search would con_____[20] that our Earth is a unique home for intelligence, distinguishing it from the millions and millions of other planets in our Galaxy.

Exercise 5   Video games

In the following text some words are jumbled. To give you some help the first letter of the word in question is given. Try to complete with words that would fit the context.

Video games have come a long way since they first (a-e p a r e d p) _____[1]. "Shoot first, ask questions later" was the usual order of the older (g-n o r t a e n i e) _____[2] of games, the so-called first person shooters. Games and graphics have become much more sophisticated today. Designers use techniques (c-a l m a b r p o e) _____[3] to those in the film industry, with publishers investing millions to put onto a disk what designers have worked out on the drawing (b-a d o r s) _____[4]. Each project requires years of development and a multi-million pound (b-d e g t u) _____[5]. First-class directors and actors are employed to make the interactive (e-p e c r n e i x e) _____[6] for the gamers as realistic as possible. The enormous sums required to produce interactive video games can only be invested by powerful multinational computer (g-a t s n i) _____[7], such as Sony, Nintendo and Microsoft. This explains why the video games industry has become big business. These companies do not only produce and (m-r e a t k) _____[8] the games they also offer the appropriate gaming machines – called consoles. The sales of consoles which are jacked into a TV set have (r-s n e i) _____[9] sharply in recent years and earned makers substantial profits. The advanced PlayStation can be used in different ways, multitasking as a games machine, TV tuner, music system and DVD (r-e c r e r o d) _____[10]. Some devices are so small that you can hold them in your hand and play games, movies and music. More money is earned from games (w-e i b e t s s) _____[11] which offer interactive gaming. Even mobile phone manufacturers are redesigning their devices from simple communication portals into (e-e n t a r t i n e t m n) _____[12] centres.
The technique has changed and so have consumers, the gamers. Gaming (a-c d s e n u i e) _____[13] are getting older and more experienced and interested in technology. In the past, the (a-e a e v r g) _____[14] controller user was seen as a pasty faced, rather lazy and unathletic, slightly

76 ◆ Science and technology

maladjusted (t-a e e e r n g) _____¹⁵. Now the average gamer has an income, a City job and a busy lifestyle. In response, machine, software and application designers are releasing indispensable gadgetry that responds to the needs of this more (m-t r a e u) _____¹⁶ market, in which female players are more numerous than ever. With consoles getting more sophisticated and internet (c-o e t n n i n o c) _____¹⁷ faster thanks to broadband, publishers hope that customers will not stop playing games once they get (b-n y e o d) _____¹⁸ their twenties. They would like to (m-i t i n n a a) _____¹⁹ their audience into their pension years and even try to reach older age brackets as well, making video gaming an accepted part of the entertainment (i-d s r t n y u) _____²⁰ of the 21st century.

Exercise 6   Synonyms

Find synonyms for the words in italics.

1. The electric car had a top speed of 80 mph and could *accelerate* from 0 to 50 mph in less than 7 seconds.   _____

2. Telework may have a lot of advantages, but how do you *assess* its social problems?   _____

3. Silicon and oxygen are the fundamental *constituents*   _____
    of rocks in the earth's crust.

4. The accident which occurred in 1986 at a nuclear power plant at Chernobyl had *disastrous* consequences.   _____

5. The Peace Corps, established by J. F. Kennedy, is looking for young people who are willing to *exceed* their own boundaries.   _____

6. Experts *predict* that there will be a significant loss of   _____
    jobs in the industrialised countries.

7. Girls achieve better results at GCSEs because they *mature* much earlier and take a school more seriously.   _____

8. HRH the Prince of Wales believes that the genetic *modification* of crops is wrong.   _____

9. Gasoline is relatively cheap in America, so living in the suburbs, without public transportation, is an attractive *option*.   _____

Science and technology 77

10. Trees are beautiful, reduce soil erosion and help *purify* the air. _____

11. In the 1950s, the basic policy of the Communist government was to *transform* China into a socialist society. _____

12. One of the Commonwealth's *unique* achievements is the cooperation between its larger and smaller members. _____

Exercise 7   Word families

Supply the missing forms.

noun	verb	adjective	adverb
_____	predict	_____	_____
access	_____	_____	---
_____	_____	confidential	_____
solution	_____	_____	---
alien	_____	_____	---
_____	speculate	_____	---
astronomy	---	_____	_____
mystery	---	_____	_____
_____	_____	fantastic	_____
_____	invade	_____	---
substance	_____	_____	_____
_____	connect	_____	---
_____	appropriate	appropriate	_____
_____	practise	_____	_____
mobility	_____	_____	---

78 ◢ Science and technology

Exercise 8   Matching words and their definitions

Match the words from list 1 with their appropriate definitions in list 2.
Please note: There are more words than definitions!

A   a blood vessel that carries blood from the heart to the body

B   a device which is put into an outlet to make a connection with an electric circuit

C   a person who receives or entertains guests socially, commercially, or officially

D   a person who takes part in an event or a game

E   a region along the coast of a body of water

F   able to be reached or easily obtained

G   an extra telephone line connected to the main line

H   being or appearing to be in all places at the same time; omnipresent

I   good at thinking up new ideas or at devising new objects or methods

J   a physical or mental defect, a damage

K   intended to be kept secret

L   lack of agreement or harmony (as between persons, things, or ideas)

M   not able to be reached or achieved

N   the inner framework of bones in vertebrate animals; it supports the body and protects softer body parts

O   the sending of radio waves; broadcast

P   the soft tissue that fills the hollow centres of most bones

Q   the waves of energy sent out by sources of heat or light, or by radioactive material

R   unable to produce plants or fruit

(1)   accessible
(2)   advanced
(3)   appropriate
(4)   artery
(5)   barren
(6)   challenging
(7)   confidential
(8)   discord
(9)   emergency
(10)   extension
(11)   host
(12)   impairment
(13)   inventive
(14)   marrow
(15)   participant
(16)   plug
(17)   radiation
(18)   scrabble
(19)   seaboard
(20)   skeleton
(21)   structure
(22)   transmission
(23)   ubiquitous
(24)   unattainable

A	B	C	D	E	F	G	H	I	J	K	L	M	N	O	P	Q	R

Crime, law and drugs

1   Word field

(to) abolish	abschaffen
abuse	Missbrauch
accusation	An-, Beschuldigung; Anklage
(to) acquit	freisprechen
addict	Süchtiger
addiction	Sucht
addictive	abhängig, süchtig machen
appeal	Berufung
armed robbery	bewaffneter Raub
(to) arrest	festnehmen
bail	Kaution, Bürgschaft
(to) betray	verraten
bloodshed	Blutvergießen
bribery	Bestechung
burglary	Einbruch, Einbruchdiebstahl
capital punishment	Todesstrafe
charge	Beschuldigung, Anklage
cocaine	Kokain
(to) combat	bekämpfen
(to) condemn	verdammen, verurteilen
confession	Geständnis
confiscate	beschlagnahmen
conspiracy	Verschwörung
(to) contract a disease	sich eine Krankheit zuziehen
convict	Verurteilter, Sträfling

80 ⟋ Crime, law and drugs

conviction	Überzeugung
counsel for the defence	Verteidiger
courier	Kurier
court	Gerichtshof
craze	Manie, Mode
credibility	Glaubwürdigkeit
cross-examination	Kreuzverhör (eines Zeugen)
custody	Gewahrsam, Haft
death penalty	Todesstrafe
defendant	Angeklagter, Beschuldigter
delinquency	Kriminalität
(to) deny	leugnen
dependence	Abhängigkeit
depressant	Beruhigungsmittel
designer drug	synthetische Droge
discourse	Unterhaltung, Vortrag
distorted	entstellt
distribution	Vertrieb
dose	Menge, Dosis
downer	Beruhigungsmittel
drug pusher	Drogenhändler
drug trafficking	Drogenhandel
drug use	Drogengebrauch
drug-related	mit Drogen in Zusammenhang stehend
emotion	Gefühl, Gefühlsregung
endeavour	Anstrengung
eradication	Ausrottung
error of justice	Justizirrtum
(to) evaluate	bewerten
evidence	Beweis
(to) exact	(dringend) fordern, eintreiben

execution	Hinrichtung
exposed	ausgesetzt
(to) facilitate	erleichtern
gaol	Gefängnis
habit	Gewohnheit
harm	Schaden
harmful	schädlich
homicide	Tötung, Mord
hooligan	Rowdy, [jüngerer] Mann, der sich in der Öffentlichkeit flegelhaft aufführt und gewalttätig wird
human rights	Menschenrechte
(to) impair	behindern
imprisonment	Haft-, Gefängnisstrafe
(to) induce	herbeiführen
inhibition	Hemmung
inmate	(Gefängnis-) Insasse, Häftling
innocent	unschuldig
intervention	Eingreifen
intoxicating	berauschend
investigation	(offizielle, polizeiliche) Untersuchung
investigator	Ermittler
judg(e)ment	Urteil
juror	der Geschworene
jury	die Geschworenen
lapse of memory	Gedächtnislücke
lawbreaker	Gesetzesbrecher
lawyer	Rechtsanwalt
lethal	tödlich
moderate	maßvoll
(to) mug	überfallen und berauben
murder	Mord
murderer	Mörder

Crime, law and drugs

narcotics	Rauschgift
narcotics agent	Rauschgiftfahnder
nausea	Übelkeit
nutrients	Nährstoffe
oath	Eid
offence	Vergehen, Verbrechen
offender	Übeltäter
(to) outlaw	für ungesetzlich erklären
overdose	Überdosis
penalty	Strafe
perjury	Meineid
perpetrator	Täter
pickpocket	Taschendieb
(to) plead	vor Gericht plädieren
precaution	Vorsicht(-smaßnahme)
preventable	vermeidbar
prior	frühere(r)
prosecution	strafrechtliche Verfolgung
prosecutor	Anklagevertreter, Staatsanwalt
racketeer	Gangster, Gauner
(to) release	freilassen
(to) relieve	erleichtern
reputation	Ruf, guter Name
research	Forschung
revenge	Rache
riot	Krawall
sentence	Urteil, verurteilen
severe	schwer wiegend, hart
shoplifting	Ladendiebstahl
suicidal	Selbstmord-, suizidal
supply route	Nachschubroute
Supreme Court	Oberster Gerichtshof (USA)

suspect	(Tat-) Verdächtiger
suspicion	Verdacht
(to) take its toll	seinen/ihren Tribut fordern
tension	Spannung
(to) testify	vor Gericht aussagen
token	Zeichen
treason	Hochverrat
treatment	Behandlung
trial	Gerichtsverfahren, Prozess
unanimously	einstimmig
unique	einzigartig
unjust	ungerecht
unlawful	ungesetzlich, rechtswidrig
unparalleled	beispiellos, einmalig
untimely	ungelegen, verfrüht, vorzeitig
violation	Verletzung (von Rechten), Missachtung
(to) vomit	erbrechen
white-collar crime	Wirtschaftsverbrechen
withdrawal treatment	Entziehungskur
witness	Zeuge
wrongdoing	Übeltat

2   Idioms and phrases

to beat s.o. up	Gangs of angry blacks broke into homes, beat people up and attacked their cars.	jdn. zusammenschlagen
to call s.o. names	The boy came crying to his mother as he was called names by his classmates.	jdn. beschimpfen
to have a violent streak	Willie T. acknowledges having a violent streak.	einen Hang zur Gewalttätigkeit haben

84 / Crime, law and drugs

to hold at gunpoint	The bank robbers held the customers at gunpoint.	mit der Waffe bedrohen
to impose punishment	Some people believe the crime rate could be brought down by imposing severer punishment.	eine Strafe verhängen
to jump a trafficlight	A black car jumped the trafficlight and went out of control.	bei Rot über die Ampel fahren
to make a living	Willie T. (26) makes a living out of selling crack.	seinen Lebensunterhalt verdienen
on the straight and narrow	Immigrant parents have always struggled to keep their children on the straight and narrow.	auf dem Pfad der Tugend
to plead guilty (innocent)	The defendant wanted to start a new page in his life: he pleaded guilty.	sich schuldig (unschuldig) bekennen
to return a verdict of (not) guilty	After a three-hour discussion the jury returned a verdict of not guilty.	auf (nicht) schuldig erkennen
to violate a law	The Conservative MP said: "We need the iron fist to prevent the thugs from violating the laws."	ein Gesetz übertreten
to work undercover	British police working undercover in Malmo warned Swedish police that there might be trouble with British hooligans.	getarnt (versteckt) arbeiten

3 Practice

Exercise 1 ### Law and order

Complete the text with words from this list:

analysis	force	prevented	themes
causes	institutions	pursued	victims
changes	nature	remediable	view
determines	obeying	responsible	
emphasis	penalties	ruling	
face	phrase	society	

The attitudes we have towards law and order depend to a substantial degree upon our assessment of what human _____[1] is really like. Some

Crime, law and drugs ✦ 85

philosophers have taken a pessimistic _____ [2]. For Thomas Hobbes human nature was such that in a state of nature, life would be, in his famous _____ [3] "nasty, solitary, brutish and short". Others were more sanguine. Rousseau, for example, believed that "man is naturally good and only by _____ [4] is he made bad". Similarly Marx, following his precept that "environment _____ [5] consciousness", believed that it was the harshness of the capitalist economic system which was _____ [6] for man's shortcomings.

For pessimists like Hobbes, chaotic anarchy could only be _____ [7] through the agency of an all-powerful state, a "Leviathan" which could impose order through overwhelming _____ [8]. For optimists like Marx the problem of lawlessness could only be solved by fundamental _____ [9] in society which would refashion human nature and produce laws based upon fairness and justice rather that the interests of the capitalist _____ [10] class.

The debate about law and order still revolves around these familiar and ultimately unresolvable _____ [11]. Conservatives tend to support the pessimistic or what they would call "realistic" _____ [12]. They believe "respect for the rules of laws is the basis of free and civilized _____ [13]" and see the problem of crime primarily from the viewpoint of the _____ [14] rather than its perpetrators. They support a deterrent strategy, i.e. stiffer _____ [15]. Individuals have free will and should be accountable for their actions. Everyone, rich and poor, has the choice of _____ [16] or breaking the law but if they take the latter course they should be in no doubt as to the penalties they must _____ [17].

Labour and the Democrats tend to take a more optimistic line. They believe that crime has social _____ [18], e.g. poverty, poor housing, unemployment, which are _____ [19] through social policy. Deterrent strategies involving greater police powers and penalties should not be _____ [20] to the point when civil liberties are unacceptably eroded. The criminal has rights too: penal policy should be humanised and more _____ [21] placed on rehabilitation rather than punishment.

Exercise 2   Cybercrime

Translate into English.

Cybercrime is the latest type of what we call "white-collar crime". The term white-collar crime refers to _____ [1] (Verstöße gegen, Verletzungen) of law by persons who use their jobs to engage in illegal activities. In our computer age incidents of high-technology theft and computer-related crime are increasing dramatically and successful _____ [2] (strafrechtliche Verfolgung) will be dependent on the computer skills of the investigators and the appropriate legislation. The US Administration is determined to fight cybercrime with the utmost energy. In the words of former Vice President Al Gore: "Unlawful activity is not _____ [3] (einzigartig) to the Internet – but the Internet has a way of magnifying both the good and the bad in our society. What we need to do is find new answers to old crimes."

The Internet is rapidly transforming the way we communicate, educate, and buy and sell goods and services. As the Internet's potential to provide unparalleled _____ [4] (Nutzen) to society continues to expand, we realize that the Internet can also serve as a powerful new medium for those who wish to _____ [5] (begehen) unlawful acts has also grown.

Unlawful _____ [6] (Verhalten) involving the use of the Internet is just as _____ [7] (untragbar, unerträglich) as any other type of illegal activity. Ensuring the safety and security of those who use the Internet is _____ [8] (so, auf diese Weise) a critical element of the Administration's overall policy regarding the Internet and electronic _____ [9] (Handel), a policy that seeks to _____ [10] (fördern) private sector leadership, technology-neutral laws and regulation, and an _____ [11] (Anerkennung, Wertschätzung) of the Internet as an important medium both _____ [12] (im Inland) and internationally. Indeed, the continued growth and _____ [13] (Heranreifen) of this new medium depends on our taking a balanced approach that _____ [14] (sicherstellt) that the Internet does not become a haven for unlawful activity. [...]

_____ [15] (Frühere, Vorige) technological advances – the automobile, the telegraph, and the telephone, for example – have brought dramatic improvements for society, but have also created new opportunities for _____ [16] (Übel-, Missetaten). The same is true of the Internet, which provides opportunities for socially beneficial _____ [17] (Anstrengungen, Bemühungen) – such as education, research, commerce and entertainment. However, individuals who wish to use a computer as a tool to _____ [18] (erleichtern) unlawful activity may find that the Internet provides a vast, inexpensive, and potentially anonymous way to commit unlawful acts, such as _____ [19] (Betrug), the sale or distribution of child pornography, the sale of guns or drugs and the unlawful distribution of computer software or other creative material protected by intellectual _____ [20] (Eigentumsrechte).

Crime, law and drugs ⁄ 87

Exercise 3 Hanging people is wrong

Only one or a couple of letters are given. Try to complete with words that would fit the context.

Every year around 100 Americans are poisoned, hanged, gassed, shot or electrocuted in US prisons. In 1972 the US Supreme Court ruled that capital punishment was "cruel and unusual punishment" and therefore unconstitutional. However, in 1976, after the federal government and 35 states had enacted new death penalty laws, the Court ruled that capital punishment did not violate the Constitution, thus confirming its legitimacy for murder convictions. The nation is still divided on this fundamental issue. Executing criminals by hanging was once the most common means of execution in the United States, but today it remains the statutory method only in Delaware, Montana, New Hampshire, and Washington.

Whether they kill for gain, or for 'poli_____[1]' ends, or both, murd_____[2] are risk-takers. Even the man who plants a bomb in a car and walks away risks his life. He may blow him_____[3] up, in making or carrying the bomb. Many have peri_____[4] in that way, and we need not weep for them. Simil_____[5], an armed man who com_____[6] a crime runs a risk of bei_____[7] shot while being pursued or when trap_____[8].

Would people prepa_____[9] to run 'immediate' risks of that kind be likely to be dete_____[10] by the more remote risk of a death-sentence? Hardly. Murderers, as well as being risk-takers, are also opti_____[11]: otherwise they would already be deterred by the thought of a life-sentence. The murderer expe_____[12] not to be caught, and if he's caught he expects his law_____[13] somehow to get him off. Neither expectation is altog_____[14] unrealistic, and neither is weakened in the sligh_____[15] by the restoration of the death sentence.

It is hard to believe in the existence of the poten_____[16] murderer who says to himself: "I'll run the risk of being blown up in the cou_____[17] of committing my crime. I'll run the risk of being caught, of being convi_____[18], and serving a life-sentence in jail. But the risk of being han_____[19] – if I am caught and if I am convicted – is too much. I wo_____[20] do it." Yet unless you think it prob_____[21] that people will react in that way, there is no case for restoration of the death pena_____[22].

It is argued that the return of hanging would actu_____[23] help the terrorist organisations by fuelling their prop_____[24] machine. If there are terrorists who would be put off by the fear of hanging, the terrorist organisation would func_____[25] just as well, or better, without them.

88 / Crime, law and drugs

Basically, however, what is at sta_____²⁶ is the principle of respect for hum_____²⁷ life. The State best upholds that princ_____²⁸ by itself respecting human life, even in the person of the most blood-thir_____²⁹ criminal convicted in its courts.

Exercise 4   Synonyms (Law)

Find synonyms for the words in italics.

1. Many people are convinced that *capital punishment* should be *abolished* in all countries.   _____

                                                                        _____

2. When someone *betrays* his country he helps its enemies.

3. As the members of the Royal Family are so rich *bribery* is simply out of the question.   _____

4. The defendant can prove that the *charges* against him are false at a preliminary hearing after his arrest.   _____

5. You should never *condemn* a person out of hand.   _____

6. The Weymouth brothers were accused of *conspiracy* to murder Mrs Jean Shivery.   _____

7. Most *convicts* serve only a fraction of their prison terms before they are released.   _____

8. There is clear *evidence* that Jim Clayton set fire to the house of the Miller family.   _____

9. The judge tried to *exact* a confession from the criminal.   _____

10. The pickpocket was sent to *gaol* for three months.   _____

11. Last year, the number of *inmates* in state and federal prisons grew by 26,000 to a record 463,000.   _____

12. The investigation proved that H.M. Swindon is *innocent*, so the police will *release* him immediately.   _____

13. Many people maintain that sometimes *law-breakers* do not receive the same punishment for the same crime.   _____

14. Miss Marple solved more than one *murder case* in the little village where she lived.   _____

Crime, law and drugs ✦ 89

15. The judge announces the *penalty* after receiving
    reports of the defendant's background.   _____

16. The defendant in a *trial* is the person who has been
    accused of a crime.   _____

17. He thought it very *unjust* when authorities wanted to
    confiscate his property.   _____

Exercise 5   Cocaine business

In the following text some words are incomplete. Only one or a couple of letters
are given. Try to complete with words that would fit the context.

Crack sold in Europe or the USA is produced from cocaine, which has been
trafficked to the countries; crack itself is rarely imported. Most of the world's
cocaine is produced in South America with Colombia being the predominant
producer. It is believed that about 40–50 tonnes of cocaine are shipped to the
UK annually.

Peru's former President Alan García once called the cocaine business "Latin
America's only successful multinational." He was right. A Latin American-
contr_____[1] operation lin_____[2] the fields of coca bushes on the tropical
eastern side of the An_____[3] in Peru and the low hills in Bolivia to the
whole-sale distri_____[4] networks in New York, Los Angeles and Spain.

Its corporate headq_____[5] is in Colombia, particularly in the cit_____[6] of
Medellin and Cali, and it is the Colombians who have set up the all-important
supply rou_____[7] and distribution chan_____[8]. By the early 1970's, the
region was smuggling a different kind of gold to the US: Santa Marta Golden,
as Colombia's top quality mari_____[9] was known. Later in the decade, the
smugglers were asked by their North American contacts to sup_____[10]
cocaine. In little more than ten years, a fash_____[11] for cocaine and the
peculiar organisational genius of a group of gang_____[12] from Medellin have
turned drug trafficking into a multi-billion dollar business.

Since it is ill_____[13], cocaine has generated super-profits, with marks-up of
up to 1,000 per cent at each link in the supply chain. These super-profits are
also one rea_____[14] that cocaine has scattered a kaleidoscope of violence
across the Andean countries. It is in Colombia, with a long trad_____[15] of
political violence, that drug-rel_____[16] bloodshed has peaked. This is because
it is here that most of cocaine's profits are ear_____[17] and it is here that
repression has been at its most effective.

For most of the past ten years, the US has atte_____[18] to fight its battle against drugs largely on Latin American soil, in a failed effort to squeeze prod_____[19]. It has done so without putting up enough ca_____[20]. The Washington government gave the Colombian narcotics police just $ 10 million a year, which is roug_____[21] what Colombia's most powerful drug baron earns in a day. Even less was spent in Peru. Trafficking networks were not serio_____[22] disrupted there, but the forcible eradi_____[23] of coca fields caused sufficient resent_____[24] to help the Maoist guerillas of Sendero Luminoso to increase their physical and political infl_____[25].

Exercise 6 Nicotine – a powerful and addictive drug

Complete the text with words from this list:

addictive	example	kidneys	quit
consumption	executive	outlawed	revenge
contracted	funded	preventable	taxes
disagreement	gathered	primarily	toll
encourage	harms	promotion	untimely

As youngsters they smoked like chimneys – as they got older their bodies took _____[1]. Rock stars like Rod Stewart, George Harrison and Charlie Watts were all heavy smokers and all of them _____[2] cancer.

News about an ageing pop star's illness or _____[3] death sheds light on the damaging effects of heavy smoking. In the early 1960s researchers established scientific proof that smoking is _____[4] and causes several diseases including cancer of the lungs and larynx. Later studies confirmed the deadly connection, adding that smoking _____ [5] the babies of women who smoke and causes disease in almost every organ in the body: cervix, _____ [6], pancreas and stomach. It kills more people than the combined _____ [7] of AIDS, cocaine, heroin, alcohol, fire, automobile accidents, homicide, and suicide. The only good news for smokers is that their health begins to improve immediately after they stop. Consequently, knowing that smoking is a _____ [8] cause of death and disease, health officials try to _____ [9] people to give up smoking.

But how best can you make people _____ [10] smoking? Experts evaluated the effectiveness of several types of tobacco control: higher taxes on cigarettes; bans on advertising and _____ [11] of tobacco products, anti-smoking education and smoking restrictions in public and work places. New York has set a radical example: smoking is _____ [12] from bars and restaurants and smokers in many states feel almost criminalised today. California _____ [13] a comprehensive anti-tobacco media campaign, _____ [14] aimed at young smokers. In a rather drastic TV advert two young boys aged 10 and 13 described what it was like to lose their father to lung cancer. In another TV ad an actor playing a tobacco _____ [15] said to his colleagues _____ [16] in a boardroom, "We need 3,000 kids to start smoking every day to replace the people who die every year from cigarettes." The campaign was successful and lung cancer rates dropped in California.

There is _____ [17] about the effectiveness of raising prices for cigarettes. Some researchers argue that increasing taxes on cigarettes is a very effective way to decrease _____ [18]. But there are others who point out that there are more smokers in European countries than in the United States, even though Europe has higher _____ [19] on cigarettes.

Probably the most effective way to keep children from taking up smoking is the _____ [20] of their parents at home. Children are likely to stay nonsmokers, when they grow up in environment where it is not normal to smoke.

Exercice 7   **Alcohol is a drug**

Translate into German.

Alcohol abuse and alcohol dependence are not only adult problems – they also affect a significant number of adolescents and young adults between the ages of 12 and 20, even though drinking under the age of 21 is illegal in every State of the USA. The US Department of Health and Human Services informs young people about the dangers of the drug alcohol.

Get the facts …
Alcohol affects your brain. Drinking alcohol leads to a loss of coordination, poor judgment, slowed reflexes, *distorted* (_____)[1] vision, memory *lapses* (_____)[2], and even blackouts.

Alcohol affects your body. Alcohol can damage every organ in your body. It is absorbed directly into your *bloodstream* (_____)[3] and can increase your risk for a variety of life-threatening diseases, including cancer.
Alcohol affects your self-control. Alcohol depresses your central nervous system, lowers your *inhibitions* (_____)[4], and *impairs* (_____)[5] your judgment. Drinking can lead to risky behaviors, such as driving when you shouldn't, or having unprotected sex.

Alcohol can kill you. Drinking large amounts of alcohol at one time or very rapidly can cause alcohol *poisoning* (_____)[6], which can lead to coma or even death. Driving and drinking also can be deadly. In 2002, 29 percent of drivers age 15 to 20 who died in traffic accidents had been drinking alcohol.

Alcohol can hurt you – even if you're not the one drinking. If you're around people who are drinking, you have an increased risk of being seriously injured, involved in car crashes, or *affected* (_____)[7] by violence. At the very least, you may have to deal with people who are sick, out of control, or unable to take care of themselves.

Before you risk it ...

Know the law. It *is illegal* (_____)[8] to buy or possess alcohol if you are under age 21.

Get the facts. One drink can make you *fail* (_____)[9] a breath test. In some States, people under age 21 can lose their driver's license, be subject to a heavy *fine* (_____)[10], or have their car permanently taken away.

Stay informed. *"Binge" drinking* (_____)[11] means having five or more drinks on one occasion. Studies show that more than 35 percent of adults with an alcohol problem developed symptoms – such as binge drinking – by age 19.

Know the risks. Alcohol is a drug. Mixing it with any other drug can be extremely dangerous. Alcohol and acetaminophen – a common *ingredient* (_____)[12] in OTC pain and fever reducers – can damage your liver. Alcohol mixed with other drugs can cause *nausea* (_____)[13], vomiting, fainting, heart problems, and difficulty breathing. Mixing alcohol and drugs also can lead to coma and death.

Keep your edge. Alcohol is a *depressant* (_____)[14], or downer, because it reduces brain activity. If you are depressed before you start drinking, alcohol can make you feel worse.

Look around you. Most teens aren't drinking alcohol. Research shows that 71 percent of people 12–20 haven't had a drink in the past month.

Know the signs ...

How can you tell if a friend has a drinking problem? Sometimes it's *tough* (_____)[15] to tell. But there are signs you can look for. If your friend has one or more of the following warning signs, he or she may have a problem with alcohol:

- Getting drunk on a regular basis
- Lying about how much alcohol he or she is using

94 ◢ Crime, law and drugs

- Believing that alcohol is necessary to have fun
- Having frequent *hangovers* (_____)[16]
- Feeling run-down, depressed, or even suicidal
- Having "blackouts" – forgetting what he or she did while drinking.

What can you do to help someone who has a drinking problem? Be a real friend. You might even save a life. Encourage your friend to stop or seek professional help.

Exercise 8   **Matching words and their definitions**

Match the words from list 1 with their appropriate definitions in list 2. Please note: There are more words than definitions!

A   stealing money or goods without using violence or force

B   a person lending money at illegally high rates of interest

C   breaking into a house and stealing things from it

D   telling lies in court

E   person who cannot live without drugs

F   route patrolled regularly by a policeman

G   imprisonment while awaiting trial

H   taking of goods by force through legal authority

I   make somebody decide not to do something

J   wilful and senseless destruction of public or private property

K   wooden framework used for hanging criminals

L   pair of metal rings for fastening round the wrists of prisoners

(1)   addict
(2)   arrest
(3)   beat
(4)   burglary
(5)   court
(6)   custody
(7)   delinquent
(8)   detention
(9)   deter
(10) enforcement
(11) gallows
(12) handcuffs
(13) loan shark
(14) perjury
(15) prostitution
(16) seizure
(17) vandalism
(18) white-collar crime

A	B	C	D	E	F	G	H	I	J	K	L

Crime, law and drugs 95

Exercise 9   Synonyms (Drugs)

Find synonyms for the words in italics.

1. The US has attempted to fight its battle against drugs largely on Latin American *soil*.   _____

2. The *dependence* caused by marijuana is not so *severe* as that resulting from heroin.   _____

3. Drugs are used to *relieve* fear, tension and to forget problems.   _____

4. Drug *racketeers* make enormous profits, pushing young people into misery.   _____

5. Drugs cannot be taken in a *moderate* way.   _____

6. Many young addicts took a *lethal* overdose to end their misery.   _____
_____

7. Drugs *induce* strong euphoric feelings.   _____

8. Many youngsters are not aware of the *harmful* consequences of drug-taking.   _____

9. Gangsters from Medellin have turned drug *trafficking* into a multi-billion dollar business.   _____

10. Drug *pushers* often approach young boys ands girls to sell them the deadly stuff.   _____

11. *Designer drugs* are developed in chemical laboratories.   _____

12. Crack cocaine is the *primary* addiction of pregnant women, although many use other drugs well.   _____

13. It is in Colombia, with a long tradition of political violence, that drug-related *bloodshed* has peaked.   _____

14. The US President promised to *combat* drug trafficking.   _____

15. Although the dependence caused by marijuana is not so severe as that resulting from heroin, it is nevertheless hard to *cure*.   _____

Exercise 10 Crossword puzzle

Try to solve the crossword puzzle.

Across
1 burglars always wipe glasses to avoid them (12)
5 lie in a court of law (7)
12 only for a time (11)
13 you say that it is not true (4)
14 Brit. special tax (3)
15 he came in from the cold (3)
17 steals things from people's handbags (10)
23 to … for president (3)
24 legal process before a judge (4)
26 girl's name (3)
27 nickname for a Conservative (4)
28 discourage (5)
29 clash between police and demonstrators (4)
30 capital punishment (12)

Down
1 people who officially take someone else's child (13)
2 Federal Bureau of … (FBI) (13)
3 money collected by the state (3)
4 stealing from a shop (11)
6 group of people in a court who decide whether the person accused is guilty (4)
7 vote (6)
8 Chairman of the House of Commons (7)
9 secret planning of a group of people (10)
10 Mr Sinatra's first name (5)
11 he saw how the accident happened (11)
16 method of curing (9)
18 American singer, formerly together with Sunny Bono (4)
19 to plan, to intend (8)
20 Romeo loved her dearly (6)
21 gaining money by trickery (5)
22 opposite of innocent (6)
25 member of the nobility; has a seat in the Upper House (4)

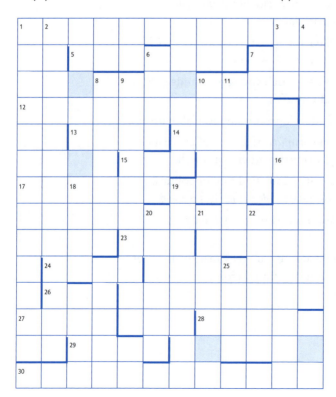

Politics in Great Britain

1   Word field

(to) abdicate	abdanken
(to) abolish	abschaffen
allegiance	Ergebenheit, Treue, Loyalität
ambassador	Botschafter
backbencher	einfaches Mitglied des Unterhauses
ballot	Stimmzettel; geheime Wahl
(to) banish	verbannen
bill	Gesetzentwurf
budget	Staatshaushalt, Etat
by-election	Nachwahl
campaign	Wahlkampf
challenger	Herausforderer
committee	Ausschuss
community	Gemeinschaft
(to) conceive	planen, ausdenken
conscience	Gewissen
constituency	Wahlkreis
constitution	Verfassung
constitutional	verfassungsmäßig
convention	Versammlung
(to) convince	überzeugen
coronation	Krönung
declaration	Erklärung, Verkündung
dependent	abhängig
(to) derive (from)	herleiten
(to) deserve	verdienen

dictatorship	Diktatur
(to) dissolve	auflösen
(to) dominate	beherrschen
electoral system	Wahlsystem
electorate	Wählerschaft
eligible (to)	berechtigt
embassy	Botschaft
emperor	Kaiser
(to) ensure	garantieren
executive	ausführende Gewalt
(to) exert	ausüben
expenditure	Ausgabe, Aufwand
(to) exploit	ausbeuten, ausnutzen
extract	Auszug
federal	Bundes…
Foreign Office	Außenministerium
foreign policy	Außenpolitik
Foreign Secretary	Außenminister
frontbencher	führender Politiker
general election	allg. Wahl
head of state	Staatsoberhaupt
hereditary	erblich, Erb-
Home Office	Innenministerium
Home Secretary	Innenminister
House of Commons (Lower House)	Unterhaus
House of Lords (Upper House)	Oberhaus
human rights	Menschenrechte
hurdle	Hindernis
impartial	unparteiisch
incompetent	unfähig

incumbent	amtierend
(to) instruct	anweisen
(to) interfere	sich einmischen
involved	kompliziert
irrelevant	unerheblich, belanglos
issue	Streitfrage
judiciary	Richterstand
legislature (legislative)	gesetzgebende Gewalt
local election	Kommunalwahl
(to) make a speech	eine Rede halten
Member of Parliament	Parlamentsabgeordneter
merit	Verdienst
minutes	Protokoll
motion	parlamentarischer Antrag
(to) nationalize	verstaatlichen
(to) negotiate	verhandeln
(to) nominate	aufstellen
obsolete	veraltet
opponent	Gegner
(to) overthrow	stürzen, umstürzen
overwhelming	überwältigend
(to) pass (a bill)	(ein Gesetz) verabschieden
patronage	Schirmherrschaft, Unterstützung
peer	Angehöriger des britischen Hochadels
peerage	Peerswürde, Adelstitel
platform	Parteiprogramm
policy	Politik, Taktik
politician	Politiker
politics	Politik, Staatskunst
poll	Wahl; Umfrage

polling booth	Wahlkabine
polling day	Wahltag
polling station	Wahllokal
precaution	Vorsichtsmaßnahme
previous	vorherig, vorhergehend
prime minister	Premierminister
proportional representation	Verhältniswahl
proposition	Vorschlag, Antrag
redundant	überflüssig
(to) reign	herrschen
(to) renounce	aufgeben
representative	Vertreter
reputation	Ruf
(to) resign	zurücktreten
(to) resist	Widerstand leisten
resolution	Beschluss
royal	königlich
session	Sitzungsperiode
shortcoming	Mangel
sovereign	Herrscher
Speaker	brit. Parlamentspräsident
splinter party	Splitterpartei
(to) stem (from)	stammen
summit	Gipfel
(to) summon	einberufen
(to) suppress	unterdrücken
term	Amtszeit, Sitzungsperiode
Tories	brit. Konservative
treaty	Vertrag
turnout	Wahlbeteiligung
tyrant	Diktator

Politics in Great Britain 101

urge	Verlangen
violation	Verletzung, Bruch
viscountcy	Viscountwürde
vote	Abstimmung
wing	Flügel

2 Practice

Exercise 1   Electoral geography of Great Britain

Translate into English or German respectively.

A major *feature* (_____)[1] of the electoral geography of Great
Britain since the *achievement* (_____)[2] of the universal adult
_____[3] (Wahlrechts) in 1928 has been the continuity in the
geography of support for the various political parties, especially Conservative
and Labour. There have been _____[4] (deutliche, erkennbare)
variations in the percentage of votes won by the parties over the last decades,
but these have not *affected* (_____)[5] the political landscape,
though its amplitude has shifted up and down as support for a particular party
either waxed or _____[6] (abnahm).
This continuity has been accounted for by proposing a class *cleavage*
(_____)[7] between the blue-collar, manual workers (or working
class), most of whom voted Labour, and the *white-collar* (_____)[8],
non-manual workers (or middle class), almost all of whom voted Conservative; the Liberal party was mainly the _____[9] (Empfänger) of
temporary protest votes, and *lacked* (_____)[10] continuity of support from particular segments of society. This class divide was generally
assumed to be uniform _____[11] (überall in) Britain; electors in
the same class were assumed to vote the same way, wherever they lived.
But the traditional class divide has been broken, and many more voters now
_____[12] (bewerten, einschätzen) parties anew at each election *in
terms of* (_____)[13] their current policies/performance/leaders,
rather than voting _____[14] (gewohnheitsmäßig) for the same
party, which was believed to occur in the past. People carefully evaluate
competing (_____)[15] party claims every time they vote. Such
political evaluation is set in the context of a general set of political
_____[16] (Einstellungen), which develop during childhood and

early adult years; but with both greater social mobility and rapid economic and social change those attiudes _____ [17] (wandeln sich) over time. Thus people are no longer so _____ [18] (eng) identified with particular parties, and they are increasingly prepared to vote in ways *inconsistent* (_____)[19] with their socialised general beliefs or *ideologies* (_____)[20] because of their evaluation of the present party leaders and policies.

Exercise 2 The British Parliament today

Fill in the blanks!

British Parliament consists of two houses: the House of Commons, which is also called the _____ [1] House, and the House of Lords or _____ [2]. This is why we speak of a two-_____ [3] system.

There are _____ [4] Members in the House of Commons, each elected in individual _____ [5] by a _____ [6] vote. General elections take place every _____ [7] years (usually); there are also _____ [8] which are held when a Member died or was _____ [9]. The monarch _____ [10] Parliament on the _____ [11] of the _____ [12] Minister.

Politics in Great Britain 103

When you are eighteen you have the right to vote or _____[13].
You go to your local _____[14] station in your constituency and
_____[15] your vote.
The main function of the House of Commons is to _____[16] government; i. e. to discuss _____[17] and budgets. Members of Parliament
(M.P.s) either belong to H_____ M_____'s[18] Government and its ruling party or to the _____[19]. The nickname for
the Conservatives is _____[20].
In the House of Lords, which originally was more important than the House
of Commons, we have _____[21] peers and life peers. In theory
the Lords could _____[22] legislation but they hardly ever do.
More important is that they are the highest Court of _____[23] in
Britain. As no _____[24] are paid, only wealthy peers can attend
the sessions all the time. If a Lord wants to become a Member of the House of
Commons he has to _____[25] his peerage.

Exercise 3   Farewell to the Lords

Complete the text with words from this list:

allegiance	dependent	interfere	peerage
balance	deserve	merits	protest
banished	dutifully	minority	seats
check	enthusiasts	motion	survive
common	exerted	mourn	urban

The tradition of the House of Lords – the upper chamber of Great Britain's
bicameral legislature – dates back to the 13th and 14th centuries. Its members
comprised representatives of the church and the nobility, in particular hundreds of hereditary peers. Until 1999 more than 1,170 members qualified to
sit in the House of Lords. In that year Parliament passed the House of Lords
Act, which disqualified all hereditary peers for membership in the House,
with the exception of 92 individuals who had been elected by their fellow
peers and were allowed to retain their seats on a temporary basis. In a farewell
tribute one commentator said:
"The character of the House of Lords will never be the same again after the
reduction of the number of hereditary _____[1]. As expected, it is
largely the most party-politically minded of the hereditaries who have been
elected to _____[2]. The 600-odd who are to be _____[3]

include most of those who have no strong _____ [4] to any party, and no particular interest in politics. In that respect, they have far more in _____ [5] with the great majority of the British people than the political _____ [6] who are to dominate the legislature from now on.

It is not our purpose to discuss the _____ [7] or shortcomings of those who have survived the cull*. Rather, this is the moment to _____ [8] the banishment of the 600 who are to be sent packing to their country estates, farms, suburban terraces and council houses. We want to say how sorry we are to see them go. We also want to thank them.

Some of the banished hereditaries, of course, have never taken their _____ [9] in the Lords. But even they _____ [10] a grateful pat on the back, if only for their humility in resisting the urge to _____ [11] where their consciences told them that they had nothing of value to contribute.

But the nation's warmest thanks are due to those who have turned up _____ [12], year after year, to listen to the arguments in the House, and vote for what they thought was right. The hereditary peers, _____ [13] on nobody's patronage for their place in the legislature, have _____ [14] an almost wholly benign influence on the life of the nation over at least the past two centuries. They have done very little harm while doing a great deal of good. They have protected _____ [15] interests – particularly those of the countryside, which in a democracy dominated by the _____ [16] masses would never have had a proper hearing without them. Certainly, there have always been a number of crackpots among them, but how much sadder a nation this will be when eccentrics are denied a hearing in public life.

Above all, the hereditary peerage has proved an effective _____ [17] on the errors and excesses of elected politicians. This week Tony Benn, who renounced his father's viscountcy in _____ [18] at the hereditary peerage, is to propose a _____ [19] in the Commons regretting how few checks and balances remain on the power of the executive in Mr Blair's Britain. With the banishment of the 600, British politics will become a business almost exclusively for professionals. And the most effective constitutional _____ [20] of them all – the disinterested vote of the fairminded amateur – will never carry the same weight again."

Exercise 4 A visit to the House of Commons

In the following text some words are incomplete. Only one or a couple of letters are given. Try to complete with words that would fit the context.

When you visit the House of Commons in London you go up to the Strangers' Gallery. There you are given a leaflet which explains the seating arrangement, the traditional procedures, etc. Besides, in a "Personal Message" the Chairman of the House, Mr Speaker, addresses the visitor. In 1992 the House of Commons broke with tradition and for the first time in its 700-year history elected a woman to be its Speaker. Ms Betty Boothroyd, Labour MP for West Bromwich West served the House as Speaker for more than eight years until her retirement in 2000; she was also the first Speaker for more than 100 years to be chosen from one of the opposition parties.

A personal message from Mr Speaker
"The scene you are loo_____¹ at today comprises a number of Members at wo_____². These Members have been ele_____³ to this House as the repre_____⁴ here of a free people. Their lin_____⁵ are many. First – they each represent their consti_____⁶ – some 50,000 citizens – and not only those who have voted for them, but also those who have voted ag_____⁷ them.

106 / Politics in Great Britain

Next, it is the du_____8 of Members to crit_____9 and control the Government of the day. Some of them, however, have been appo_____10 as the Queen's Ministers, and they have to subm_____11 to this criticism and answer it. All of them are gui_____12 by the traditions of which the Speaker is guar_____13. These traditions go back in an unbro_____14 chain for over six hundred years. The strongest of them is that the House of Commons poss_____15 freedom of debate – the right to spe_____16 for or against any proposal.

This House displ_____17 its work, for better or wo_____18, to the critical scrutiny of people not only from this country but from all ov_____19 the world. For that reason I wel_____20 your visit here today."

Exercise 5 **How to be a new MP**

Complete the text with words from this list:

applicants	elected	meeting	room
arena	improving	memory	sharing
character	institution	modest	sounds
contribute	job	Opposition	speaker
crowds	longer	palace	supporter
decide	lucky	Prime	things
distinguished	maiden	reminded	
ease	matter	rituals	

When newcomers to the Commons step into the _____1, many find that they are not the _____2 gladiators they thought they were. For a start, they are no _____3 heroes. Cheering _____4 and back-slapping constituency supporters dim in the _____5 as they enter the most adaptable and mercurial _____6 in the land. They can be long or short, gentle or tough, _____7 or pompous; the House will accommodate them with the _____8 of an elephant swallowing a gnat.

At the first _____9 of their Parliamentary Party, usually in a large committee _____10, they listen to eulogies for the _____11 Minister, or consoling words for the Leader of the _____12. The new MP has no time to waste since he has to consider the job he was _____13 to do and to learn to find his way round Westminster. This is less easy than it _____14 because the Chamber, although

the central and most dramatic focal point, is but one part of the a _____ 15
which covers ten acres with five miles of corridors and 2,000 rooms.

The new Member's first _____ 16 is to find his room but, unless
he is _____ 17, he may find himself with only a desk and filing cabinet, _____ 18 a corridor with a dozen others. Conditions are slowly
_____ 19 but Parliament like the public schools seem to assume
that Spartan life is good for _____ 20. Those who complain are
_____ 21 by an impatient public of the queue of _____ 22
for their job.

Few, but very few, Members impress the House with a _____ 23
speech. Yet it is just at that moment, when the new Member is most derisive
of the Parliamentary _____ 24, that he is helped by them. For one
of the most revered is that a maiden speaker, no _____ 25 how
poor his speech, is complimented by the following _____ 26.

Thereafter, feeling baptised, new Members _____ 27 as best they
can. Only they can make their value judgment and _____ 28 their
role – to be a loyal party _____ 29, rebel, constituency man, headline catcher, champion of the needy, friend of the greedy, conscience of the
party, or all _____ 30 to all men.

Exercise 6   **The case against the "first-past-the-post"-system**

Translate into German.

The core idea behind representative government is that it enables all sections
of society to have a say in the formation and conduct of government. This ful-
fils a basic right which all are held to have and, we have good reason to believe,
makes it more likely that government will be carried out in the interests of,
and with the general consent of, the governed.

Critics maintain that because our present system is insufficiently representative it offends against basic human rights and delivers the wrong kind of
government: FPTP discriminates against smaller parties. A party with thin
national support might poll a substantial number of votes but win very few
seats. Thus in 1983, despite the fact that 26 % of votes cast went to the SDP-
Liberal Alliance and that their candidates came second in 313 contests, they
won only twenty-three contests outright: 3.5 % of the seats in the House of
Commons. Over a quarter of the voting population, therefore, received mini-
mal representation.

108 / Politics in Great Britain

Exercise 7   Synonyms

Find synonyms for the words in italics.

1. Edward VIII had to *abdicate* because he wanted to _____
   marry Mrs Wally Simpson, a divorced American
   woman.

2. I cannot understand the Prime Minister's *attitude* _____
   towards self-rule for Northern Ireland.

3. The Prime Minister must *convince* Parliament that the _____
   proposed law is really necessary.

4. The following *extracts* are derived from a parliamen- _____
   tary debate on "The cost of monarchy".

5. The monarch has *effectively* no political power. _____

6. The Queen is an impartial observer who has to *ensure* _____
   fair play in the democratic process.

7. The *House of Commons* is more important than the _____
   House of Lords.

8. The opposition tries to convince the public that the
   present government is *incompetent*. _____

9. All polling-stations will be *instructed* to close the _____
   doors at 10 p.m.

10. The main *issue* in the last election was the financial _____
    situation of the country.

11. In Britain, the Queen and the Prime Minister play an
    important role to *maintain* democracy. _____

12. After more than six months in Parliament the M.P. for
    Fulham managed to *make* a speech for the first time. _____

13. The opposition wants to prove that the government is
    a *menace* to the country. _____

14. Our main political *opponent* in this matter is the _____
    Right Honorable Member for Erith-South.

15. The *platform* of a political party is what they say they _____
    will do if they are elected.

16. A *rebellion* is a violent, organized action by people who are trying to change their country's political system.

17. I'm sure the opposition will *reject* any plan of the government to raise the taxes.

18. A *tyrant* is a cruel, unjust or oppressive ruler.

Exercise 8   Opposites

Find opposites for the words in italics.

1. Most people have come to *accept* the notion that a fair social policy aims at redistributing wealth downwards.

2. Many Londoners have gone off to seek a *better* life in the suburbs.

3. The Home Office cannot *deny* the immigrants the right of abode any longer.

4. The charge is that he and his policies are *hostile* to the nation's poor.

5. England is, in effect, *insular* and maritime.

6. The English Channel protected the island from the destructions of *major* wars.

7. People who behave badly abroad are an embarrassment and a *nuisance* to contemporary Britain.

8. Many politicians *object to* the State Department's efforts to negotiate an international production freeze.

9. Lord Craigavon's *successors* had adequate reasons for not talking his language.

10. Many of our institutions were strange and *singular* but others had to adjust themselves to us.

11. Other nations earned our *contempt* for their inclination to revolution.

12. The *central* question now is whether Britain's uniqueness, so often a source of strength in the past, has become a handicap.

110 ✦ Politics in Great Britain

Exercise 9   Matching words and their definitions

Match the words from list 1 with their appropriate definitions in list 2. Please note: There are more words than definitions!

A   person who is against another person in a fight, a struggle, a game or an argument

B   formal expression of one's opinion or choice e. g. by ballot or show of hands

C   meeting between the heads of two or more governments, esp. of the world's most powerful countries

D   number of people who take part in a ballot

E   main policies and aims of a political party, esp. as stated before an election

F   small enclosure or compartment for a specific purpose, for example for voting at elections

G   draft of a proposed law, to be discussed by a parliament

H   diplomat sent from one country to another either as a permanent representative or on a special mission

I   judges of a country collectively

J   official note that records a decision or comment

K   passage selected (from a poem, book, film, piece of music, etc.)

L   formal proposal to be discussed and voted on at a meeting

(1)   ambassador
(2)   bill
(3)   booth
(4)   budget
(5)   community
(6)   declaration
(7)   extract
(8)   judiciary
(9)   minute
(10) motion
(11) opponent
(12) platform
(13) summit
(14) term
(15) turnout
(16) vote

A	B	C	D	E	F	G	H	I	J	K	L

Politics in Great Britain 111

ercise 10   Word families

Supply the missing forms.

noun (abstract)	noun (concrete)	verb	adjective
presidency	president	preside	presidential
politics	_____	---	_____
_____	_____	represent	_____
election	_____	_____	_____
_____	---	_____	conceptual
_____	dictator	_____	_____
_____	_____	speak	---
tyranny	_____	_____	_____
_____	---	continue	_____
_____	---	_____	various

ercise 11   Crossword puzzle

Try to solve the crossword puzzle.

Across
1   all the people who have the right to vote (10)
5   to say that something is very bad and
    unacceptable (7)
8   to include (7)
9   trust (10)
12 legal process before a judge (5)
14 either – ... (2)
15 meeting of a group (7)
17 German word for "sound" (3)
18 to hit with a stick (4)
19 he lives in a country (10)
22 art of making formal speeches in public (7)
23 girl's name (3)
24 first woman of them all (3)
25 a long seat of wood or metal (5)

Down
2   to take something away (10)
3   to set free (7)
4   formal party (9)
6   member of the nobility; has a seat in the Upper
    House (4)
7   formal proposal (6)
10 opp. of yes (2)
11 worn by a king or queen (5)
13 to ... for president (3)
16 Mr Newton's first name (5)
20 boy's name (3)
21 money collected by the state (3)

112 ❘ Politics in Great Britain

Politics in the US

1 Word field

(to) adjourn	unterbrechen; verschieben
administration	Regierung, Verwaltung
(to) advocate	unterstützen
(to) affirm	jdm. etwas versichern
affirmative action	„positive Einwirkung, Maßnahme", bestimmt zur Unterstützung von Minderheiten
Afro-Americans	politisch korrekte Bezeichnung für Schwarze in den USA
aide	Berater
(to) allege	behaupten, dass …
allegiance	Loyalität, Treue
allies	Alliierte, Verbündete
(to) allot	jdm. eine Arbeit/einen Raum zuteilen
amendment	Änderung, Ergänzung; Zusatzartikel zur Verfassung
(to) appoint	berufen, ernennen
approval	Anerkennung, Billigung
(to) arouse	erwecken, erregen
asset	Pluspunkt, Vorzug
backlog	Rückstand
ballot	Abstimmung
barred	ausgesperrt, abgesperrt
birthright	Geburtsrecht
blatant	offensichtlich, eklatant
budget	Etat, Haushaltsplan
bulwark	Bollwerk
campaign	Aktion, Feldzug, Wahlkampf
candid	offen, ehrlich

Politics in the US

carnage	Blutbad
caucus	Parteiausschuss für Wahlangelegenheiten
challenger	Herausforderer, Herausforderin
chamber	Sitzungssaal, Kammer
Charter	Charta, Satzung
citizenship	Staatsbürgerschaft
commander-in-chief	Oberkommandeur
(to) conceal	verbergen
(to) concede	zugeben, eingestehen
condescending	herablassend
confederation	Bündnis
(to) confirm	bestätigen
(to) conform	sich einfügen
Congress	Kongress – Parlament, bestehend aus Repräsentantenhaus und Senat
congressman	Kongressabgeordneter
constitutional	verfassungsmäßig
constraint	Zwang
contender	Kandidat, Bewerber
contention	Streit, Debatte
convention	Versammlung; Brauch
(to) crush	zusammendrücken, niederschlagen
defiance	Auflehnung, Aufsässigkeit, Trotz
Delegate	Delegierter, Abgesandter
(to) denounce	anprangern, entlarven
despair	Verzweiflung
(to) detain	in Haft nehmen
determination	Entschlossenheit
dignity	Würde
diplomacy	Diplomatie, Verhandlungsgeschick
disgrace	Schande

Politics in the US / 115

(to) dismiss	jdn./etwas abtun
(to) dispel	Zweifel zerstreuen
(to) disrupt	stören, unterbrechen
(to) dissipate	allmählich verschwinden
donation	Geldspende
(to) draft	(milit.) einberufen
elector	Wähler, Wahlmann
electoral college	Wahlmännergremium
eligible	infrage kommen
(to) enact	(ein Gesetz) erlassen
endowment	finanzielle Ausstattung, Stiftung
enforcement	Durchsetzung (eines Rechts oder Gesetzes)
entrenched	verwurzelt
executive	ausführende Gewalt
expectation	Erwartung, Hoffnung
(to) falter	stocken
(to) frame s.o.	jdm. etwas anhängen
frontier	Grenze, Grenzgebiet
front-runner	Spitzenreiter
fund-raising	Wohltätigkeits-, Benefiz-
(to) gather	sammeln
hateful	hasserfüllt
impeachment	Amtsenthebungsverfahren
inaugural address	Amtsantrittsrede
inauguration	Amtseinführung
(to) incapacitate	außer Gefecht setzen
indictment	Anklageerhebung
(to) infringe	verletzen, gegen etwas verstoßen
insignificance	Unwichtigkeit, Belanglosigkeit
(to) insist	bestehen auf
jeopardy	Gefahr, Risiko
judicial	gerichtlich

116 Politics in the US

judiciary	Richterstand
legacy	Vermächtnis
legislation	Gesetzgebung
legitimacy	Rechtmäßigkeit
liberation	Befreiung
mandate	Auftrag
Medicare	staatliche Gesundheitsfürsorge für Senioren
naturalization	Einbürgerung
(to) negotiate	verhandeln, aushandeln
oath	Eid
oath-taking	Eid ablegen
objection	Einwand
obstacle	Hindernis
(to) obtain	bekommen, erhalten
opponent	Gegner
outmoded	altbacken, altmodisch
(to) override	sich über Einwände hinwegsetzen
(to) participate	teilnehmen, sich beteiligen
party convention	Parteitag
peril	Gefahr
(to) pledge	versprechen, geloben
plot	Verschwörung
polling	Wahl, Abstimmung
preamble	Einleitung
precaution	Vorkehrung, Vorsichtsmaßnahme
precinct	Wahlkreis, Wahlbezirk
predecessor	Vorgänger
(to) prescribe	verschreiben, verordnen
(to) preside	den Vorsitz haben
presidency	Präsidentschaft
presidential election	Präsidentschaftswahlen
primaries	Vorwahlen

Politics in the US 117

primarily	vorwiegend, hauptsächlich
rally	Massenversammlung, Treffen, Zusammenkunft
(to) ratify	ratifizieren, bestätigen, genehmigen
re-election	Wiederwahl
relentless	unnachgiebig
(to) reprieve	begnadigen
residency	Wohnsitz
resignation	Kündigung, Rücktritt, Amtsniederlegung
resumption	Wiederaufnahme
(to) reveal	zeigen, zum Vorschein bringen
(to) run for (president)	kandidieren (für die Präsidentschaft)
solemn	feierlich
sovereignty	höchste Gewalt, Oberhoheit
staunch	standhaft, zuverlässig
(to) stipulate	verlangen, fordern
succession	Folge, Nachfolge
successor	Nachfolger
summit	Gipfel, Gipfeltreffen
supplement	Ergänzung
supporter	Anhänger
sustained	anhaltend
target	Ziel
tiresome	mühsam
turmoil	Tumult
turnout	Wahlbeteiligung
undecided	unentschlossen
(to) vacate	räumen
valedictorian	Abschiedsredner
(to) verify	nachprüfen, überprüfen
vested with	bevollmächtigt sein, etwas zu tun
vice-president	Vizepräsident

118 / Politics in the US

warrant	Haftbefehl
(to) waver	ins Wanken geraten, wanken
winner-takes-all	der Sieger erhält alles

2 Idioms and phrases

to trail in the polls	The challenger of the incumbent President is trailing in the polls by more than 20 percent.	bei den Meinungs-umfragen hinterher-hinken
to address s.o.	At the convention the chairman addressed an audience of 15,000 people.	zu jdm. sprechen
the days are numbered	There was a general feeling among the delegates that the glory days of the party might be numbered.	die Tage sind gezählt
to be at a crossroads	The resigning Secretary of State said that America was at a crossroads.	am Scheideweg stehen
to suit s.o.	The voters turn their attention to domestic issues that have always suited the Democratic party.	jdm. gelegen kommen
to give s.o. the go-ahead	In 1791 Thomas Jefferson gave the French architect, Pierre Charles L'Enfant, the go-ahead to lay out a new city: Washington.	jdm. grünes Licht geben
to range from ... to	World issues range from the menace of outdated nuclear reactors to the refugee problem.	reichen von ... bis
to cast one's vote	Delegates cast their votes to nominate their presidential candidate.	seine Stimme abgeben
to fare better	The party members hope the new presidential nominee will fare better than four years ago.	besser abschneiden
to swear in	The US President must be sworn in on Inauguration Day.	vereidigen
to go a bridge too far	Soon it became clear that with his taxcut promises the President had gone a bridge too far.	sich zu weit vorwagen

Politics in the US ◢ 119

to come into force	The new regulation cannot come into force until Congress has approved of it.	in Kraft treten
to be taken aback	The electorate has been taken aback at the scale of the changes brought about by the new social programme.	bestürzt, stark betroffen sein
to cover an issue	Both candidates covered the issue of abortion in depth.	ein Thema behandeln

3 Practice

Exercise 1 The Queen in Philadelphia

In the following text some words are incomplete. Only one or a couple of letters are given. Try to complete with words that would fit the context.

On an official visit to the United States in 1976 Queen Elizabeth II made a speech in Philadelphia. This is an excerpt:

"It seems to me that Independence Day, the Fourth of July, should be celebrated as much in Britain as in America. Not in rejoicing at the separ_____[1] of the American colonies from the British crown, but in sinc_____[2] gratitude to the foun_____[3] fathers of this great republic for hav_____[4] taught Britain a very valuable lesson.

We lost the American colonies because we lac_____[5] that statesmanship 'to know the right time and the manner of yiel_____[6] of what is impossible to keep'. But the lesson was lea_____[7]. In the next century and a half we kept more clo_____[8] to the principals of Magna Carta which have been the common heri_____[9] of both our countries.

We learnt to resp_____[10] the rights of others to govern them_____[11] in their own ways. This was the outc_____[12] of experience learnt the hard way in 1776. Without that great act in the cause of liberty perf_____[13] in Independence Hall 200 years ago, we could never have transf_____[14] an Empire into a Commonwealth.

Ultim_____[15], peace brought the renewal of friends_____[16], which has continued and gro_____[17] over the years and has played a vital pa_____[18] in world affairs. Together we have fou_____[19] in two world wars in the defe_____[20] of our common heritage of freedom. Together we have striven to keep the peace so dearly won. Together as friends and alli_____[21] we can

120 ✦ Politics in the US

face the uncertainties of the fut_____²², and this is something for which we
in Britain can also celebrate the Fourth of July.
This morning I saw the Liberty Bell. It came here over 200 years ago when
Philadelphia, after London, was the larg_____²³ English-speaking city in the
world. It was cast to commem_____²⁴ Pennsylvania's Charter of Privileges,
but is better known for its association with the Declaration of Indep_____²⁵.
Today to mark the two hundredth annive_____²⁶ of that declaration, it gives
me greatest plea_____²⁷, on behalf of the British people, to present the new
bell to the people of the United States of America. It comes from the same
foundry as the Liberty Bell, but written on the side of this bell are the words
'Let Freedom Ring'."

Exercise 2   **Presidential versus Parliamentary Government**

Complete the text with words from this list:

Chancellor	delay	looking	republic
combined	elections	policy	separates
contrast	exercise	power	single
correcting	follows	practised	stable
cut off	goals	relationship	stated
defended	likelihood	removable	term

In an essay published in 1879, Woodrow Wilson, who would one day serve as
US President (1913–1921), argued for the transformation of the American
system of presidential government into one resembling a parliamentary system.
The continued fascination of American observers with the parliamentary system, especially as it is _____¹ in Britain, is an established fact. Critics
are _____² to the parliamentary system as a means of _____³
what is seen as an excessive concentration of _____⁴.
The differences between a parliamentary and a presidential system of government may be easily _____⁵. They relate mainly to the nature of the
executive and to the executive's _____⁶ with the legislature. In a
presidential system like that of the United States, there is a _____⁷
executive who is elected by the voters for a fixed _____⁸, and his
office is separated from the legislature.
In _____⁹, the executive of a British-type parliamentary system is
a multi-member Cabinet whose members are chosen by, chosen from, remain

members of and are always _____ [10] by the legislature. An additional feature of the parliamentary system is that it _____ [11] the offices of titular chief of state (King in a monarchy, President in a _____ [12]) from the office of Head of Cabinet, i. e. the Prime Minister (or Premier or _____ [13]). In contrast, in a presidential system, the two offices are _____ [14] in a single person.

A British-style parliamentary system has been _____ [15] on the grounds that the executive can usually have its programs enacted with minimum _____ [16] and with no chance of deadlock. Second, and more often stressed, is the fact that under this system government _____ [17] forms a coherent, integrated whole. There is no _____ [18] that programs will be enacted only to have the funds _____ [19], or that funds will be appropriated but not spent, or that complex planning _____ [20] will be frustrated because only part of a program can be gotten through the legislature.

The case for the presidential system can be stated as _____ [21]: First, the presidential system provides _____ [22] government; Cabinet overthrows and unanticipated _____ [23] are unknown. Effective government is therefore more likely. Second, the executive, being secure in office, is able to _____ [24] bold and decisive leadership.

Exercise 3   The Democratic and the Republican Party

Complete the text with words from this list:

amalgamation	professional	strong	until
era	reelection	succeeded	vice-president
fought	representation	support	victories
growth	reunited	tariffs	war
presidential	strength	themselves	woman

The Democratic Party

The Democratic Party is the descendant of the Anti-Federalist and Democratic-Republican parties.

From Thomas Jefferson's election in 1800 through James Buchanan's election in 1856, the party was strong, gathering its _____ [1] mainly from farmers, small businessmen, and the _____ [2] classes. In this period, Democrats opposed a central bank, protective _____ [3], and internal improvements at federal expense. Southern planters in the party promoted expansionism, which led the United States to _____ [4] with Mexico (1846).

Party _____ [5] declined after the Civil War until 1932, when Franklin D. Roosevelt was elected. After that, it remained strong _____ [6] 1952. In 1960, Democratic candidate John F. Kennedy won the presidential election beginning "the New Frontier" _____ [7] that stressed US world responsibilities for peace and economic _____ [8] at home. Lyndon B. Johnson _____ [9] Kennedy with an ambitious program of domestic legislation.

In the 1976 elections, the Democratic candidate, Jimmy Carter, was elected president. Carter lost his bid for _____ [10] in 1980, which was followed by party losses in the 1984 and 1988 presidential elections. In 1984 the Democrats became the first major party to choose a _____ [11] (Geraldine Ferraro) for its vice-presidential candidate.

The Republican Party

The Republican Party is also known as the G.O.P., or Grand Old Party.

It was organized in 1854 as an _____ [12] of Whigs and Free Soilers with businessmen, workers, and professional people who formerly had called _____ [13] Independent Democrats, Know-Nothings, Barnburners, and Abolitionists. John C. Fremont was the party's first _____ [14] candidate in 1856.

Its first successful candidate was Abraham Lincoln, elected in 1860. The party was particularly _____ [15] in the period from the Civil War to 1932. After 1932, Dwight Eisenhower (1952, 1956) and Richard Nixon (1968, 1972) each won election _____ [16] but both had to work with largely Democratic Congresses. When Ronald Reagan was elected president in 1981, the Republican _____ [17] in Congress increased substantially. In 1989 George Bush, who had served as _____ [18] under Ronald Reagan, became the 41st president. The years of his presidency saw the Berlin wall come down, Germany was _____ [19] and the Gulf War against Iraque's Saddam Hussein was _____ [20]. His son, George W. Bush, was elected president in 2000 and re-elected in 2004.

Politics in the US 123

Exercise 4   The office of President

Translate into German.

Americans don't want a president to become too powerful; yet the country certainly wants him to have ample power to cope with all emergencies. In fact, Congress and the public constantly push at the President new authority to handle new problems.

One reason Presidents find it hard to surrender power is because it was largely forced on them by farmers, businessmen, working people who wanted government to act in a time of dire economic depression or military crisis. These groups turned to the one institution that seemed to be able to act.

The nation definitely prefers a President who is "a man of the people", a rather ordinary person with whom it can identify. But the nation doesn't want this man to be too ordinary. They not only want extraordinary ability and uncommonly gifted leadership, but they also want him to be better than they themselves are – to be someone they can look up to and respect.

Exercise 5   "The new frontier" by John F. Kennedy (= Nomination acceptance speech before the Democratic National Convention, July 15, 1960)

Complete the text with words from this list:

ask	doubts	opportunities	solved
assembly	edge	overcome	votes
back	explored	peace	whether
challenges	instead	questions	within
common	motto	rhetoric	young
conquer	need	social	

I stand today facing West on what was once the last frontier. From the lands that stretch 3000 miles behind me, the pioneers of old gave up their safety, their comfort, and sometimes their lives to build a new world here in the West.

They were not the captives of their own _____[1], the prisoners of their own price tags. Their _____[2] was not "every man for himself" – but "all for the _____[3] cause". They were determined to make that new world strong and free, to _____[4] its hazards and its hardships, to _____[5] the enemies that threatened from without and _____[6].

124 ◆ Politics in the US

Today some would say that those struggles are over – that all the horizons have been _____ [7] – that all the battles have been won – that there is no longer an American frontier.

But I trust that no one in this vast _____ [8] will agree with those sentiments. For the problems are not all _____ [9] and the battles are not all won – and we stand today on the _____ [10] of a new frontier – the frontier of the 60's – a frontier of unknown _____ [11] and perils – an a frontier of unfulfilled hopes and threats.

Woodrow Wilson's New Freedom promised our nation a new political and _____ [12] framework, Franklin Roosevelt's New Deal promised security and succor to those in _____ [13]. But the New Frontier of which I speak is not a set of promises – it is a set of _____ [14]. It sums up not what I intend to offer the American people, but what I intend to _____ [15] of them. It appeals to their pride, not to their pocketbook – it holds out the promise of more sacrifice _____ [16] of more security.

But I tell you the New Frontier is here, _____ [17] we seek it or not. Beyond that frontier are the uncharted areas of science and space, unsolved problems of _____ [18] and war, unconquered pockets of ignorance and prejudice, unanswered _____ [19] of poverty and surplus. It would be easier to shrink _____ [20] from that frontier, to look to the safe mediocrity of the past, to be lulled by good intentions and high _____ [21] – and those who prefer that course should not cast their _____ [22] for me, regardless of party.

But I believe the times demand invention, innovation, imagination, decision. I am asking each of you to be new pioneers on that Frontier. My call is to the _____ [23] in heart, regardless of age – to the stout in spirit, regardless of party – to all who respond to the Spiritual call: "Be strong and of good courage; be not afraid, neither be thou dismayed."

Exercixe 6   **Inaugural Addresses**

In these excerpts from inaugural addresses of four US presidents a couple of letters are missing at the beginning or the end of a word. Try to complete the words.

In a land of great wea_____ [1], families must not live in hopeless po_____ [2]. In a land rich in harvest, children just must not go hungry. In a land of healing miracles, neighbours must not suffer and die unatt_____³. In a great land of learning and scholars, young people must be taught to read and write.

For the more than 30 years that I have served this Nation, I have believed that this injustice to our people, this wa_____⁴ of our resources, was our real enemy. For 30 years or more, with the resources I have had, I have vigilantly fought against it. I have learned, and I know, that it will not sur_____⁵ easily.

But change has given us new weapons. Before this generation of Americans is finished, this enemy will not only retreat – it will be con_____⁶.

Justice requires us to remember that when any citizen denies his fellow, saying, "His color is not mine," or "His beliefs are strange and different," in that moment he betr_____⁷ America, though his fore_____⁸ created this Nation.

Lyndon Baines Johnson, Democrat, 36th president of the United States (1963–69).
Inaugural Address, January 20, 1965

So, as we begin, let us take _____tory⁹. We are a nation that has a government – not the other way around. And this makes us _____cial¹⁰ among the nations of the Earth. Our Government has no power except that _____nted¹¹ it by the people. It is time to check and _____erse¹² the growth of government which shows signs of having grown beyond the consent of the governed.

It is my intention to curb the size and influence of the Federal establishment and to demand recognition of the _____ction¹³ between the powers granted to the Federal Government and those reserved to the States or to the people. All of us need to be _____inded¹⁴ that the Federal Government did not create the States; the States created the Federal Government.

Ronald Reagan, Republican, 40th president of the United States (1981–89).
First Inaugural Address, January 20, 1981

And once again, we have _____olved[15] for our time a great debate over the role of government. Today we can declare: Government is not the problem, and government is not the solution. We – the American people – we are the solution. Our _____nders[16] understood that well and gave us a democracy strong enough to _____ure[17] for centuries, flexible enough to face our common _____llenges[18] and advance our common dreams in each new day.

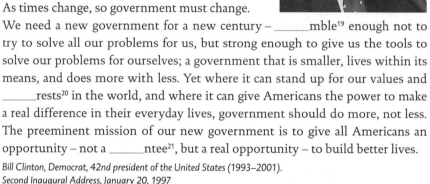

As times change, so government must change. We need a new government for a new century – _____mble[19] enough not to try to solve all our problems for us, but strong enough to give us the tools to solve our problems for ourselves; a government that is smaller, lives within its means, and does more with less. Yet where it can stand up for our values and _____rests[20] in the world, and where it can give Americans the power to make a real difference in their everyday lives, government should do more, not less. The preeminent mission of our new government is to give all Americans an opportunity – not a _____ntee[21], but a real opportunity – to build better lives.

Bill Clinton, Democrat, 42nd president of the United States (1993–2001).
Second Inaugural Address, January 20, 1997

What you do is as im_____[22] as anything government does. I ask you to seek a common good beyond your comf_____[23]; to defend needed reforms against easy atta_____[24]; to serve your nation, beginning with your neighbor. I ask you to be citizens: citizens, not spec_____[25]; citizens, not subjects; responsible citizens, building com_____[26] of service and a nation of character. Americans are gener_____[27] and strong and decent, not because we believe in ourselves, but because we hold beliefs beyond ourselves. When this spirit of citizenship is missing, no government program can repl_____[28] it. When this

spirit is present, no wrong can stand against it. After the Declaration of Independence was signed, Virginia statesman John Page wrote to Thomas Jefferson: "We know the race is not to the swift nor the battle to the strong. Do you not think an angel rides in the whirlwind and directs this storm?"

Politics in the US / 127

Much time has passed since Jefferson arrived for his inau_____[29]. The years and changes accumulate. But the themes of this day he would know: our nation's grand story of cour_____[30] and its simple dream of dignity.

George W. Bush, Republican, 43rd president of the United States (2001–).
First Inaugural Address, January 20, 2001

xercise 7   **US politics after 9/11: America's political mission**

Translate into English or German respectively.

Every year in January the US president delivers a keynote speech to a joint session of Congress, in which he reports on the "State of the Union", outlining the principal policies of his government in view of current events. This excerpt is taken from the State of the Union address delivered by President George W. Bush in January 2004.

"I know that some people question if America is really in a war at all. They view terrorism more as a crime, a problem to be solved mainly with law enforcement and *indictments* (_____)[1]. After the World Trade Center was first attacked in 1993, some of the guilty were indicted and tried and _____[2] (verurteilt, überführt), and sent to prison. But the matter was not settled. The terrorists were still training and plotting in other nations, and drawing up more *ambitious* (_____)[3] plans. After the chaos and _____[4] (Blutbad) of September the 11th, it is not enough to serve our enemies with legal papers. The terrorists and their supporters _____[5] (erklärten) war on the United States, and war is what they got.

Some in this chamber, and in our country, did not support the liberation of Iraq. *Objections* (_____)[6] to war often come from principled motives. But let us be candid about the consequences of leaving Saddam Hussein in power. We're seeking all the facts. Already, the Kay Report identified dozens of weapons of mass destruction-related program activities and significant amounts of equipment that Iraq *concealed* (_____)[7] from the United Nations. Had we failed to act, the dictator's weapons of mass destruction programs would continue to this day. Had we failed to act, Security Council resolutions on Iraq would have been revealed as empty _____[8] (Drohungen), weakening the United Nations and encouraging *defiance* (_____)[9] by dictators around the world. Iraq's torture chambers would still be filled with victims, terrified and innocent. The killing fields of Iraq – where hundreds of thousands of men and women and children *vanished* (_____)[10] into the sands – would still be known only to the killers. For all who love freedom and peace, the world without Saddam Hussein's regime is a better and safer place. [...]

From the beginning, America has _____[11] (gesucht) international support for our operations in Afghanistan and Iraq, and we have gained much support. There is a difference, however, between leading a coalition of many nations, and _____[12] (sich unterwerfen) to the objections of a few. America will never seek a permission slip to defend the security of our country.

We also hear _____[13] (Zweifel) that democracy is a realistic goal for the greater Middle East, where freedom is rare. Yet it is mistaken, and *condescending* (_____)[14], to assume that whole cultures and great religions are *incompatible* (_____)[15] with liberty and self-government. I believe that God has planted in every human heart the desire to live in freedom. And even when that desire is *crushed* (_____)[16] by tyranny for decades, it will rise again.

As long as the Middle East remains a place of tyranny and despair and anger, it will continue to produce men and movements that threaten the safety of America and our friends. So America is pursuing a forward strategy of freedom in the greater Middle East. We will _____[17] (herausfordern) the enemies of reform, confront the allies of terror, and expect a higher standard from our friend. To cut through the barriers of hateful propaganda, the Voice of America and other broadcast services are expanding their programming in Arabic and Persian – and soon, a new television service will begin providing *reliable* (_____)[18] news and information across the region. I will send you a proposal to double the budget of the National Endowment for Democracy, and to focus its new work on the development of free elections, and free markets, free press, and free labour unions in the Middle East. And above all, we will finish the historic work of democracy in Afghanistan and Iraq, so those nations can light the way for others, and help transform a troubled part of the world.

America is a nation with a mission, and that mission comes from our most basic beliefs. We have no desire to _____[19] (herrschen, beherrschen), no ambitions of empire. Our aim is a democratic peace – a peace founded upon the _____[20] (Würde) and rights of every man and woman. America acts in this cause with friends and allies at our side, yet we understand our special calling: This great republic will lead the cause of freedom."

Politics in the US 129

Exercise 8   Synonyms

Find synonyms for the words in italics.

1. The American two-party system was not *conceived* by the Founding Fathers. _____

2. The American electoral system is complicated and to a large extent *obsolete*. _____

3. The first *hurdle* in any presidential election are the primary elections. _____

4. During the primaries the *challenger* of the President must make himself known to the voters. _____

5. The opposition often criticizes the President without *compassion*. _____

6. The opinion polls show that the President and his wife are *perceived* as "people who like elegance and parties". _____

7. Today women *constitute* 44 per cent of the US labour force. _____

8. In their *fight* for independence the American colonists defeated the British army. _____

9. The president's decision met with *harsh* criticism from all sides. _____

10. American youths were *noted* for the acceptance of the traditional American way of life. _____

11. The turning point in modern American history came with the *assassination* of President Kennedy in 1963. _____

12. Then came the Vietnam War – with the result that the golden image of America was *shattered*. _____

13. US soldiers were sent to fight on foreign *soil*. _____

14. One of the most *striking* characteristics of American youths is their interest in careers. _____

130 / Politics in the US

Exercise 9   Matching words and their definitions

Match the words from list 1 with their appropriate definitions in list 2.
Please note: There are more words than definitions!

A main ideas and aims of a political party

B ceremony introducing s.o. into an office

C a combination of events happening by chance

D sth. one receives by right from former generations
   or from an older member of the family

E fundamental law of a state

F that cannot be taken away

G difficult and demanding task

H act of making a foreigner a citizen of a country

I programme of things to be done

J sth. given in return for service or merit

K US election in which voters select candidates for
   the coming presidential election

L to form an idea or plan in the mind

M meeting of members of a political party

N to start or establish an organization, institution, etc.

O holding the specified official position

P overwhelming majority of votes for one side in an
   election

(1) agenda
(2) ballot
(3) campaign
(4) candidate
(5) challenge
(6) coincidence
(7) conceive
(8) constitution
(9) convention
(10) delegate
(11) found
(12) heritage
(13) inauguration
(14) incumbent
(15) issue
(16) landslide
(17) naturalization
(18) platform
(19) poll
(20) precinct
(21) primary
(22) reward
(23) unalienable
(24) vote

A	B	C	D	E	F	G	H	I	J	K	L	M	N	O	P

Immigration

1 Word field

abode	Aufenthaltsort, Wohnsitz
(to) absorb	aufnehmen
(to) accommodate	unterbringen
adverse	ungünstig, nachteilig, widrig
alien	fremd, ausländisch; Ausländer
(to) alienate	entfremden
ancestor	Vorfahr
ancestry	Abstammung
appalling	erschreckend, entsetzlich
aspiration	Bestrebung, Hoffnung, Ehrgeiz
(to) assassinate	ein Attentat auf jdn. verüben, ermorden
(to) assemble	versammeln
(to) assert	auf etwas bestehen
(to) assimilate	sich anpassen
asylum	Asyl
asylum seeker	Asylsucher, Asylant
(to) attain	erreichen
barge	Lastschiff
barred from	ausgeschlossen von
belongings	Hab und Gut
bilingual	zweisprachig
(to) blend	vermischen, verschmelzen
(to) blur	verschwimmen
boarder	Pensionsgast
boatload	Schiffsladung
brutish	brutal, roh

132 / Immigration

bundle	Bündel
citizen	Staatsbürger
(to) clutch	sich klammern an
collection centre	Sammellager
commonplace	alltäglich, normal
(to) conceive	entwerfen
contagious	ansteckend, direkt übertragbar
contagious disease	ansteckende Krankheit
(to) counsel	beraten
(to) cram	stopfen, hineinpacken, hineinzwängen
cramped	eingeengt, beengt
dedicated	engagiert
densely	dicht
deportation	Ausweisung
deprivation	Entbehrung
(to) deprive	jdm. etwas nehmen
deprived	benachteiligt
descendant	Nachkomme
despair	Verzweiflung
desperate	verzweifelt
(to) detain	festhalten, warten lassen
disconcerting	beunruhigend
discrepancy	Widerspruch, Unstimmigkeit
discrimination	nachteilige Behandlung
disparity	Ungleichheit
diversity	Verschiedenheit
doorway	Eingang
(to) emigrate	auswandern
entry procedure	Einreise-, Aufnahmeverfahren
equal opportunities	Chancengleichheit
equality	Gleichheit
essence	Wesen, Substanz

ethnic	ethnisch, völkisch
ethnicity	Ethnie (= Menschengruppe – insbesondere Stamm oder Volk – mit einheitlicher Kultur)
examination	Untersuchung
famine	Hungersnot
ferry boat	Fährschiff
filthy	schmutzig
flight (from)	Flucht (vor)
flood	Flut, Überschwemmung
forebears	Vorfahren
freedom of worship	Religionsfreiheit
garment	Kleidungsstück, Bekleidung
gateway	Tor
harassment	Belästigung
hate, hatred	Hass
heritage	Erbe
homeland	Heimat
homeless	heimatlos, obdachlos
horde	Horde, Masse
hostility	Feindseligkeit
(to) humiliate	erniedrigen, demütigen
immigrant	Einwanderer
immigration act	Einwanderungsgesetz
immigration bill	Einwanderungsgesetz
immigration quota	Einwanderungsquote
(to) imprint	einprägen
incidence	Vorkommen
incident	Zwischenfall
indignation	Entrüstung
influx, inflow	Zustrom
insulation	Isolierung
interpreter	Dolmetscher

134 / Immigration

(to) intimidate	einschüchtern
landmark	Wahrzeichen
(to) line up	sich anstellen
(to) lock up	einsperren
low-status job	niedrige Arbeit
(to) lure	anlocken
mainstream	Hauptrichtung, vorherrschende gesellschaftspolitische, kulturelle Richtung
managerial	Manager-
managerial skills	Managerfähigkeiten
means	Mittel
melting pot	Schmelztiegel
memento	Andenken
migration	Wanderung
minority	Minderheit
misfit	Außenseiter
mobility	Beweglichkeit, Mobilität
(to) mould	formen
multiculturalism	Multikulturalität, kulturelle Vielfalt
multi-racial	vielrassig
myth	Mythos, Ammenmärchen
native	einheimisch
native language	Muttersprache
nativism	Nativismus (= betontes Festhalten an bestimmten Elementen der eigenen Kultur)
naturalization	Einbürgerung
newcomer	Neuankömmling
(to) oppress	bedrücken, unterdrücken
oppression	Unterdrückung
ordeal	schwere Prüfung, Qual, Tortur
outlaw	Geächteter
penniless	mittellos

(to) persecute	verfolgen
Pilgrims	Pilger(väter)
pledge	Versprechen, Gelöbnis
(to) populate	bevölkern, besiedeln
population	Bevölkerung
possession	Besitz
poverty	Armut
prejudiced (against)	voreingenommen (gegenüber)
prejudice	Voreingenommenheit, Vorurteil
pressure	Druck
(to) process	abfertigen
processing centre	Aufnahmelager
prospect	Aussicht
pursuit	Streben
quay	Kai
refuge	Zuflucht
refugee	Flüchtling
relative	Verwandter
reservation	Vorbehalt
resistance	Widerstand
(to) restore	wiederherstellen
restriction	Beschränkung, Einschränkung
(to) reveal	zeigen, offenbaren
riches	Reichtum, Reichtümer
right of abode	Aufenthaltsrecht
screening	Untersuchung
(to) scrutinise	genau untersuchen
search	Suche
(to) seek	suchen
self-improvement	Weiterbildung, Weiterkommen
shelter	Unterkunft
(to) shunt	verschieben, abschieben

singularity	Eigenartigkeit
steerage	Zwischendeck
sweatshop	Ausbeuterbetrieb
(to) tackle	anpacken, (ein Problem) angreifen
tension	Spannung
thug	Schlägertyp, Rowdy
tide	Flut, Strom
(to) toil	hart arbeiten, schuften
tolerance	Toleranz, Nachsicht
(to) trigger	etwas auslösen
troublemaker	Unruhestifter
truism	Binsenweisheit
underprivileged	benachteiligt
undocumented	ohne Ausweispapiere
uninhabitable	unbewohnbar
uprooted	entwurzelt
vicious	boshaft, gemein
violation	Verletzung, Vergehen
virtue	Tugend
wage	Lohn
weakness	Schwäche
(to) withstand	aushalten, überstehen
worship	Verehrung, Anbetung
xenophobia	Ausländerfeindlichkeit
yearning	Sehnsucht

Immigration 137

2   Idioms and phrases

to add insult to injury	The government added insult to injury by announcing a quicker immigration check for first-class passengers at Heathrow Airport.	das Ganze noch schlimmer machen
to admit s.o.	From 1892 to 1954 millions of immigrants were admitted into the US.	jdn. hereinlassen
to whisk s.o. to safety	Authorities whisked the victims to safety.	jdn. in Windeseile in Sicherheit bringen
to be desperate for	The new arrivals were desperate for a job and a place to sleep.	dringend suchen nach
to claim asylum	The number of people claiming asylum is on the increase.	Asyl beantragen
to collect s.o.	After the medical examination the immigrant waited to be collected by a relative or friend.	jdn. abholen
to cope with	Thousands couldn't cope with the different living conditions in their new homeland.	fertig werden mit
to declare open season on s.o.	To observers from abroad it seemed almost as if Germans had declared open season on foreigners living within their borders.	die Jagd auf jdn. freigeben
in search of	Immigrants came in flight from tyranny or in search of riches.	auf der Suche nach
to get away with	The police are determined to do everything possible so that hooligans don't get away with their attacks on foreigners.	ungeschoren davonkommen
to grow fluent in a language	Right-wing politicians have grown fluent in the language of xenophobia.	lernen, eine Sprache fließend zu sprechen
to stand by	A Vietnamese told the police that ordinary Germans stood by while he was being attacked by a gang of thugs.	danebenstehen; untätig zusehen

138 / Immigration

to not run free	Xenophobia has not run free in Germany: thousands have marched to protest the violence.	nicht kritiklos hinnehmen
to be at fault	It was as if the victims of discrimination were at fault, and not those persecuting them.	selber die Schuld tragen
to vie (with sb.) for sth.	The steamship lines vied with each other for the patronage of European emigrants to the United States.	wetteifern mit jdm.
to be on guard	Hundreds of US border control agents are on guard for a record number of illegal Mexican aliens.	auf der Hut sein; Vorkehrungen treffen

3   Practice

Exercise 1   US immigration

Complete the text with words from this list:

advanced	descended	increasing	plantations
biased	deterioration	influx	pot
brought	earliest	involved	primarily
call	economic	join	quota
control	encouraged	native	ranged
denigrate	established	naturalization	rate
derived	forced	persecution	values

The population of the USA is _____[1] largely from European immigrants. The _____[2] Indians diminished rapidly as white settlement _____[3] and live mostly in the SW and W. The _____[4] pioneers along the Atlantic coast were chiefly from the British Isles. An early mass _____[5] to the country was of blacks from Africa, transported to work the _____[6] of the South. In the 19th century a tide of immigration began bringing more than 40,000,000 persons into the country up to 1960.

Before 1890 immigrants were _____[7] Anglo-Saxon Protestants from the British Isles, Germany, and Scandinavia. Immigration after 1890 _____[8] mainly Roman Catholics and Jews from eastern and southern Europe, _____[9] to leave because of famine, lack of social and

Immigration 139

_____[10] opportunities, political notability, or religious _____[11].
Once a particular group of immigrants settled in an area, they urged others
from their homeland to _____[12] them.
The Homestead Act of 1862 _____[13] potential emigrants; the steam-
ship lines vied for their patronage; Northern Pacific Railroad agents offered
land bargains; and young American industries sent out a _____[14]
for workers.
The _____[15] of immigration corresponded to economic cycles in
the United States; _____[16] when prosperity was high. Attitudes of
native Americans toward immigrants _____[17] from eagerness to
exploit them and fear that they would _____[18] the quality of life in
the United States, to pride in the strength the country had _____[19]
from its ethnic mix. Earlier settlers were often racially _____[20]
against those who followed. There were many who blamed immigrants for
rising crime rates, labour unrest, and the _____[21] of cities.
Chinese immigration was restricted in 1882 and Japanese in 1908; mech-
anisms to _____[22] immigration included restrictions on _____[23]
and denial of elective office to foreign-born. Restrictive policies won out with
the passage of the Johnson Act (1924), which _____[24] a national
origins quota favoring northwestern Europeans. The _____[25] system, reaffirmed (1952) in the Immigration and Nationality Act, was abolished
in 1965. The polyglot of subcultures that immigration _____[26]
to the United States offers to the mainstream a variety of life styles and
_____[27], encouraging cultural borrowing. The strong ethnicity of
some immigrants has resisted the melting _____[28].

Exercise 2   Ellis Island

*In the following text some words are incomplete. Only one or a couple of letters
are given. Try to complete with words that would fit the context.*

Ellis Island was opened as the first official Federal immigration centre in 1892
when the ti_____[1] of immigration from southern and eas_____[2] Europe
began to flood the country. By that time, the older immigrants from northern
Europe and their children were calling for restri_____[3] to bar the newcomers
– "brutish, ill-smelling alien hordes", as a New York journalist descr_____[4]
them at the turn of the century.
But the doors were ke_____[5] open and between 1892 and 1954 – when the
processing centre fina_____[6] shut – 17 million men, women and children

became Americans at Ellis Island. Most were poor. Immigrants who trav_____⁷ first- and second-class were allowed to land dire_____⁸ in New York. Only steerage passe_____⁹ had to be processed first at Ellis Island.

Barges would coll_____¹⁰ them from steamships and ferry them to the island. They marc_____¹¹ up to the quay, thousands each week, men in black sui_____¹², women in shawls, aprons and felt slip_____¹³, children tightly clutching them, and everyone carr_____¹⁴ bundles and bask_____¹⁵ with mementoes from home – sausages, wine, plants, olive oil, kitc_____¹⁶ ware.
For most, the immigration rout_____¹⁷ was terrifying. Each boatload of people was met by an inter_____¹⁸ and led to the main building. There everyone had to lea_____¹⁹ his possessions and climb a long flight of stairs to the great hall for the examination which would deter_____²⁰ whether America would accept or rej_____²¹ him.
Signs in nine languages – English, German, Italian, Polish, Russian, Scandinavian, Greek, Hebrew, and Magyar – told those immigrants who could re_____²² what to do. In the great hall they lined up and an inspe_____²³ examined each in turn, scrutinising eyes, hair, skin, sear_____²⁴ for any signs of illness, especially contagious dise_____²⁵.
If the immigrant had a medical problem, he was shunted into a wire pen for furt_____²⁶ tests. If he was healthy, he was passed on to a legal inspector and

Immigration 141

quizzed: 30 questions in two minutes. More than 80 per cent pas_____[27] the test and were sent to another building to make travel arran_____[28] or wait for a relative or friend. Those who did not pass were held in cramped, often filt_____[29] cages for more questioning. Event_____[30] 2 per cent of them were sent back home.

Annotation
After laying in ruins for twenty years, the building on Ellis Island ("The Isle of Hope, the Isle of Tears"), where desperate immigrants had landed in the New World, was restored and turned into a museum (Ellis Island Immigration Museum). In September 1990 Vice-President Dan Quayle dedicated the museum and the American Immigrant Wall of Honour – a copper coating over the Sea Wall that contains 200,000 immigrant names.

Exercise 3   **A nation of immigrants**

Translate into English or German respectively.

The search for *freedom of worship* (_____)[1] has brought people to America from the days of the _____[2] (Pilgerväter) to modern times. In our own days, for example, anti-Semitic and anti-Christian *persecution* (_____)[3] in Hitler's Germany and the Communist _____[4] (Weltreich) have driven people from their homes to seek _____[5] (Zuflucht) in America. Not all found what they sought immediately. [...]
The second great force behind immigration has been political _____[6] (Unterdrückung). America has always been a refuge from tyranny. As a nation conceived in liberty, it has held out to the world the _____[7] (Versprechen) of respect for the *rights of man* (_____)[8]. Every time a revolution has failed in Europe, every time a nation has *succumbed* (_____)[9] to tyranny, men and women who love freedom have _____[10] (versammelt) their families and their belongings and set sails across the seas. *Nor* (_____)[11] has this process come to an end in our own day. [...]
The economic factor has been more *complex* (_____)[12] than the religious and political factors. From the very beginning, some have come to America in search of *riches* (_____)[13], some in _____[14] (Flucht vor) poverty and some because they were bought and sold and had no choice. [...]
The immigrants who came for economic reasons *contributed* (_____)[15] to the strength of the new society in several ways. Those who came from countries with advanced political and economic institutions brought with them faith in those institutions and _____[16] (Erfahrung) in making them work. They also brought technical and managerial _____[17]

142 / Immigration

(Fähigkeiten, Fertigkeiten) which contributed greatly to economic growth in the new land. *Above all* (_____)[18], they helped give America the extraordinary social mobility which is the essence of an open society. [...]
These were the major forces that *triggered* (_____)[19] this massive migration. Every immigrant served in American society that had attracted him in the first place. The motives of some were *commonplace* (_____)[20]. The motives of others were noble. Taken together they add up to the strengths and weaknesses of America.

From: Kennedy, John F.: A Nation of Immigrants. (First published in 1958)

Annotation
On January 20, 1961 John F. Kennedy entered the White House as the 35th President of the United States of America; on November 22, 1963 he was assassinated in Dallas.

Exercise 4   Arrival in the New World

Translate into German.

From 1882 to 1902 more than two million immigrants sailed to New York from Bremen alone. The fare was $ 33, and after paying for himself and possibly his family, the refugee from poverty and oppression arrived in New York penniless. When he got off the ferry from Ellis Island, he would make his way to the Lower East Side to find work and a floor to sleep on.
In time these few square miles of New York's Lower East Side became more densely populated than even the worst section of Bombay. And the imagery of the ordeal of the journey and the arriving became imprinted in the mind of those immigrants whose children have now inherited New York.
Two parents, six children and six boarders had to cram into a typical two-roomed flat of that time. Rent for these rooms, without ventilation, daylight or running water ran from 2 dollars a week. In 1890, sweatshop wages for a 14-hour day were around three dollars a week for women, not more than ten for men. That year, the turnover of the garment trade in New York was worth $ 88 million.

Immigration / 143

Exercise 5 Immigration myths

Complete the text with words from this list.

account	decreased	indicate	perception
burden	earnings	lack	self-employed
concern	employed	native-born	throughout
confined	evidence	opposite	welfare
continually	generous	percentage	workforce

Regardless of the reasons for immigrating, myths still abound regarding immigrants once they arrive in the United States. Now's the time to separate some of this fact from fiction.

Myth Number 1: Immigrants take jobs away from Americans

Nothing could be further from the truth. Studies have shown that quite the _____[1] is true: Immigrants create jobs. Specifically various recent studies have shown that: Immigrants are more likely to be _____[2] and start new businesses. Small businesses, 18 percent of which are started by immigrants, _____[3] for up to 80 percent of the new jobs available in the United States each year. Slightly more than 10 percent of the US Industrial _____[4], or roughly 2.2 million Americans, are _____[5] by foreign companies doing business in the United States.

Myth Number 2: America is being overrun by immigrants

This, unfortunately, is another case where _____[6] is out of sync with reality.

To be sure, the number of immigrants living in the United States is larger than ever before, but these numbers are relatively small as a _____[7] of the population. More importantly, the percentage of immigrants in the total population has _____[8]. So far, no single decade has topped 1901–1910 for immigration admissions. Further, even though the United States has one of the world's most _____[9] refugee resettlement programs, less than 1,5 percent of the world's refugee population finds its way to the United States. Perhaps the misperception regarding numbers of immigrants rests in the fact that in the 1980s, three-quarters of all immigrants entering the United States settled in just six states: California, New York, Texas, Florida, New Jersey, and Illinois.

Myth Number 3: Most immigrants are a drain on the US economy

New immigrants must prove that they won't be a _____[10] before they are allowed to enter the United States. Compared to the _____[11] population, immigrants are more likely to be employed, save more of their

144 / Immigration

_____ [12], and are more likely to start new businesses. Immigrants collectively earn $ 240 billion a year, pay $ 90 billion a year in taxes, and receive $ 5 billion in _____ [13]. Immigrants have a slightly higher per capita income than natives and a slightly lower household income.

Myth Number 4: Immigrants aren't really interested in becoming part of American society

All _____ [14] points to the contrary. Immigrants are very interested in being part of our society. In fact, the grandparents and parents of immigrant children have expressed some _____ [15] that their youngsters are assimilating too quickly.

Immigrants want to learn and speak English. Reports from _____ [16] the United States _____ [17] that the demand for classes in English as a second language far outstrips supply. After 15 years in America, 75 percent of Spanish-speaking immigrants speak English on a regular basis. The children of immigrants, although bilingual, prefer English to their native tongue at astounding rates. Immigrants and refugees intermarry outside their group at a rate of 1 in 3. The rate is even higher, 1 out of 2, for their children.

Myth Number 5: Immigrants contribute little to American society

Besides their significant economic contributions, immigrants _____ [18] have helped shape and mold the fabric of our society.

Immigrants recognize the value of an education. While many _____ [19] a high school education, they are just as likely as natives to hold a college degree: 20 percent. They are less likely than natives to be _____ [20] to a state prison. Among the five states with the most immigrants – California, Florida, Illinois, New York, Texas – only New York has a greater share of immigrants in its prisons than in its general population.

Exercise 6   Is multiculturalism working?

Translate into English or German respectively.

The faces of America and Britain are changing – *literally* (_____)[1]. In both countries people are worrying about the social changes und *upheavals* (_____)[2] brought about by immigration. The debate concentrates on the question whether cultural differences should be _____ [3] (geduldet) or minimized. Should ethnic and racial boundaries be erased through assimilation of immigrants by blurring differences to achieve a _____ [4] (Schmelztiegel), or should racial and ethnic differences be maintained to create a stronger pluralistic society? The nations are still undecided.

A recent *survey* (_____)⁵ conducted in the United States included the following statement: "Some people say that it is better for America if different racial and ethnic groups _____⁶ (aufrechterhalten, beibehalten) their distinct cultures. Others say it is better if groups change so that they blend into the larger society as in the idea of a melting pot." People were asked to *rank* (_____)⁷ their opinions on a scale ranging from "maintaining distinct cultures" (pluralism) to "blending into the larger society" (assimilation). Roughly one-third of Americans thought pluralism was the best route, one-third *endorsed* (_____)⁸ assimilation, and one-third found themselves somewhere in between.

By tradition, the United States prefers to think of itself as a melting pot of nations where people from many different cultures, races, and religions have been assimilated and *moulded* (_____)⁹ into "the first universal nation". People who sailed across the Atlantic to the New World in the late 19th and early 20th centuries thought of themselves as Americans, as members of a _____¹⁰ (wahrlich, wahrhaft) multicultural society. After World War II and during the succeeding decades, however, ethnic diversifycation intensified, because the US government dropped racially based quotas on immigration. The number of coloured immigrants from Asia, Africa and Central and South America rose _____¹¹ (beträchtlich). America's white face started to change: the "browning of America" set in. The new generations of Asian and Hispanic immigrants were not willing to assimilate into American society, they wanted to keep their own identity, their _____¹² (Bräuche) and traditions and their own language. By 2050 one-third of the people living in the USA will claim Asian or Hispanic *roots* (_____)¹³. To accommodate immigrants the government developed the concept of multiculturalism according to which ethnic or cultural groups have the right to remain _____¹⁴ (getrennt) rather than integrate into the mainstream culture of the country they *adopt* (_____)¹⁵ as their homeland. The system of "Bilingual education" in schools reflects this idea. Children of immigrants were taught in English and in their _____¹⁶ (Muttersprache), in most cases Spanish. After heated debates about the merits of bilingual education the tables turned against the system. The majority of people in California were _____¹⁷ (überzeugt) that bilingual education had done more harm than good, so they voted for the *abolition* (_____)¹⁸ of the system in 1998, demanding "English First" for all school children. Assimilation or multiculturalism *is still on the agenda* (_____

146 / Immigration

_____)[19] and opinions are divided. Today criticism of multiculturalism even comes from the members of ethnic _____[20] (Minderheiten) who argue that immigrants must integrate into their host country instead of demanding special privileges. "If you don't want to integrate, why come in the first place?"

Exercise 7   Synonyms

Find synonyms for the words in italics.

1. Every time a revolution has failed in Europe, men and women who love freedom have *assembled* their families and their *belongings* and set sails across the seas.   _____ _____

2. Not all immigrants found what they sought *immediately*.   _____

3. The *search* for freedom of worship has brought people to America from the days of the Pilgrims to modern times.   _____

4. Those immigrants who came from countries with *advanced* political and economic institutions brought with them *faith* in those institutions and experience in making them work.   _____ _____

5. Sociologists study migration for several reasons: to analyze the *effects* it has on preexisting social structures; and to locate and *predict* migration trends.   _____ _____

6. The numbers of native Indians *diminished* rapidly as white settlement advanced.   _____

7. The earliest pioneers along the Atlantic coast were *chiefly* from the British Isles.   _____

8. An early mass influx to the country was of blacks from Africa, transported to *work* on the plantations of the South.   _____

9. In the 19th century a *tide* of immigration began bringing more than 40,000,000 persons into the country up to 1960.   _____

Immigration ⏐ 147

10. The 1924 Johnson Act *established* quotas for immi- _____
gration based on the *number* of former nationals of _____
each country in the United States.

11. The contributions of the immigrants *invigorated* the _____
nation's life and economic growth. _____

12. Intermarriage produced a population of *diverse* blood. _____

13. Subversives and some groups *considered* politically _____
unreliable were declared *ineligible*. _____

14. The McCarran-Walter Act, or Immigration and
Nationality Act (1952), codified US immigration *laws* _____
and was *amended* in 1965. _____

Exercise 8   Matching words and their definitions

*Match the words from list 1 with their appropriate definitions in list 2. Please note:
There are more words than definitions!*

A   condition of being kept down by an unjust
government

B   boat which carries people across a river, channel,
etc.

C   to give way to superior force

D   severe test of character or endurance

E   to receive from those who have lived earlier

F   person who lives as a lodger with a family

G   firm employing underpaid workers

H   to have a different (religious) opinion

I   something handed down from ancestors or predecessors

J   fear or hatred of foreigners

K   former immigration station in New York Bay

L   to make somebody feel ashamed or disgraced

(1)   alienate
(2)   asylum
(3)   boarder
(4)   deprive
(5)   dissent
(6)   Ellis Island
(7)   famine
(8)   ferry
(9)   gateway
(10) humiliate
(11) influx
(12) inherit
(13) legacy
(14) oppression
(15) ordeal
(16) succumb
(17) sweatshop
(18) xenophobia

A	B	C	D	E	F	G	H	I	J	K	L

148 ✦ Immigration

Exercise 9   Word families

Supply the missing forms.

noun (abstract)	noun (concrete)	verb	adjective
presidency	president	preside	presidential
_____	---	number	_____
_____	_____	take refuge	---
diversity	---	---	_____
_____	---	admit	_____
_____	---	adopt	_____
_____	---	_____	approvable
industry	_____	_____	1. _____
			2. _____
hostility	---	---	_____
_____	---	_____	legal
_____	---	populate	_____
_____	settler	_____	---
suspicion	---	_____	_____

Civil rights

1 Word field

(to) accumulate	ansammeln
arson	Brandstiftung
aspiration	Bestreben, Ziel
(to) assassinate	ermorden
authority	Behörde, Amtsgewalt
(to) bestow	jdm. etwas verleihen
bigotry	Fanatismus, Intoleranz, Scheinheiligkeit
challenge	Herausforderung
citizen	Staatsbürger
citizenship	Staatsbürgerschaft
civil rights	Bürgerrechte
civil rights movement	Bürgerrechtsbewegung
clash	Zusammenstoß
common virtue	gemeinsame Tugend
conciliation	Versöhnung
(to) condemn	verurteilen, verdammen
consciousness	Bewusstsein
(to) cope with	fertig werden mit
(to) degrade	erniedrigen
delinquency	Kriminalität
deprivation	Benachteiligung
(to) deride	verspotten, sich lustig machen
desegregation	Aufhebung der Rassentrennung
determination	Entschlossenheit
dictatorship	Diktatur
dignity	Würde

150 Civil rights

discrimination	Benachteiligung
dispossessed	Besitzlose
disturbance	Unruhe
diversity	Vielfalt
endowed	ausgestattet sein, besitzen
enforcement	Durchsetzung
enfranchised	wahlberechtigt
(to) enrol	sich einschreiben
enterprise	Vorhaben
equal opportunities	Chancengleichheit
eruption	Ausbruch
exclude	ausschließen
facility	Einrichtung, Anlage
fierce	heftig, ungestüm
hate, hatred	Hass
heritage	Erbe
indignity	Demütigung
inferior	minderwertig
inferiority	Minderwertigkeit
injustice	Ungerechtigkeit
insoluble	unlösbar
intractable	hartnäckig
juvenile	jugendlich
(to) launch	starten
legacy	Vermächtnis
legal aid	Rechtshilfe
legislation	Gesetzgebung
liberation	Befreiung
looting	Plündern
migration	Wanderung
minority	Minderheit
non-violent	gewaltlos

Civil rights ✦ 151

obstacle	Hindernis
odds	Chancen, Wahrscheinlichkeit
opponent	Widersacher, Gegner
outbreak	Ausbruch
perseverance	Beharrlichkeit
prejudice	Vorurteil
primary	Haupt-
(to) prohibit	verbieten
pursuit	Streben, Verfolgen
quintessential	wesentlich
race relations	Rassenbeziehungen
racial tension	Rassenspannung
rampage	Randale
random	willkürlich
refusal	Ablehnung, Weigerung
resistance	Widerstand
Reverend	Pfarrer
right to vote	Stimmrecht, Wahlrecht
(to) segregate	absondern, trennen
segregation	Rassentrennung
self-esteem	Selbstachtung, Selbstwertgefühl
stake	Einsatz
(to) be at stake	auf dem Spiel stehen
superiority	Überlegenheit
Supreme Court	Oberstes Bundesgericht der USA
(to) wage	zu Felde ziehen
unalienable	unveräußerlich
unconstitutional	verfassungswidrig
violent	gewalttätig
weary	müde, erschöpft

2 Idioms and phrases

to be at a disadvantage	Ethnic minorities are still at a disadvantage in society.	benachteiligt sein
to take action	The government must take action to fight crime in the ghettos.	Maßnahmen ergreifen
to try s.o.'s patience	Racial incidents in her Los Angeles neighbourhood had tried Mrs Cooper's patience so hard that she decided to move back to her hometown in the South.	jds. Geduld auf die Probe stellen
to spread the word	Many migrants spread the word about better job opportunities and living conditions in the North.	es weitersagen
to encourage s.o. to do sth.	The speaker said he hoped that the conference would encourage black Americans to discover their African heritage.	jdn. darin bestärken
to pave the path	After South Africa's formal abolition of apartheid the path was paved for readmission to international sport.	den Weg bahnen
to read s.o. his rights	Cedric Holloway was ordered out of the car, handcuffed and read his rights.	jdn. über seine Rechte aufklären
to set s.o. apart	Blacks say that they feel discrimination more than any other group because their colour immediately sets them apart.	jdn. (von jdm.) unterscheiden
to be anxious to do	The city council is anxious to improve living conditions in the ghettos.	darauf bedacht sein, etwas zu tun
to urge s.o. to do	The new law urges large companies to offer more jobs to minority groups.	jdn. drängen, etwas zu tun
to drop out of school	Many more black students drop out of school than whites.	vorzeitig die Schule verlassen
to be scheduled to do	The motel where Martin Luther King was killed was scheduled to open as a museum in June, but construction delays postponed the opening for three months.	(laut Plan) tun sollen

Civil rights 153

| to bring home to s.o. | Controversy over a new civil rights bill is bringing home to Americans the deepening divisions between blacks and whites. | jdm. etwas bewusst machen |
| to give rise to | The court's ruling gave rise to a heated discussion on racial equality. | eröffnen, zu etwas führen |

3 Practice

Exercise 1 The life of Martin Luther King

Complete the text with words from this list:

against	disobedience	imprisoned	refused
awarded	employment	less	resigned
backgrounds	entered	married	role
boycott	entitled	movement	seating
capital	equality	passed	sniper
closed	face	pastorate	sought
demonstration	facilities	presidency	

Martin Luther King was born on January 15, 1929, the second of three children of the Reverend Martin and Mrs Alberta King. He attended public elementary and high schools as well as private Laboratory High School of Atlanta University. While attending Boston University, he met Coretta Scott whom he _____ [1] in June 1953. Early in 1954, King accepted his first _____ [2] at the Dexter Avenue Baptist Church in Montgomery. He had been a resident in Montgomery _____ [3] than one year when Mrs Rosa Parks defied the ordinance regulating segregated _____ [4] on municipal transportation.

In the aftermath of the successful _____ [5], and urged by prominent black Baptist ministers in the South to assume a larger _____ [6] in the struggle for black civil rights, King accepted the _____ [7] of the newly formed Southern Christian Leadership Conference (SCLC). In January 1960, he _____ [8] his Montgomery pastorate and moved to Atlanta, Georgia, where the SCLC had its headquarters.

On February 1, 1960 four black students _____ [9] a variety store, made several purchases, and then sat down at the lunch counter and ordered coffee. They were _____ [10] service because of their race, but undaunted they remained in their seats until the store _____ [11]. This was the beginning of the sit-in _____ ¹². As a direct result of the sit-ins, lunch counters across the South began to serve blacks, and other public _____ ¹³ were desegregated.

The most critical direct action _____ ¹⁴ began in Birmingham, Alabama, on April 3, 1963, under the leadership of Dr. King. The demonstrators demanded fair _____ ¹⁵ opportunities, and desegregation of public facilities. King was arrested, and while _____ ¹⁶, wrote his celebrated "Letters from a Birmingham jail" to fellow clergymen critical of his tactics of civil _____ ¹⁷. The Birmingham demonstrations did not bring the concessions that the marchers _____ ¹⁸, but the protest was important because it compelled the American people to _____ ¹⁹ the problem of southern discrimination.

On August 28, 1963, more than 250,000 Americans from many religious and ethnic _____ ²⁰ converged on Washington, staging the largest demonstration in the history of the nation's _____ ²¹. At the March on Washington King gave one of the greatest speeches in American history, _____ ²² "I Have A Dream".

In 1964 The Civil Rights Act was _____ ²³ by Congress. It protected citizens _____ ²⁴ discrimination in voting, education, and the use of public facilities. In the same year King was _____ ²⁵ the Nobel Peace Prize in Oslo, Norway. He continued to work to integrate housing, jobs and schools, to make the dream of racial _____ ²⁶ a reality. On April 4, 1968, he was assassinated by a _____ ²⁷ as he stood on a balcony in Memphis, Tennessee, where he had gone to support a strike of sanitation workers.

Exercise 2 Martin Luther King: Nobel prize acceptance speech (Oslo 10. 12. 1964)

In the following text some words are incomplete. Only one or a couple of letters are given. Try to complete with words that would fit the context.

I must ask why this prize is awarded to a movement which is beleaguered and committed to unrelenting struggle: to a movement which has not won the very peace and brotherhood which is the essence of the Nobel Prize.

Civil rights ◢ 155

After contem_____[1], I conclude that this award which I received on beh_____[2] of that movement is profound recognition that nonvi_____[3] is the answer to the crucial political and moral question of our time – the need for man to overc_____[4] oppression and violence without resorting to oppression and violence.

Civili_____[5] and violence are antithetical concepts. Negroes of the United States, foll_____[6] the people of India, have demons_____[7] that nonviolence is not sterile passi_____[8], but a powerful moral force which makes for social transf_____[9]. Sooner or later, all people of the world will have to discover a way to live toge_____[10] in peace, and thereby transform this pending cosmic elegy into a creative psalm of brotherh_____[11].

If this is to be achi_____[12], man must evolve for all human conf_____[13] a method which rejects revenge, aggre_____[14] and retaliation. The foundation of such a method is love. [...]

I refuse to acc_____[15] the idea is mere flotsam and jetsam (Treibgut) in the river of life which surr_____[16] him. I refuse to accept the view that mankind is so tragic_____[17] bound to the starless midnight of racism and war that the bright dayb_____[18] of peace and brotherhood can never become a reality.

I refuse to accept the cynical not_____[19] that nation after nation must spiral down a militaristic stairw_____[20] into the hell of thermonuclear destr_____[21]. I believe that unarmed truth and uncondit_____[22] love will have the final word in reality. This is why right temporarily defe_____[23] is stronger than evil triumphant.

I believe that even amid today's mortar bursts and whining bullets, there is still hope for a brighter tomo_____[24]. I believe that woun_____[25] justice, lying prostrate (ausgestreckt) on the blood-flowing streets of our nations, can be lifted from this dust of shame to reign supreme among the children of men.

Exercise 3   **The legacy of Rosa Parks**

Translate into English or German respectively.

The quintessential story of the 20th Century is the story of the triumph of freedom – of democracy over *dictatorship* (_____)[1], free enterprise over state socialism, of tolerance over _____[2] (Fanatismus, Scheinheiligkeit). It was a fight waged on the beaches of Normandy, on the islands of the South Pacific, at Checkpoint Charlie, behind the *Iron Curtain* (_____)[3], and countless known and unknown, large and small villages, across the globe. Here, at home, a fight *waged* _____[4] in classrooms, lunch counters, and on public buses in the segregated South. For us, what has always been *at stake* _____[5] is whether we could keep moving on that stony road, closer to the ideals of our Founders – whether we really could be a country where we are all equal, not only *endowed* (_____ _____)[6] by our creator with – but in fact living with – the rights to life, liberty, and the pursuit of happiness.

Forty-four years ago, Rosa Parks reminded us all that we were a long way from those ideals; that for millions of Americans, our history was full of weary years – our sweet land of liberty bearing only bitter fruit and silent tears. And so she sat, anchored to that seat, as Dr. King said, "by the *accumulated* _____[7] indignities of days gone by, and the countless *aspirations* (_____)[8] of generations yet unborn." Rosa Parks said, "I didn't get on that bus to get *arrested* _____[9]. I got on that bus to go home." In so many ways, Rosa Parks brought America home, to our Founders' dream.

When Rosa Parks got on that bus in Alabama, I was a nine-year-old boy, living in Arkansas, going to segregated schools, riding public buses every single day, where all the colored people sat _____[10] (im hinteren Teil). My family got a television when I was nine years old, just a few months before it became worldwide news that Mrs Parks had gotten on the bus. I thought it was a *pretty* (_____)[11] good deal, and so did my friends. And we couldn't anything we could do, *since* (_____)[12] we couldn't even vote. So, we began to sit on the back of the bus when we got on.

We must never, ever forget about the power of ordinary people that stand in the fire for the cause of human _____[13] (Würde), and to touch the hearts of people that have almost turned to stone.

I thank the Congress for honoring Rosa Parks. But remember, my fellow Americans, freedom's work is never done. There are still people who are discriminated against. There are still people that because of their human condition are looked down on, derided, *degraded* (_____)[14], demeaned, and we should all remember the powerful example of this one citizen. And those of us with greater authority and power should *attempt* (_____)[15] every day, in every way, to follow her lead."

Excerpts from President Clinton's remarks when he bestowed the Congressional Gold Medal on civil rights legend Rosa Parks.

Civil rights ❘ 157

Exercise 4   Desegregation of Schools

In the following text some words are incomplete. Only a couple of letters are given. Try to complete with words that would fit the context.

This is a story of hope; of perseverance; of refusal to give up no matter how big the obs_____[1]; no matter how fierce the opponent; no matter how unfair the odds. In America, the story is called Brown vs. the Board of Education. Not a very catchy title but one that many Americans know and I would like to share it with you today. The story begins with a little girl.

Not so long ago, Linda Carol Brown was an 8-year-old African American girl who att_____[2] a segregated all black public primary school in the United States. At the time the law in many states pro_____[3] interracial education. In order to get an education little Linda Brown had to walk through a dangerous railroad yard and across the tracks to catch the bus every morning. The bus took her to a school that was 21 blocks away from her home. The bus would arrive at the school 30 minutes before the building opened every morning, and she would be for_____[4] to wait outside the locked schoolhouse even in bitter cold, driving rain and snow.

The little girl's father was not sati_____[5] with the system. He wanted to enrol his daughter in an all-white school which was only five blocks away from his home. He dema_____[6] to know why the Board of Education had the right to exc_____[7] his daughter from the nearby school simply because of her race. When Mr Brown tried to enrol his daughter in the all white school, the Board of Education ref_____[8] to admit her and forced her to stay in the segr_____[9] school.

And so the Brown family and other African American families began a co_____[10] case against the authorities to fight inju_____[11] in the American education system. At that time, the law said that blacks and whites could be forced to use separate fac_____[12] – separate schools, separate toilets, separate drinking fountains, separate entr_____[13], separate park benches, separate everything – as long as the facilities were equal. But everyone knew that was a lie – because the separate facilities were never equal; nor were they ever meant to be. The separate facilities were int_____[14] to be a means of one race maintaining dominance and supe_____[15] over another. You and I both know that is never acceptable in a democracy because in any democracy, every citizen has the same right to the bene_____[16] of society and the law must protect those rights.

So what happened? The Brown family was joined by other families from their state and other states who were equally deter_____[17] to stop the practice of

158 / Civil rights

giving black Americans an inferior education. Armed with determination and cou_____[18] and secure in the knowledge that they had right on their side they took their case to the highest court in the United States. And they won. It was a victory for African Americans, a victory for democracy and a victory for human rights everywhere.

Remarks by Robyn E. Hinson-Jones, Consul General, US Consulate General General, Lagos. Delivered at Benson Idahosa University, Benin-City. February 4, 2004

Exercise 5   Synonyms

Find synonyms for the words in italics.

1. M. L. King's march on Washington was organized to draw the public's attention to the *appalling* conditions of the negroes.

2. Blacks have been denied civil rights (e. g. the *right to vote*) for too long.

3. M. L. King, who had always fought with means of non-violent *resistance,* was assassinated in 1968.

4. "We must fight for the liberation of *oppressed* people everywhere."

5. Sweatshop employers *intimidated* their illegal workers.

6. Cultural *diversity* is one of the main characteristics of a multi-racial society.

7. Riots broke out in one of the most *deprived* estates in Los Angeles.

8. US President John F. Kennedy was *assassinated* in 1963.

9. Many blacks are still *barred* from equal opportunities at work.

10. The *rage* among middle-class blacks has been increasing.

11. Racial discrimination is often more *subtle* than face-to-face confrontation.

12. Blacks of all ages and economic backgrounds tell similar stories of racial *humiliation.*

Civil rights 159

13. The last half century has seen *crucial* changes in the   _____
life of the Afro-Americans.

14. The Supreme Court's decision outlawing segregation
in the public schools *enhanced* the Blacks' sense of   _____
dignity.

15. Segregation and discrimination are strange paradoxes
in a nation *founded* on the principle that all men are   _____
created equal.

Exercise 6   Opposites

Find opposites for the words in italics.

1. After 45 minutes of questioning, the police *accepted*   _____
his statement that he had not taken part in the riot.

2. This is no time for *apathy* and complacency.   _____

3. We blacks are too *cowardly* to face the fact that our   _____
leaders have been lying to us for years.

4. The *decline* of agriculture has drawn large numbers of   _____
Blacks to urban centres.

5. Nobody can *deny* that the decisions of the Supreme   _____
Court have had an enormous influence on US politics.

6. We, the Blacks, are the most *despised* children of the   _____
great Western house.

7. Despite the striking advances in racial equality, the
gains remain *fragile* and partial.   _____

8. Stokely Carmichael's militant Black Power movement
terrified the American nation.   _____

9. Among Northern whites there was a sense of
superiority in discussions of race.   _____

10. Even a *superficial* look at history reveals that no social   _____
advance rolls in automatically.

11. But black Americans say *segregation's* legacy is still   _____
alive today.

12. Economic racism, in which money and social status
are used as barriers, is more frequent than the *overt*   _____
racism of the past.

160 / Civil rights

Exercise 7 Matching words and their definitions

Match the words from list 1 with their appropriate definitions in list 2. Please note: There are more words than definitions!

A opinion formed before one has adequate knowledge or experience

B district outside the central part of a town or city

C condition of being kept down by unjust or cruel government

D violent and sudden attack

E mental, emotional, nervous strain

F public, often organized rally or march protesting against or supporting somebody or something

G violent outburst of lawlessness by the people in a district

H greater number or part

I kill somebody violently, for political reasons

J section of a town lived in by underprivileged classes, or people who are discriminated against

K distinction in one's attitude to people, usually in a negative sense

L difficult, demanding or stimulating task

M cultural achievements that have been passed on from earlier generations

N move from one place to go to live or work in another

(1) assassinate
(2) assault
(3) challenge
(4) condemn
(5) demonstration
(6) discrimination
(7) diversity
(8) enforcement
(9) ghetto
(10) heritage
(11) loot
(12) majority
(13) migrate
(14) oppression
(15) prejudice
(16) rampage
(17) random
(18) riot
(19) suburb
(20) tension
(21) violate

A	B	C	D	E	F	G	H	I	J	K	L	M	N

Civil rights **/** 161

Exercise 8   Word families

Supply the missing forms.

noun (abstract)	verb	adjective
presidency	preside	presidential
_____	_____	annoying
conciliation	_____	_____
_____	defy	_____
_____	hate	_____
_____	---	inferior
irritation	_____	_____
_____	_____	legal
_____	obey	_____
_____	persist	_____
pursuit	_____	_____
_____	_____	repentant
_____	resent	_____
resistance	_____	_____
_____	_____	separate [it]
slavery	_____	_____

Exercise 9   Crossword puzzle

Try to solve the crossword puzzle.

Across
4 Hindernis
5 Vorurteil
7 ermorden
8 Hass
10 heftig, ungestüm
12 Diktatur
14 Tugend
15 Wanderung
17 ausstatten
19 wahlberechtigt
21 Einsatz
22 Versöhnung
24 Kriminalität
27 hartnäckig

Down
1 Bewusstsein
2 Zusammenstoß
3 zu Felde ziehen
5 Haupt-
6 Vorhaben
9 Einrichtung, Anlage
11 Ausbruch
12 erniedrigen
13 Demütigung
16 ansammeln
18 Vermächtnis
20 ausschließen
23 Ablehnung, Weigerung
25 fertig werden (mit)

162 Civil rights

30 verbieten
31 starten
34 Unruhe
35 sich einschreiben
36 Bewegung
37 Minderheit

26 Behörde, Amtsgewalt
28 willkürlich
29 Plündern
32 Brandstiftung
33 müde, erschöpft

Key

1 Environment

Exercise 1 What we are doing to our environment

1 sewage; 2 detergents; 3 yields; 4 predicted; 5 poisoning; 6 attention;
7 heating; 8 burning; 9 temperature; 10 increase; 11 expands; 12 levels;
13 Droughts; 14 Agriculture; 15 Amazon; 16 released; 17 desert;
18 attempts; 19 global; 20 reduction

Exercise 2 The vital importance of our oceans

1 surface; 2 Ströme, Strömungen; 3 mäßigen; 4 enormous; 5 accustomed;
6 unzerstörbar; 7 verschwenderisch; 8 erschöpft, ausgelaugt; 9 jeopardized,
endangered, put into danger; 10 zu erhalten; 11 weggeworfen; 12 habitat;
13 livelihood; 14 Häfen; 15 stellen dar; 16 Not(lage); 17 exploiting

Exercise 3 Global warming

1 comprehensive; 2 revealed; 3 findings; 4 maintain; 5 worst; 6 consequence;
7 rapid; 8 response; 9 greenhouse; 10 conclusions; 11 Scientists; 12 temperature; 13 whether; 14 spreading; 15 planet's; 16 Climatologists; 17 evidence;
18 certainly; 19 likely; 20 remotely

Exercise 4 How can we save our atmosphere?

1 ozone; 2 rays; 3 shield; 4 cancer; 5 emissions; 6 reduced; 7 quantity;
8 raising; 9 renewable; 10 nuclear; 11 threat; 12 nitrate; 13 efficient;
14 chemical-free; 15 fertilizers; 16 decreasing; 17 livestock; 18 substitutes;
19 aerosol; 20 recommendation; 21 intensify; 22 network; 23 atmosphere

164 ❘ Key: Environment

Exercise 5 Too many people

1 derives; 2 economies; 3 survival; 4 rural; 5 decline; 6 present; 7 followed;
8 East; 9 birthrate; 10 pollution; 11 particular; 12 rapid; 13 issue; 14 republic;
15 pregnant; 16 trend; 17 levels; 18 prevent; 19 increase; 20 abortions

Exercise 6 Synonyms

1 improvements, breakthroughs; 2 devices, gadgets; boring, repetitive,
monotonous; 3 fragile, sensitive, feeble equilibrium; 4 burning; 5 cleaner,
cleanser, washing-powder; 6 decline, reject; illness; 7 non-returnable; 8 waste
management; 9 rubbish-heaps; 10 waters, oceans; rubbish, refuse, trash, litter,
junk; 11 dangers, perils, risks; 12 toxic, noxious; 13 contaminating; 14 clean,
cleanse; 15 spoil, devastate; 16 waste water; 17 menace, danger

Exercise 7 Word families

noun (abstract)	noun (concrete)	verb	adjective
presidency	president	preside	presidential
environment	environmentalist	---	environmental
erosion	---	erode	erosive
pollution	pollutant	pollute	polluting, polluted
survival	survivor	survive	surviving
nutrition	nutrient	---	nutritious nutritional
nourishment	---	nourish	nourishing
waste	---	waste	wasteful
---	inhabitant	inhabit	inhabitable
science	scientist	---	scientific
purification	---	purify	pure

Exercise 8 Matching words and their definitions

A	B	C	D	E	F	G	H	I	J	K	L	M	N
19	1	4	11	2	9	5	13	6	12	10	8	18	15

Exercise 9 — Crossword puzzle

P	O	L	L	U	T	E				J									S
R	E	N		P			U	R	B	A	N	I	S	E					O
O	A	T	H	R	E	A	T	E	N					E					I
T	D	R		C			K		R	E	V	E	A	L					L
E		E	D	K	V									E					D
C	O	N	T	A	M	I	N	A	T	E		T	I	M	B	E	R		R
T		T	S	G	N							O		E					A
	S	E	A		I		G					R							N
D	P	D	I	S	I	N	T	E	G	R	A	T	E		E				C
I	I		T		G		A	E		A			Q		E				E
S	U	L	P	H	U	R			N		F	A	L	L	O	U	T		
P	L		O				C				R		I		I				
O		D	U	N	P	R	E	D	I	C	T	A	B	L	E				B
S	P	E	C	I	E	S			A		G		Y		I				I
A		S				T	I	D	E		E				B				O
L	A	Y	E	R		A			R	E	S	O	U	R	C	E	S		S
		U	I			A					A				I				P
		P	O	L	L	U	T	I	O	N					U				H
C	O	A	S	T		I		I			T	C	L	I	M	A	T	E	
		N				O													R
	E	C	O	L	O	G	Y		N	A	T	U	R	A	L	G	A	S	E

Exercise 10 — Word square

1 unpredictable; 2 uninhabitable; 3 biodegradable; 4 biodiversity;
5 contaminate; 6 composition; 7 widespread; 8 conclusive; 9. combustion;
10 centigrade; 11 untreated; 12 depletion; 13 biosphere; 14 vigorous;
15 survival; 16 delicate; 17 creature; 18 abundant; 19 vicious; 20 variety;
21 surface; 22 sulphur; 23 fertile; 24 concern; 25 climate; 26 chimney;
27 balance; 28 advance; 29 vapour; 30 threat; 31 supply; 32 carbon;
33 bleach; 34 ailing; 35 waste; 36 dense; 37 coast; 38 birth; 39 tide; 40 rate

166 Key: Environment

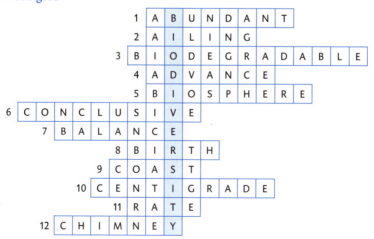

Exercise 11   Word grid

Key: World affairs / 167

2 World affairs

xercise 1 A world of disparities

1 primarily; 2 common; 3 malnutrition; 4 literacy; 5 rose; 6 place;
7 industrial; 8 subsistence; 9 experienced; 10 relieve; 11 plight; 12 donation;
13 subsidies; 14 poverty; 15 market; 16 obligations; 17 responsibility;
18 property; 19 disparity; 20 development

xercise 2 The plight of working children

1 famine; 2 harvest; 3 brunt; 4 borrow; 5 advance; 6 debt; 7 slavery;
8 estimated; 9 harvest; 10 care; 11 trade; 12 carpets; 13 lung; 14 burns;
15 human; 16 helpful; 17 experience; 18 tolerate; 19 passed; 20 labour

xercise 3 The day that changed the world: Hiroshima

1 course; 2 warfare; 3 populated; 4 target; 5 altitude; 6 mushroom;
7 height; 8 vicinity; 9 horrifying; 10 glance; 11 devastations; 12 arsenals;
13 deteriorated; 14 engaged; 15 fission; 16 disarmament; 17 proliferation;
18 negotiations; 19 limitation; 20 arms

xercise 4 The day that changed the world: 9/11

1 attack; 2 order; 3 entführte; 4 Einschlag; 5 collapsed; 6 Ansprache; 7 Böse;
8 victims; 9 Entschlossenheit; 10 entschlossenen; 11 issues; 12 citizens;
13 besorgt; 14 Ministerium; 15 folglich; 16 measures; 17 delays;
18 dauerhaften; 19 assassination; 20 Gefühl, Einstellung

xercise 5 Amnesty: fighting for human rights

1 treatment; 2 impartial; 3 penalty; 4 donations; 5 volunteers; 6 graduate;
7 research; 8 abuses; 9 founded; 10 prisoners; 11 newspaper; 12 tortured;
13 opinions; 14 effective; 15 appealed; 16 frustrated; 17 injustices;
18 Supporters; 19 distinguishing; 20 chairman

168 ✦ Key: World affairs

Exercise 6   Synonyms

1 analyze, determine, evaluate; 2 classify, rate, order; 3 sources, causes;
4 seemingly, supposedly, presumably; scarcity, lack, shortage, inadequacy;
5 substantially, significantly, dramatically; 6 acceptable, adequate, reasonable,
satisfactory; 7 definitive, final; 8 wages, income, pay; 9 intense, violent, brutal,
cruel; 10 overcrowded, blocked, choked; 11 contain, embrace, comprise;
12 current, existing; 13 provide for, sustain; 14 chiefly, largely, mainly,
primarily, above all

Exercise 7   Opposites

1 conserved, saved; 2 birth, emergence, creation, rise; 3 release, freeing;
4 keeping to, respect for; 5 expense; 6 encouraged, inspired, motivated;
7 secondary, minor, subordinate; 8 understandable, logical, clear; 9 soldiers,
servicemen; 10 eager, zealous, anxious, keen

Exercise 8   Matching words and their definitions

A	B	C	D	E	F	G	H	I	J	K	L	M	N	O	P
21	5	3	7	16	1	10	13	15	20	8	19	12	9	16	14

Exercise 9   Word families

noun (abstract)	noun (concrete)	verb	adjective
presidency	president	preside	presidential
deterrence	deterrent	deter	deterrent
operation	operator	operate	operative
alliance	ally	ally	allied
armament	---	arm	armed
---	volunteer	volunteer	voluntary
protection	protector	protect	protective
grief	---	grieve	grievous
explosion	---	explode	explosive
endurance	---	endure	endurable
objection	objector	object	objectionable

navigation	navigator	navigate	navigable
invasion	invader	invade	---
deceit	---	deceive	deceitful
defiance	---	defy	defiant
courage	---	encourage	courageous
conspiracy	conspirator	conspire	conspiratorial
conquest	conqueror	conquer	---
captivity	captive	captivate	captive
blood	---	bleed	bloody

Exercise 10 Word square

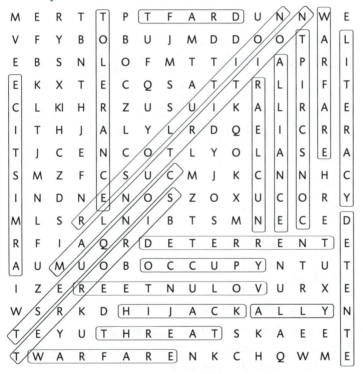

Exercise 11 Crossword puzzle

W		D	I	S	P	A	R	I	T	Y		B	A	L	A	N	C	E		E	
E		I		U								O							R	A	N	K
A	S	S	A	S	S	I	N	A	T	I	O	N		B	L	A	S	T		D
P	A	T		N			N		D			E		P		U
O	R	A	D	E	F	I	C	I	E	N	C	Y		N		I		R
N	M	I		I			O		D			T		T		I
	A	N		C		M	A	L	N	U	T	R	I	T	I	O	N
	M		A	B	U	S	E		A			M		F		G
	D	E	S	E	R	T		P		B	W		E		U
F	N		O	P	R	E	D	O	M	I	N	A	N	T	L	Y
E	T		R		R		U	D			T
E		A	R	H	A	R	V	E	S	T		V
D	E	C	I	S	I	V	E		E		S		I
R	S		L	D	A	I	R	Y	P	R	O	D	U	C	E
P	O	V	E	R	T	Y	D		R		E		I
P	S		S	L	U	R	E		S		N
S	S	C	A	R	C	E	I	A	P	I
R	E	W	T	D	E	C	E	N	T
U	S	C	A	L	E	D	N	R	Y
R	O	G	R	I	G	A
A	R	S	E	N	A	L	E	A	D	E	Q	U	A	T	E
L	V	C	T	L	E
I	L	L	I	T	E	R	A	C	Y	F

3 Consumer/Health

Exercise 1 "Big Brother" in our supermarkets

1 detail; 2 habits; 3 provided; 4 collect; 5 item; 6 scanned; 7 replace; 8 adapts;
9 record; 10 left; 11 stolen; 12 loyalty; 13 target; 14 maintain; 15 totalitarian;
16 stored; 17 profit; 18 messages; 19 flood; 20 junk

Key: Consumer/Health | 171

Exercise 2 Glass against plastic

1 decades; 2 moved; 3 direction; 4 supermarket; 5 encourage; 6 dropped;
7 easily; 8 significant; 9 popularity; 10 substitution; 11 response; 12 manufacturer's; 13 changed; 14 shopkeepers; 15 preference; 16 contents; 17 taste;
18 image; 19 convenient; 20 recycled; 21 used; 22 durability; 23 output;
24 increase; 25 bottles; 26 returnable; 27 difference; 28 outside; 29 material;
30 estimated; 31 delivering; 32 washing; 33 spectacular

Exercise 3 Teenage obesity

1 adolescents; 2 fett(leibig); 3 customers; 4 mit der Behauptung; indem sie
behaupteten; 5 die verbunden sind; 6 lawsuit; 7 weight; 8 Fertiggerichte;
9 diet; 10 performance; 11 Ernährungswissenschaftler; 12 imbalance;
13 exercise; 14 Folgekrankheiten; 15 vividly; 16 carbohydrates; 17 stärke-
haltige; 18 harm; 19 ausreichend, genügend; 20 benefits

Exercise 4 School meals: Pupils' health at risk

1 lunches; 2 evidence; 3 damaging; 4 sales; 5 fizzy; 6 lunchtime; 7 compelled;
8 introduced; 9 recruits; 10 recent; 11 provided; 12 catering; 13 healthy;
14 bags; 15 choice; 16 authorities; 17 diet; 18 diabetes; 19 habits; 20 vegetable; 21 wholemeal; 22 making; 23 offer; 24 nutritional

Exercise 5 The British National Health Service (NHS)

1 taxation; 2 patient; 3 care; 4 cabinet; 5 precedent; 6 prescriptions; 7 exami-
nations; 8 discouraged; 9 preventive; 10 cancer; 11 demand; 12 transplants;
13 emerge; 14 geriatric; 15 bearable; 16 dismantle; 17 cover

Exercise 6 Synonyms

1 devalue, think little of; 2 recognizable, noticeable; 3 trader, dealer; 4 judge,
assess; 5 false, wrong, inexact; 6 aim, purpose; 7 faithfulness, fidelity;
8 confirm; 9 favourable; 10 notion, idea, belief; 11 profit; 12 confusing,
puzzling; 13 goods, articles, products, merchandise; 14 forced, obliged;
15 rival; 16 contrive, devise; 17 mislead, cheat, fool, delude; 18 wealth,

172 / Key: Consumer/Health

affluence, economic well-being; 19 assortment; 20 depression, slump, slack period; 21 reply, answer, return; 22 conspicuous, stunning; 23 violation, offence against; 24 enormous, huge, immense

Exercise 7 Word families

noun (abstract)	noun (concrete)	verb	adjective
presidency	president	preside	presidential
advantage	---	---	advantageous
benefit	---	benefit	beneficial
compulsion	---	compel	compulsory
consumption	consumer	consume	consumptive
creation	creature, creator	create	creative
difference	---	differ	different
economy	economist	economize	economic
employment	employer, employee	employ	---
influence	---	influence	influential
response	---	respond	responsive
science	scientist	---	scientific
speciality	---	specialize	special
succession	successor	succeed	successive

Exercise 8 Matching words and their definitions

A	B	C	D	E	F	G	H	I	J	K	L
12	11	13	15	5	6	8	7	1	10	9	2

Key: Work ⏐ 173

Exercise 9 Crossword puzzle

A	D	V	E	R	T	I	S	I	N	G
N	W	A	N	T	E	D	F	N	O	C
T	N	P	R	E	V	I	E	W	N	O
P	U	R	C	H	A	S	E	R	P	M
S	T	O	C	K	L	C	C	I	R	P
A	C	T		A	U	E	U	T	O	E
L	S	E	A	L	A	R	S	I	F	T
A	A	C	H	E	T	N	T	N	I	I
R	E	T	I	R	E	I	O	G	T	T
Y	R	I	O	T		B	M	I	N	I
M	A	O	M	I	S	L	E	A	D	V
C	O	N	S	U	M	E	R	E	V	E

4 Work

Exercise 1 Upheaval in the labour lovement

1 abzuwenden; 2 trug bei; 3 unskilled workers; 4 praktisch; 5 disadvantaged; 6 indem sie verhandelten; 7 schließlich; 8 campaign; 9 disease; 10 Rückständigkeit; 11 vernichteten; 12 workforce; 13 behauptet; 14 relationship; 15 nach und nach, im Großen und Ganzen; 16 Mittel; 17 verankert; 18 Collective bargaining; 19 disputes; 20 verfolgen

Exercise 2 When one job is not enough

1 completed; 2 increased; 3 economic; 4 divorces; 5 poverty; 6 insufficient; 7 decently; 8 observed; 9 lifestyle; 10 pleasant; 11 accustomed; 12 beyond; 13 vacation; 14 expression; 15 diversion; 16 opportunities; 17 employment; 18 supplement; 19 earnings; 20 regenerate

Exercise 3 A safer place to work

1 cotton; 2 exactly; 3 clocks; 4 deducted; 5 contrast; 6 picking; 7 injury; 8 breadwinner; 9 pioneers; 10 proposed; 11 enquiry; 12 conditions; 13 survey; 14 exploitation; 15 chairman; 16 safety; 17 principle; 18 experience; 19 required; 20 determine

174 / Key: Work

Exercise 4 Young people's life-skills

1 essential; 2 research; 3 commissioned; 4 develop; 5 varying; 6 extent;
7 emerged; 8 aesthetic; 9 sufficiently; 10 rated; 11 perceived; 12 acquire;
13 gender; 14 stressed; 15 commitment; 16 requisite; 17 attach; 18 promote;
19 implications; 20 prospects

Exercise 5 Synonyms

1 strikebreaker; 2 trade; 3 assembly line; 4 patron, client; 5 sack, fire; 6 labour
exchange; 7 labour, workers; 8 finished products; 9 talks; 10 staff; 11 walkout,
industrial action

Exercise 6 Opposites

1 general, overall; 2 employed, hired; 3 dismiss, sack, fire; 4 lowering,
reducing, decreasing; 5 hire, employ; 6 victories, success, achievements;
7 boom, growth; 8 slowed down, decreased, dropped; 9 poor, badly off;
10 temporary; 11 kept, preserved, retained; 12 disadvantage, damage,
detriment

Exercise 7 Crossword puzzle

		A	L	I	E	N	A	T	I	O	N
	M	O	O	N	A	O	R	T	A	R	
D	A	D	V	E	R	T	I	S	E	D	F
I	N	T	E	R	V	I	E	W	L	E	O
S	P	R	O	D	U	C	E	A	I	R	R
P	O	A	P	P	R	E	N	T	I	C	E
U	W	I	T	N	E	S	S		D	A	M
T	E	N	A	C	I	O	U	S	E	T	A
E	R	E	T	I	R	E	N	C	A	N	N
	N	E	G	O	T	I	A	T	I	O	N

Key: Work 175

Exercise 8 Word families

noun (abstract)	noun (concrete)	verb	adjective
presidency	president	preside	presidential
application	applicant	apply	applicable
attendance	---	attend	attentive
bankruptcy	---	---	bankrupt
benefit	beneficiary	benefit	beneficial
business	businessman businesswoman	busy	busy
competition	competitor	compete	competitive
conveyance	---	convey	---
cooperation	cooperator	cooperate	cooperative
employment	employer	employ	---
execution	executive	execute	executive
industry	industrialist	industrialize	industrial
labour	labourer	labour	laborious
nation	---	nationalize	national
vacancy	---	vacate	vacant

Exercise 9 Matching words and their definitions

A	B	C	D	E	F	G	H	I	J	K	L
4	15	1	6	14	8	5	11	18	2	12	7

176 / Key: Science and technology

5 Science and technology

Exercise 1 **Stem cells – We can rebuild you**

1 diseased; 2 research; 3 treatments; 4 sentence; 5 matures; 6 material;
7 raises; 8 sufferers; 9 limitations; 10 transform; 11 tissue; 12 purified;
13 radiation; 14 chromosome; 15 repair; 16 memory; 17 arteries; 18 attack;
19 potential; 20 transplant; 21 concerns; 22 cloning; 23 object

Exercise 2 **Concorde: The dream of supersonic flight**

1 nightmare; 2 crashed; 3 accelerate; 4 celebrities; 5 jetliners, jets, jet aero-
planes, jet planes; 6 unattainable; 7 considerably; 8 inventive; 9 design;
10 estimated; 11 took shape; 12 drawing-board; 13 speed of sound;
14 awarded; 15 assumed; 16 inseparable; 17 unpredictable; 18 compared to;
19 modifications; 20 successor

Exercise 3 **The wireless debt**

1 praktisch, eigentlich; 2 ständig, dauernd; 3 Benutzer; 4 Nützlichkeit;
5 -zelle, -kabine; 6 Wechselgeld; 7 übertroffen; 8 Notfall; 9 Aufenthaltsort;
10 Zahlungen; 11 schriftliche Arbeit, schriftliche Aufgaben; 12 eher, lieber;
13 günstigen, positiven; 14 Erzieher; 15 Rechtschreibung; 16 umfangreich,
beträchtlich; 17 sammeln an, häufen an; 18 Vorsichtsmaßnahmen, Schutz;
19 Verträge; 20 Verpflichtungen

Exercise 4 **Is there life on other planets?**

1 universe; 2 inhabited; 3 fiction; 4 simulated; 5 panic; 6 humans;
7 uninhabitable; 8 advanced; 9 equator; 10 craters; 11 agency; 12 devices;
13 explorations; 14 discoveries; 15 mysteries; 16 transmitted; 17 emitted;
18 encounters; 19 failed; 20 confirm

Exercise 5 **Video games**

1 appeared; 2 generation; 3 comparable; 4 boards; 5 budget; 6 experience;
7 giants; 8 market; 9 risen; 10 recorder; 11 websites; 12 entertainment;
13 audiences; 14 average; 15 teenager; 16 mature; 17 connection; 18 beyond;
19 maintain; 20 industry

Key: Science and technology ✦ 177

Exercise 6 Synonyms

1 speed up; 2 evaluate, judge, calculate; 3 elements, components, factors, ingredients; 4 catastrophic, fateful, fatal; 5 surpass, pass beyond, overstep; 6 forecast, prognosticate, prophesy; 7 grow up; 8 change, alteration, mutation, variation; 9 choice, alternative; 10 clean, cleanse; 11 change, convert; 12 singular, particular, extraordinary, matchless

Exercise 7 Word families

noun	verb	adjective	adverb
prediction	predict	predictable	predictably
access	access	accessible	---
confidence	confide	confidential	confidentially
solution	solve	soluble; solvent	---
alien	alienate	alien	---
speculation	speculate	speculative	---
astronomy	---	astronomical	astronomically
mystery	---	mysterious	mysteriously
fantasy, fantasist	fantasise	fantastic	fantastically
invasion	invade	invasive	---
substance	substantiate	substantial	substantially
connection	connect	connective	---
appropriateness	appropriate	appropriate	appropriately
practice	practise	practical	practically
mobility	mobilise	mobile	---

Exercise 8 Matching words and their definitions

A	B	C	D	E	F	G	H	I	J	K	L	M	N	O	P	Q	R
4	16	11	15	19	1	10	23	13	12	7	8	24	20	22	14	17	5

178 / Key: Crime, law and drugs

6   Crime, law and drugs

Exercise 1   Law and order

1 nature; 2 view; 3 phrase; 4 institutions; 5 determines; 6 responsible;
7 prevented; 8 force; 9 changes; 10 ruling; 11 themes; 12 analysis; 13 society;
14 victims; 15 penalties; 16 obeying; 17 face; 18 causes; 19 remediable;
20 pursued; 21 emphasis

Exercise 2   Cybercrime

1 violations; 2 prosecution; 3 unique; 4 benefit(s); 5 commit; 6 conduct,
behaviour; 7 intolerable; 8 thus; 9 commerce; 10 promote; 11 appreciation;
12 domestically, at home; 13 maturation; 14 ensures; 15 Prior, Earlier;
16 wrongdoing; 17 endeavors [AE], endeavours [BE]; 18 facilitate; 19 fraud;
20 property rights

Exercise 3   Hanging people is wrong

1 political; 2 murderers; 3 himself; 4 perished; 5 Similarly; 6 commits;
7 being; 8 trapped; 9 prepared; 10 deterred; 11 optimists; 12 expects;
13 lawyer(s); 14 altogether; 15 slightest; 16 potential; 17 course; 18 convicted;
19 hanged; 20 won't; 21 probable; 22 penalty; 23 actually; 24 propaganda;
25 function; 26 stake; 27 human; 28 principle; 29 thirsty

Exercise 4   Synonyms (Law)

1 the death penalty, the death sentence; done away with; 2 double-crosses,
sells out; 3 corruption; 4 accusations, allegations; 5 blame, denounce; 6 plot,
secret plan; 7 prisoners, inmates; 8 proof; 9 demand, wrench, squeeze;
10 prison, jail; 11 prisoners, convicts; 12 guiltless, not guilty; set free, free,
discharge; 13 criminals, delinquents, offenders; 14 killing, homicide;
15 punishment; 16 inquiry, inquisition, law-suit; 17 unfair, biased

Key: Crime, law and drugs / 179

rcise 5   Cocaine business

1 controlled; 2 links; 3 Andes; 4 distribution; 5 headquarters; 6 cities;
7 routes; 8 channels; 9 marijuana; 10 supply; 11 fashion; 12 gangsters;
13 illegal; 14 reason; 15 tradition; 16 related; 17 earned; 18 attempted;
19 production; 20 cash; 21 roughly; 22 seriously; 23 eradication;
24 resentment; 25 influence

rcise 6   Nicotine – a powerful and addictive drug

1 revenge; 2 contracted; 3 untimely; 4 addictive; 5 harms; 6 kidneys; 7 toll;
8 preventable; 9 encourage; 10 quit; 11 promotion; 12 outlawed; 13 funded;
14 primarily; 15 executive; 16 gathered; 17 disagreement; 18 consumption;
19 taxes; 20 example

rcise 7   Alcohol is a drug

1 entstellter, verzerrter; 2 Gedächtnislücken, Aussetzer; 3 Blutkreislauf;
4 Hemmungen; 5 beeinträchtigt; 6 Vergiftung; 7 verwickelt in, betroffen von;
8 verstößt gegen das Gesetz; 9 nicht bestehen; 10 Geldstrafe; 11 „Saufgelage";
12 Bestandteil; 13 Übelkeit; 14 Beruhigungsmittel; 15 schwierig; 16 Kater

rcise 8   Matching words and their definitions

A	B	C	D	E	F	G	H	I	J	K	L
18	13	4	14	1	3	6	16	9	17	11	12

rcise 9   Synonyms (Drugs)

1 earth, ground; 2 addiction; serious, grave; 3 ease, get rid of; 4 gangsters;
5 reasonable, temperate, modest; 6 deadly, fatal; 7 arouse, provoke, cause;
8 dangerous, hazardous, perilous; 9 trade, dealing; 10 dealers, traffickers,
peddlers; 11 synthetic drugs; 12 chief, major, principal, number one;
13 killing, massacre, slaughter; 14 fight against, battle; 15 remedy, heal

Exercise 10 — Crossword puzzle

F	I	N	G	E	R	P	R	I	N	T	S
O	N	P	E	R	J	U	R	Y	B	A	H
S	V		S	C	U		F	W	A	X	O
T	E	M	P	O	R	A	R	I	L	Y	P
E	S	D	E	N	Y	V	A	T	L		L
R	T		A	S	P	Y	N	N	O	T	I
P	I	C	K	P	O	C	K	E	T	R	F
A	G	H	E	I	J	O	F	S	G	E	T
R	A	E	R	R	U	N	R	S	U	A	I
E	T	R	I	A	L	C	A	P	I	T	N
N	I	D	A	C	I	E	U	E	L	M	G
T	O	R	Y	Y	E	I	D	E	T	E	R
S	N	R	I	O	T			R	Y	N	
D	E	A	T	H	P	E	N	A	L	T	Y

7 Politics in Great Britain

Exercise 1 — Electoral geography of Great Britain

1 Merkmal; 2 Erlangung; 3 franchise, suffrage, vote; 4 significant; 5 betroffen, beeinträchtigt; 6 waned; 7 Kluft, Spaltung; 8 Büro …; 9 recipient; 10 hatte keine; 11 throughout, all over; 12 evaluate; 13 hinsichtlich; 14 habitually; 15 konkurrierende; 16 attitudes; 17 vary, change; 18 closely; 19 unvereinbar, widersprüchlich; 20 Denkweisen

Exercise 2 — The British Parliament today

1 Lower; 2 Upper House; 3 chamber; 4 650; 5 constituencies; 6 majority; 7 five; 8 by-elections; 9 removed; 10 dissolves; 11 advice; 12 Prime; 13 suffrage; 14 polling; 15 cast; 16 control; 17 bills; 18 Her Majesty's; 19 opposition; 20 Tories; 21 hereditary; 22 delay; 23 Appeal; 24 fees; 25 resign

Key: Politics in Great Britain ◢ 181

ercise 3   Farewell to the Lords

1 peerage; 2 survive; 3 banished; 4 allegiance; 5 common; 6 enthusiasts;
7 merits; 8 mourn; 9 seats; 10 deserve; 11 interfere; 12 dutifully; 13 dependent; 14 exerted; 15 minority; 16 urban; 17 check; 18 protest; 19 motion;
20 balance

ercise 4   A visit to the House of Commons

1 looking; 2 work; 3 elected; 4 representatives; 5 links; 6 constituents;
7 against; 8 duty; 9 criticize; 10 appointed; 11 submit; 12 guided; 13 guardian;
14 unbroken; 15 possesses; 16 speak; 17 displays; 18 worse; 19 over;
20 welcome

ercise 5   How to be a new MP

1 arena; 2 distinguished; 3 longer; 4 crowds; 5 memory; 6 institution;
7 modest; 8 ease; 9 meeting; 10 room; 11 Prime; 12 Opposition; 13 elected;
14 sounds; 15 palace; 16 job; 17 lucky; 18 sharing; 19 improving; 20 character; 21 reminded; 22 applicants; 23 maiden; 24 rituals; 25 matter; 26 speaker;
27 contribute; 28 decide; 29 supporter; 30 things

ercise 6   The case against the "first-past-the-post"-system

Argumente gegen das Mehrheitswahlsystem
Die Grundidee einer Regierungsform, die das Volk vertritt, besteht darin, dass
alle Gruppen der Gesellschaft bei der Bildung und Führung der Regierung ein
Mitspracherecht haben. Damit wird ein Grundrecht erfüllt, das alle besitzen
(sollen), und – es gibt gute Gründe für diese Annahme – dadurch wird es
wahrscheinlicher, dass die Regierung im Interesse und mit allgemeiner Zu-
stimmung der Regierten geführt wird.
Kritiker behaupten, dass unser gegenwärtiges System, weil es nicht ausreichend repräsentativ ist, gegen grundlegende Menschenrechte verstößt und
eine falsche Art von Regierung an die Macht bringt: Das Mehrheitswahlrecht
benachteiligt kleinere Parteien. Eine Partei mit schwacher landesweiter Gefolg-
schaft mag zwar eine beträchtliche Zahl an Wählerstimmen gewinnen, sie
wird aber nur sehr wenige Sitze erringen. So gewann 1983 die SDP-Liberal
Allianz (Wahlbündnis zwischen Sozialdemokraten und Liberalen), obwohl sie
26 % der abgegebenen Stimmen auf sich vereinigte und in 313 Wahlkreisen an

182 / Key: Politics in Great Britain

die zweite Stelle kam, nur 23 Direktmandate, d. h. 3,5 % der Sitze im Unterhaus. Damit wurde über ein Viertel der Wählerschaft nur unzureichend vertreten.

Exercise 7 **Synonyms**

1 resign, step down; 2 view, opinon; 3 assure, persuade; 4 excerpts, passages; 5 virtually, practically; 6 guarantee, secure; 7 Lower House; 8 useless, incapable; 9 directed, ordered; 10 matter, topic, problem; 11 keep up, sustain; 12 deliver; 13 threat; 14 adversary; 15 programme, manifesto; 16 revolt, revolution; 17 turn down, refuse; 18 dictator, despot

Exercise 8 **Opposites**

1 refuse; 2 worse; 3 grant, allow, permit; 4 favourable/friendly towards, in favour of, supporting; 5 continental; 6 minor; 7 joy, delight, pleasure; 8 agree with, approve of, consent to; 9 predecessors; 10 ordinary, usual, common; 11 respect; 12 unimportant, minor, marginal

Exercise 9 **Matching words and their definitions**

A	B	C	D	E	F	G	H	I	J	K	L
11	16	13	15	12	3	2	1	8	9	7	10

Exercise 10 **Word families**

noun (abstract)	noun (concrete)	verb	adjective
presidency	president	preside	presidential
politics	politician	---	political
representation	representative	represent	representative
election	elector	elect	electoral
concept	---	conceive	conceptual
dictatorship	dictator	dictate	dictatorial
speech	speaker	speak	---
tyranny	tyrannt	tyrannize	tyrannical

| continuity | --- | continue | continuous |
| variety | --- | vary | various |

Exercise 11 — Crossword puzzle

E	L	E	C	T	O	R	A	T	E
R		C	O	N	D	E	M	N	P
E	M	I	N	V	O	L	V	E	E
C	O	N	F	I	D	E	N	C	E
E	T	R	I	A	L	A	O	R	R
P	I	U	S	E	S	S	I	O	N
T	O	N	C	A	N	E	S	W	
I	N	H	A	B	I	T	A	N	T
O	R	A	T	O	R	Y	A	D	A
N	E	V	E	B	E	N	C	H	X

8 Politics in the US

Exercise 1 — The Queen in Philadelphia

1 separation; 2 sincere; 3 founding; 4 having; 5 lacked; 6 yielding; 7 learnt;
8 closely; 9 heritage; 10 respect; 11 themselves; 12 outcome; 13 performed;
14 transformed; 15 ultimately; 16 friendship; 17 grown; 18 part; 19 fought;
20 defence; 21 allies; 22 future; 23 largest; 24 commemorate; 25 Independence; 26 anniversary; 27 pleasure

Exercise 2 — Presidential versus Parliamentary Government

1 practised; 2 looking; 3 correcting; 4 power; 5 stated; 6 relationship; 7 single;
8 term; 9 contrast; 10 removable; 11 separates; 12 republic; 13 Chancellor;
14 combined; 15 defended; 16 delay; 17 policy; 18 likelihood; 19 cut off;
20 goals; 21 follows; 22 stable; 23 elections; 24 exercise

184 / Key: Politics in the US

Exercise 3   The Democratic and the Republican Party

1 support; 2 professional; 3 tariffs; 4 war; 5 strength; 6 until; 7 era; 8 growth;
9 succeeded; 10 reelection; 11 woman; 12 amalgamation; 13 themselves;
14 presidential; 15 strong; 16 victories; 17 representation; 18 vice-president;
19 reunited; 20 fought

Exercise 4   The office of President

Das Präsidentenamt

Die Amerikaner wollen nicht, dass ein Präsident zu mächtig wird; jedoch
(andererseits) will das Land ganz sicher, dass er weit reichende Befugnisse hat,
um mit allen Notsituationen fertig zu werden. Tatsächlich schieben der Kon-
gress und die Öffentlichkeit dem Präsidenten ständig neue Vollmachten zu,
damit er neue Probleme bewältigen kann.
Ein Grund, warum es Präsidenten schwer finden, Macht abzugeben, liegt
darin, dass sie ihnen größtenteils von Farmern, Geschäftsleuten und Arbeitern
aufgezwungen wurde, die wollten, dass die Regierung in der Zeit einer schwe-
ren wirtschaftlichen oder militärischen Krise handlungsfähig war. Diese Gruppen wandten sich an die eine Institution, die in der Lage schien zu handeln.
Das Land möchte mit Sicherheit lieber einen Präsidenten, der ein „Mann des
Volkes" ist, ein eher gewöhnlicher Mensch, mit dem es sich identifizieren
kann. Aber das Land möchte auch nicht, dass dieser Mann zu gewöhnlich ist.
Die Menschen erwarten (von ihm) nicht nur außergewöhnliche Fähigkeiten
und eine ungewöhnliche Führungsstärke, sie wollen auch, dass er besser ist als
sie selber – dass er jemand ist, zu dem sie aufsehen und den sie respektieren
können.

Exercise 5   "The new frontier" by John F. Kennedy (= Nomination acceptance speech
before the Democratic National Convention, July 15, 1960)

1 doubts; 2 motto; 3 common; 4 overcome; 5 conquer; 6 within; 7 explored;
8 assembly; 9 solved; 10 edge; 11 opportunities; 12 social; 13 need; 14 challenges; 15 ask; 16 instead; 17 whether; 18 peace; 19 questions; 20 back;
21 rhetoric; 22 votes; 23 young

Key: Politics in the US ⁄ 185

xercise 6   Inaugural Addresses

1 wealth; 2 poverty; 3 unattended; 4 waste; 5 surrender; 6 conquered;
7 betrays; 8 forebears; 9 inventory; 10 special; 11 granted; 12 reverse;
13 distinction; 14 reminded; 15 resolved; 16 founders; 17 endure;
18 challenges; 19 humble; 20 interests; 21 guarantee; 22 important;
23 comfort; 24 attacks; 25 spectators; 26 communities; 27 generous;
28 replace; 29 inauguration; 30 courage

xercise 7   US politics after 9/11: America's political mission

1 Anklage[erhebung]en, Anklageschriften; 2 convicted; 3 ehrgeizige;
4 carnage, bloodbath; 5 declared; 6 Einwände; 7 versteckte, verbarg; 8 threats;
9 Aufsässigkeit, Auflehnung; 10 verschwanden; 11 sought; 12 submitting;
13 doubts; 14 herablassend; 15 unvereinbar; 16 niedergeschlagen;
17 challenge; 18 verlässliche, zuverlässige; 19 dominate; 20 dignity

xercise 8   Synonyms

1 devised; 2 outmoded, out of date; 3 obstacle; 4 competitor, rival, contender,
opponent; 5 pity, sympathy; 6 seen, regarded, looked upon; 7 make up,
account for; 8 battle, combat; 9 severe, strong; 10 known, famous; 11 killing,
murder, violent death, homicide; 12 destroyed, broken to pieces, smashed;
13 earth, ground, land; 14 astonishing, remarkable, outstanding

xercise 9   Matching words and their definitions

A	B	C	D	E	F	G	H	I	J	K	L	M	N	O	P
18	13	6	12	8	23	5	17	1	22	21	7	9	11	14	16

186 / Key: Immigration

9 Immigration

Exercise 1   US Immigration

1 descended; 2 native; 3 advanced; 4 earliest; 5 influx; 6 plantations;
7 primarily; 8 involved; 9 forced; 10 economic; 11 persecution; 12 join;
13 encouraged; 14 call; 15 rate; 16 increasing; 17 ranged; 18 denigrate;
19 derived; 20 biased; 21 deterioration; 22 control; 23 naturalization;
24 established; 25 quota; 26 brought; 27 values; 28 pot

Exercise 2   Ellis Island

1 tide; 2 eastern; 3 restrictions; 4 described; 5 kept; 6 finally; 7 travelled;
8 directly; 9 passengers; 10 collect; 11 marched; 12 suits; 13 slippers;
14 carrying; 15 baskets; 16 kitchen; 17 routine; 18 interpreter; 19 leave;
20 determine; 21 reject; 22 read; 23 inspector; 24 searching; 25 disease;
26 further; 27 passed; 28 arrangements; 29 filthy; 30 eventually

Exercise 3   A nation of immigrants

1 Religionsfreiheit; 2 Pilgrims; 3 Verfolgung; 4 empire; 5 refuge; 6 oppression;
7 promise; 8 Menschenrechte; 9 sich unterworfen; 10 assembled; 11 Und
nicht/Auch nicht; 12 umfassend; 13 Reichtum; 14 flight from; 15 trugen bei;
16 experience; 17 skills; 18 Vor allem; 19 löste aus; 20 gewöhnlich

Exercise 4   Arrival in the New World

Ankunft in der Neuen Welt
Von 1882 bis 1902 schifften sich allein in Bremen mehr als zwei Millionen
Einwanderer nach New York ein. Die Überfahrt kostete 33 Dollar, und nach-
dem er sein eigenes Ticket und vielleicht das seiner Familie bezahlt hatte, kam
der Auswanderer, der auf der Flucht vor Armut und Unterdrückung war, in
New York völlig mittellos an. Sobald er die Fähre von Ellis Island verließ,
machte er sich gewöhnlich in Richtung Lower East Side auf, um sich Arbeit
und eine Schlafmöglichkeit zu suchen.
Mit der Zeit wurden diese wenigen Quadratmeilen der New Yorker East Side
noch dichter bevölkert als die schlimmsten Bezirke Bombays. Und die Erinne-
rungen an die leidvolle Überfahrt und die Ankunft prägten sich tief bei den
Einwanderern ein, deren Kinder nun New York geerbt haben.

Die beiden Eltern, sechs Kinder und sechs Logiergäste mussten sich in eine für die damalige Zeit typische 2-Zimmer-Wohnung drängen. Die Miete für diese Räume ohne Frischluftzufuhr, Tageslicht oder fließendes Wasser betrug 2 Dollar und mehr pro Woche. 1890 betrugen die Wochenlöhne bei einem 14-Stunden-Arbeitstag in einem der Ausbeutungsbetriebe der Textilbranche für Frauen ungefähr drei Dollar, für Männer höchstens zehn. Im selben Jahr belief sich der Umsatz der Bekleidungsindustrie auf 88 Millionen Dollar.

Exercise 5   Immigration myths

1 opposite; 2 self-employed; 3 account; 4 workforce; 5 employed; 6 perception; 7 percentage; 8 decreased; 9 generous; 10 burden; 11 native-born; 12 earnings; 13 welfare; 14 evidence; 15 concern; 16 throughout; 17 indicate; 18 continually; 19 lack; 20 confined

Exercise 6   Is multiculturalism working?

1 wörtlich, buchstäblich; 2 Umwälzungen; 3 tolerated; 4 melting pot; 5 Untersuchung, Umfrage; 6 maintain, keep; 7 einstufen; 8 unterstützten, hießen gut; 9 geformt; 10 truly, genuinely; 11 considerably; 12 customs; 13 Wurzeln; 14 separate; 15 annehmen, auswählen; 16 mother tongue; 17 convinced; 18 Abschaffung; 19 steht immer noch auf der Tagesordnung; 20 minorities

Exercise 7   Synonyms

1 collect, gather, property, possessions, things; 2 at once, instantly, instantaneously, promptly; 3 pursuit, quest; 4 progressive, liberal, tolerant; confidence, trust; 5 consequences, repercussions; forecast, foresee, foretell, prognosticate; 6 decreased; 7 mainly, primarily, principally; 8 labour, toil, slave; 9 inflow, stream, rush; 10 fixed, installed; amount; 11 strengthened, stimulated; 12 mixed, varied; 13 regarded, viewed; unsuitable, unfit; 14 regulation, legislation, statute; adjusted, improved, corrected

188 ✦ Key: Civil rights

Exercise 8   Matching words and their definitions

A	B	C	D	E	F	G	H	I	J	K	L
14	8	6	15	12	3	17	5	13	18	16	10

Exercise 9   Word families

noun (abstract)	noun (concrete)	verb	adjective
presidency	president	preside	presidential
number	---	number	numerous
refuge	refugee	take refuge	---
diversity	---	---	diverse
admission, admittance	---	admit	admissible, admitted
adoption	---	adopt	adopted, adoptive
approval	---	approve	approvable
industry	industrialist	industrialize	1. industrial 2. industrious
hostility	---	---	hostile
legalisation, legality	---	legalize	legal
population	---	populate	populous, populated
settlement	settler	settle	---
suspicion	---	suspect	suspicious

10 Civil rights

Exercise 1   The life of Martin Luther King

1 married; 2 pastorate; 3 less; 4 seating; 5 boycott; 6 role; 7 presidency;
8 resigned; 9 entered; 10 refused; 11 closed; 12 movement; 13 facilities;
14 demonstration; 15 employment; 16 imprisoned; 17 disobedience;
18 sought; 19 face; 20 backgrounds; 21 capital; 22 entitled; 23 passed;
24 against; 25 awarded; 26 equality; 27 sniper

Key: Civil rights ✦ 189

xercise 2 Martin Luther King: Nobel prize acceptance speech (Oslo 10.12.1964)

1 contemplation; 2 behalf; 3 nonviolence; 4 overcome; 5 Civilization;
6 following; 7 demonstrated; 8 passivity; 9 transformation; 10 together;
11 brotherhood; 12 achieved; 13 conflict; 14 aggression; 15 accept; 16 sur-
rounds; 17 tragically; 18 daybreak; 19 notion; 20 stairway; 21 destruction;
22 unconditional; 23 defeated; 24 tomorrow; 25 wounded

xercise 3 The legacy of Rosa Parks

1 Diktatur; 2 bigotry; 3 Eisernen Vorhang; 4 wogte, wurde ausgefochten;
5 auf dem Spiel stand; 6 ausgestattet; 7 angestauten, angesammelten; 8 Zielen,
Hoffnungen, Bestrebungen; 9 verhaftet (zu werden); 10 in the back; 11 ziem-
lich; 12 da, weil; 13 dignity; 14 erniedrigt; 15 versuchen

xercise 4 Desegregation of Schools

1 obstacles; 2 attended; 3 prohibited; 4 forced; 5 satisfied; 6 demanded;
7 exclude; 8 refused; 9 segregated; 10 court; 11 injustice; 12 facilities;
13 entrances; 14 intended; 15 superiority; 16 benefits; 17 determined;
18 courage

xercise 5 Synonyms

1 awful, dreadful, horrible, terrible; 2 suffrage, franchise; 3 opposition;
4 suppressed, persecuted; 5 scared, frightened; 6 variety; 7 destitute,
disadvantaged, underprivileged; 8 killed, murdered, shot dead; 9 excluded;
10 fury, indignation, anger; 11 refined, crafty, cunning, insidious;
12 contempt; 13 decisive, important; 14 strengthened, increased, supported,
reassured; 15 established, built, created

xercise 6 Opposites

1 rejected; 2 commitment; 3 courageous, brave; 4 boom, growth; 5 admit,
acknowledge, concede; 6 respected, admired, praised; 7 solid, sound; 8 calmed
down, appeased, pacified; 9 inferiority; 10 thorough; 11 integration's,
desegregation's; 12 hidden, secret, concealed

190 / Key: Civil rights

Exercise 7   Matching words and their definitions

A	B	C	D	E	F	G	H	I	J	K	L	M	N
15	19	1	2	20	5	9	12	14	18	6	3	10	13

Exercise 8   Word families

noun (abstract)	verb	adjective
presidency	preside	presidential
annoyance	annoy	annoying
conciliation	conciliate	conciliatory
defiance	defy	defiant
hate, hatred	hate	hateful
inferiority	---	inferior
irritation	irritate	irritable
legality	legalize	legal
obedience	obey	obedient
persistence	persist	persistent
pursuit	pursue	pursuant
repentance	repent	repentant
resentment	resent	resentful
resistance	resist	resistant
separation	separate	separate [it]
slavery	enslave	slavish

Exercise 9 Crossword puzzle

```
C           C                                           W
O  B  S  T  A  C  L  E        P  R  E  J  U  D  I  C  E        A
N                 A              R                       N     G
S           A  S  S  A  S  S  I  N  A  T  E        H  A  T  R  E  D
C                 H                 M                          E
I                 F                 A              F  I  E  R  C  E
O        D  I  C  T  A  T  O  R  S  H  I  P                 P     R
U        E        C           Y           N     V  I  R  T  U  E  E
S        M  I  G  R  A  T  I  O  N     E  N  D  O  W        I     P
N        R        C     L           I        L     S        T
E  N  F  R  A  N  C  H  I  S  E  D     G     E     E        I
S        D        U     T     X        N     G              O
S  T  A  K  E     M     Y     C  O  N  C  I  L  I  A  T  I  O  N
                  U     L           T        C              R
      D  E  L  I  N  Q  U  E  N  C  Y     Y     A           E
                  A     D     O           U           F
I  N  T  R  A  C  T  A  B  L  E     P  R  O  H  I  B  I  T     U
         A        E     O     E              H              S
L  A  U  N  C  H        O           W        O              A
         R        D  I  S  T  U  R  B  A  N  C  E     E  N  R  O  L
         S        O           I           A        I
         O  M  O  V  E  M  E  N  T     M  I  N  O  R  I  T  Y
         N              G           Y     Y
```

word family	dt. Bedeutung	English sentence	synonyms/opposites
(to) abandon **abandonment**	*aufgeben* *Aufgabe, Verlassen*	In developing countries more and more small farmers abandon their land and invade the great cities.	= give up, desert ≠ reclaim
(to) abdicate **abdication**	*abdanken* *Abdankung*	Edward VIII had to abdicate because he wanted to marry Mrs Wally Simpson, a divorced American woman.	= resign, step down
(to) abolish **abolition**	*abschaffen* *Abschaffung*	President Lincoln's aim was to abolish slavery.	= do away with ≠ introduce, institute
above all	*vor allem*	Most immigrants have come to America seeking a better life for themselves and, above all, for their children.	= mainly especially, in particular
(to) abstain **abstention** **abstinent** [adj]	*sich enthalten* *Stimmenthaltung, Abstinenz* *abstinent*	The leader of the opposition told his party colleagues to abstain from voting.	= refrain
abundance **abundant**	*Fülle, Reichtum* *reichlich vorhanden*	Silicon is one of the earth's most abundant elements.	= plenty, plentiful, abounding, replete ≠ rare, scarce, deficient, lacking, insufficient
(to) accelerate	*beschleunigen*	The immigrants accelerated the economic growth of the country.	= quicken, speed, facilitate ≠ slow down, decrease, drop
(to) accept **acceptance/acceptability** **acceptable** [adj]	*annehmen* *Annahme/Annehmbarkeit* *hinnehmbar*	Most Americans accept that a fair social policy consists of redistributing wealth downwards.	≠ refuse, reject, turn down

word family	dt. Bedeutung	English sentence	synonyms/opposites
access/accession accessible [adj]	*Zugang* *erreichbar*	Black Americans fought hard to gain access to university education.	= admission, admittance, entrance, entry
(to) achieve achievement	*leisten* *Leistung*	People think that the achievements of a nation's sports-men reflect the success of the nation they represent.	= accomplishment, performance, triumph
(to) acquire acquisition, acquirement acquisitive [adj]	*erwerben, sich aneignen* *Erwerb, Anschaffung* *gewinnsüchtig*	For thousand of years one of man's problem has been to acquire leisure time.	= obtain, gain, secure
act **(to) actualize** actuality actual [adj] actually [adv]	*Gesetz, Maßnahme* *verwirklichen* *Wirklichkeit* *wirklich, tatsächlich, eigentlich* *tatsächlich*	Despite the restrictions of immigration acts, the num-ber of undocumented foreigners has increased. The actual state of relations between the two commu-nities needed to be glossed over. Do illegal aliens actually play a useful role in the US labour force?	= law, regulation, measure, statue = real, true, genuine, definite = in fact, really, indeed
(to) adapt adaptation adaptable	*anpassen* *Anpassung* *anpassungsfähig*	Workers have to adapt to continuous changes brought about by computers and other new technologies.	= adjust
addiction **(to) be addicted to** addicted [adj] addictive [adj]	*Sucht* *abhängig sein von* *süchtig* *Sucht erzeugend*	Crack cocaine is the primary addiction of pregnant women, although many use other drugs as well.	= dependence
adequacy adequate [adj]	*Angemessenheit* *ausreichend, genügend, angemessen*	Members of minority groups are often confronted with negative stereotype images even if they have job skills and adequate education.	= sufficient, satisfactory ≠ insufficient

word family	dt. Bedeutung	English sentence	synonyms/opposites
(to) adhere adherence adhesion adherent [adj]	*festhalten* *Festhalten* *Haften, Haftvermögen* *verbunden*	Employers should adhere to civil rights laws.	= stick to, keep to
(to) adjust adjustment adjustable [adj]	*anpassen, sich einstellen* *Anpassung, Abstimmung*	Many immigrants were unable to adjust to the British way of life.	= adapt
(to) administer	*verwalten, leiten,* *sich kümmern um*	The Commonwealth Secretariat administers the programmes of cooperation.	= supervise, direct, manage
(to) advance advances advancement advanced [adj]	*vorrücken, vordringen* *Fortschritte* *Förderung, Fortschritt* *fortschrittlich*	The general's army managed to advance even further. Recent advances in science and technology have made it possible for man to influence his environment. A number of immigrants came from countries with advanced political and economic institutions.	= move forward = progress, improvement, breakthrough = progressive, liberal, civilized
adverse [adj]	*widrig, feindlich*	The settlers had to cope with adverse weather conditions.	= hostile, unfavourable, bad ≠ favourable, nice, good, pleasant, agreeable
(to) advocate advocate	*befürworten, verteidigen* *Befürworter, Verfechter*	The Prime Minister seems to advocate a reduction of defence costs. Advocates of televising Parliament point out that the presence of the cameras may encourage members to behave themselves better than they do now.	= support, defend, recommend ≠ critic

word family	dt. Bedeutung	English sentence	synonyms/opposites
(to) affect affection affectionate [adj]	sich auswirken auf, angreifen Zuneigung liebevoll, zärtlich	Ultraviolet light does affect people.	= trouble, harm, touch, worry, bother, concern
(to) afflict	treffen, heimsuchen, plagen	The skill shortage afflicts not only laid-off workers.	= hit, trouble, bother
affluence affluent [adj]	Überfluss reich, reichlich	One of the most pleasant and potentially most dangerous by-products of our affluent society is the spare time at our disposal.	= rich, wealthy, well-to-do, prosperous; ≠ poor, badly off
agriculture	Landwirtschaft	In the USA, agriculture has always played a major role.	= farming
ahead of	vor, voraus	We must consider thoroughly, ahead of time, how we intend to recycle remains.	≠ behind
(to) alert alertness alert [adj]	warnen Wachsamkeit wachsam	The president advised the public to stay alert.	= watchful, vigilant, wide-awake
alliance	Bündnis	Nearly all UN member states formed an alliance to fight against the dictator.	= union, partnership
almost	fast, beinahe	Almost five percent of the population of Britain are of Commonwealth ethnic origin.	= nearly, practically, more or less, approximately, virtually
already [adv]	schon	Robots already paint cars.	≠ not yet
although	obwohl, obgleich	The workers accepted the pay increase, although their union bosses had recommended a walk-out.	= despite the fact that, whereas, whilst

word family	dt. Bedeutung	English sentence	synonyms/opposites
(to) amend	ändern, berichtigen, verbessern, novellieren	The McCarran-Walter Act was amended in 1965.	= adjust, improve, correct
annually [adv]	jährlich	The Pulitzer Prize is awarded annually since 1917.	= every year, yearly
apathy	Teilnahmslosigkeit	This is not a time for apathy and complacency.	≠ commitment
appalling [adj]	entsetzlich, erschreckend	People in the slums live in the most appalling urban living conditions.	= horrible, shocking, dreadful, awful, terrible
(to) appear	scheinen, erscheinen	Sometimes it appears that all TV programmes are one super-commercial.	= seem, look like
appearance	Erscheinung		
apparent [adj]	sichtbar		
apparently [adv]	scheinbar	An apparently satisfactory calorie intake hides a wide-spread deficiency of essential vitamins.	= seemingly, supposedly, presumably
appliance	Gerät, Vorrichtung	Household appliances relieve housewives from dull work.	= device, apparatus, gadget
(to) apply (to)	zutreffen auf, gelten für	The criticism of the low moral standards of the House of Windsor only applies to the younger members of the Royal Family.	= be true for
(to) apply	verwenden, sich bewerben		
application	Verwendung, Anwendung, Bewerbung		
applicable [adj]	passend		
(to) appreciate	(hoch-)schätzen	Since we highly appreciate the quality of your product, we would like to do business with your company.	= value, esteem
appreciation	Anerkennung		≠ hate, look down on, frown at
appreciative [adj]	anerkennend		

word family	dt. Bedeutung	English sentence	synonyms/opposites
appropriate [adj]	angemessen, passend	Is our nation's historic commitment to mass public education appropriate in its current form?	= suitable, correct, proper
approximately [adv]	annähernd, ungefähr, etwa	Recent surveys have shown that watching TV takes up approximately a quarter of the leisure of the average member of the public.	= about, more or less, close to, roughly
(to) argue	behaupten, argumentieren, Gründe (für und wider) anführen, streiten, rechten	Some economists argue that governments spend too much money, that they are living beyond their means.	= maintain
argument argumentation	Argument; Wortwechsel, Streit Argumentation		
arguable [adj]	fragwürdig, diskutabel	It is arguable that Scotland was united as a nation under Edward I of England.	= debatable, disputable, doubtful, dubious, question-able, uncertain
armistice	Waffenstillstand	In Ulster an armistice was declared by several terrorist organizations.	= truce, cease-fire
arms	Waffen (Pl.)	We must make every effort to reduce the production of nuclear arms.	= weapons
(to) arouse	erregen, erwecken	The new course leading to the Post-Graduate Certificate in Education has aroused enormous interest.	= stimulate, excite
(to) assassinate assassination	ermorden Ermordung, Attentat	US President John F. Kennedy was assassinated in 1963. The turning point came with the assassination of President Kennedy.	= kill, murder = killing, murder, violent death, homicide

word family	dt. Bedeutung	English sentence	synonyms/opposites
(to) assemble (1)	versammeln, sich versammeln	Every time a revolution has failed in Europe, men and women who love freedom have assembled their families and set sails across the seas.	= collect, gather, rally
assembly	Versammlung		
(to) assemble (2)	montieren	By the mid-1920s, a Ford Model T could be assembled in fewer than 30 seconds.	= put together, manufacture, produce
(to) assert	behaupten, beteuern	In the third century BC the astronomer Aristarchus of Samos asserted that the earth moved around the sun.	= declare, maintain, claim, argue
assertion	Behauptung		
(to) assess	beurteilen, einschätzen, bewerten	The commonest way to assess a country's degree of development is by reference to its Gross National Product (GNP).	= analyze, determine, evaluate
(to) be at risk	auf dem Spiel stehen	The destruction of sea life puts our oceans at risk.	= be at stake
(to) put at risk	gefährden		= endanger; ≠ protect, save
(to) attain	erlangen, erreichen, erzielen	The objective of a party is to govern. To attain this it must win every possible vote.	= accomplish, achieve
attempt	Versuch	Shouldn't some attempt be made to find alternative sources of leisure entertainment for young football hooligans?	= effort
(to) attend (1)	besuchen, teilnehmen	Children must be given adequate attention by their parents.	≠ neglect, disregard
attention	Aufmerksamkeit		
attentive [adj]	aufmerksam		
(to) attend (2)	begleiten, aufwarten		
attendance	Bedienung, Pflege		
attendant [adj]	begleitend		

word family	dt. Bedeutung	English sentence	synonyms/opposites
aware [adj] (to) be aware of awareness	bewusst bewusst sein Bewusstsein	The general public all over the world must become more aware of the importance of our environment.	= conscious, mindful, attentive
badly [adv]	dringend	We badly need another scientific breakthrough.	= urgently, rapidly, right away
balance	Gleichgewicht	The earth's biosphere is in a state of delicate balance.	= equilibrium
bald [adj]	bloß, nackt	Advertising is no longer a matter of simple encouragement and bald facts.	= bare, sheer, mere
ballot	Wahlgang, Abstimmung; Wahlzettel, -schein	With a secret ballot people select a candidate in an election.	= vote
bareness bare [adj] barely [adv]	Nacktheit, Blöße; Kargheit bloß, nackt kaum, knapp	Mexico City's population will double within barely two decades.	= just about, not quite, hardly
(to) be barred from	ausgeschlossen sein von	Members of minority groups are still barred from equal opportunities at work.	= excluded from
because of	wegen, aufgrund	Because of the Chernobyl disaster everyone became aware of the dangers of atomic power plants.	= due to, owing to
belongings	Habe, Habseligkeiten	With all their belongings they emigrated to the US.	= property, possession
(to) benefit benefit	nützen Nutzen, Vorteil	The Internet provides unparalleled benefits to society.	= advantage, profit ≠ disadvantage, damage
beneficent [adj]	gütig, wohltätig		

word family	dt. Bedeutung	English sentence	synonyms/opposites
(to) betray betrayal	verraten Verrat	When someone betrays his country he helps its enemies.	= sell out, double-cross
boastfulness	Prahlerei	Sport is often connected with boastfulness.	≠ modesty
boom	Hochkonjunktur, Aufschwung	When business goes extremely well we talk about a boom.	≠ depression, slack period, slump
both … and	sowohl … als auch	Unionists found this language both distasteful and unrewarding.	= as well as; ≠ neither … nor
briefness brevity brief [adj]	Kürze Kürze, Prägnanz kurz (zeitig)	The new hazards are neither local nor brief.	= momentary, temporary, transitory, transient
by and large	im Großen und Ganzen	By and large, the Republican party supports the interests of manufacturing and commercial enterprises.	= on the whole, in general, basically
capital punishment	Todesstrafe	Capital punishment should be abolished in all countries.	= death penalty
casualties	Verluste	No casualties were reported.	= victims, losses
certainty certain [adj] certainly [adv]	Gewissheit gewiss, sicher sicher, gewiss	To try to fight alcohol by banning it would certainly be useless and inappropriate.	= clearly, definitely, indeed
(to) challenge	ablehnen, infrage stellen	The new plans which make promotion for women more difficult must be challenged.	= oppose, reject, question, fight against
challenger	Herausforderer	The challenger of the President must make himself known to the voters.	= competitor, rival

word family	dt. Bedeutung	English sentence	synonyms/opposites
chance	Möglichkeit	The chances of the individual to discover and develop his talents in a larger school are much greater.	= opportunity, possibility
(to) change	ändern	We have to change our production processes.	≠ stick to, hold on to, maintain, keep
charge	Beschuldigung, Anklage	The defendant can try to prove that the charges against him are false at a preliminary hearing after his arrest.	= accusation
(to) chase	jagen, hetzen	Inflation is often described as being caused by too much money chasing too few goods.	= pursue
chiefly [adv]	hauptsächlich	Professional sports developed chiefly in England and the United States.	= mainly, notably, particularly, primarily, specifically
clear	klar, deutlich, offensichtlich	Agreement cannot be reached on even so clear-cut an issue.	= obvious, evident
(to) combat combat combatant [adj]	bekämpfen Kampf kämpfend	The US President promised to combat drug trafficking.	= fight against
combustion	Verbrennung	Fossil fuel combustion is responsible for the earth's warming.	= burning
(to) comfort comfort comfortable [adj]	trösten Trost, Bequemlichkeit bequem, behaglich	The special relationship with the USA has been a source of comfort and security for Britain.	= support, relief
(to) commence	anfangen, beginnen	Slum clearance is due to commence in six months' time.	= begin, start

word family	dt. Bedeutung	English sentence	synonyms/opposites
commerce commercial [adj]	Handel, Verkehr kaufmännisch, Handel-	Commerce between England and the USA has grown steadily.	= business, trade
commodities	Waren, Handelsgüter	British standards for consumer goods exist for a limited range of commodities.	= goods, merchandise, products
commonly [adv]	häufig	People commonly declare that the new technology is a threat to their employment.	= generally, usually, frequently, very often
community	Gemeinschaft	Bicycle paths, community gardens and organic food stores can now be found in most major US cities.	≠ private
compassion	Mitgefühl	Tim often criticizes Susan without compassion.	= pity, sympathy, feelings
(to) compel compulsion compelling [adj] compulsory [adj] compulsive [adj]	zwingen Zwang zwingend verpflichtend zwingend	No manufacturer is compelled to give a quality mark or guarantee seal. Specialists have found no compelling evidence that terrorist attacks would cease if the media stopped covering them.	= force, oblige = convincing, clear, forceful
(to) compensate compensation	entschädigen Ausgleich	The army has to compensate farmers for damage done to their land during manoeuvres.	= repay, refund, reimburse
(to) comply compliance compliant [adj]	folgen, (eine Regel) einhalten, sich fügen Einwilligung fügsam	The cost of complying with all environmental regulations has amounted to 1.5 percent of the US gross domestic product.	= observe, keep, follow ≠ disregard, neglect
(to) be composed of compostion	bestehen aus, sich zusammensetzen aus	Genetic material is composed of two nucleic acids, deoxyribonucleic acid and ribonucleic acid.	= consist of

word family	dt. Bedeutung	English sentence	synonyms/opposites
(to) comprehend comprehension comprehensible [adj] comprehensive [adj]	begreifen, umfassen Verständnis, Fassungskraft verständlich umfassend	He was unable to comprehend the idea that anyone would willingly hand back an American passport.	= understand, grasp, see, take in
(to) conceal concealment	verstecken, verbergen Verheimlichung	The experienced newspaper reader tends to suspect concealed advertising in advice columns on shopping.	= hide, cover, camouflage
(to) concede concession	zugestehen, einräumen Zugeständnis	The father conceded that his son had been taking drugs for three years.	= admit
(to) conceive conceivable [adj] conception conceit conceited [adj]	planen, sich ausdenken, begreifen denkbar (geistige) Vorstellung Eingebildetheit eingebildet	The American two-party system was not conceived by the Founding Fathers. Some of his statements make him appear a bit conceited.	= devise, invent ≠ modest humble
(to) concern	interessieren, beschäftigen	Each nation is naturally concerned with its own pressing problems.	= occupied with, worried about
(to) condemn	verdammen, verurteilen	You should never condemn a person out of hand.	= denunciate, reprehend ≠ praise, applaud, glorify
(to) confide confidence confident [adj]	gestehen, anvertrauen Vertrauen zuversichtlich	The industry was confident that the one million mark would soon be surpassed.	= certain, sure, convinced, positive
confidential [adj]	vertraulich	We require confidential information about Smith & Co.	≠ public, open

word family	dt. Bedeutung	English sentence	synonyms/opposites
(to) confine confinement	begrenzen Beschränkung	The "ignition" function of advertising slogans is not confined to the English language.	= limit, restrict
congested [adj]	überfüllt, übervölkert, verstopft	Already Mexico City, Sao Paolo and Shanghai are among the largest, most congested cities on earth.	= overcrowded, blocked, choked
consensus	Übereinstimmung	There is no global consensus on the issue of cloning.	= assent, consent, agreement
(to) conserve conservation conservative [adj]	erhalten Schutz, Erhalt konservativ, zurückhaltend	WWF works in more than 100 countries around the globe to conserve the diversity of life on earth.	= keep, maintain, preserve, sustain ≠ fritter, squander, waste
(to) consider consideration	betrachten, ansehen Erwägung, Überlegung, Berücksichtigung	Some groups were considered politically unreliable.	= regard, view
considerable [adj] considerate [adj] considerably [adv]	beträchtlich rücksichtsvoll beträchtlich, erheblich	A considerable number of the USA's top athletes go to college on a scholarship. Developing countries differ considerably from one another.	≠ small, insignificant = substantially, significantly, dramatically
(to) consign consignment	etwas senden Lieferung	You have to sign here and acknowledge receipt of the consignment.	= shipment
(to) consist consistency consistence consistent [adj]	bestehen Beständigkeit Beschaffenheit beständig	A computer system consists of hardware and software.	= be composed of, be made up of
(to) console consolation	trösten Trost	Men of the lower classes also lacked rights, but they could console themselves by feeling superior to women.	= comfort, cheer up, solace

word family	dt. Bedeutung	English sentence	synonyms/opposites
(to) consolidate consolidation	festigen Festigung	After World War II, the Soviet Union was beginning to consolidate its power in Eastern European countries.	= unify, compact, concentrate, integrate
(to) conspire conspiracy	sich verschwören Verschwörung	Sir Walter Raleigh was imprisoned in the Tower of London after being accused of conspiracy.	= plot, secret plan
constant [adj] constancy	ständig, fortwährend Beständigkeit	In his inaugural address the president called race relations "America's constant curse".	= continuous, lasting ≠ temporary, momentary, fleeting, transient
(to) constitute constitution constituency constituent [adj] constitutional [adj]	bilden, ausmachen, errichten Einrichtung, Verfassung Wahlkreis wesentlich verfassungsmäßig	Women constitute about half of the US labour force.	= make up, account for
(to) constrain constraint	einschränken Einschränkung, Zwang	The system was devised to constrain central power.	= curb, check, restrict
(to) construct	bauen, entwerfen	Frederic Dent was appointed to construct the clock.	= build, manufacture, devise
contempt contemptible [adj] contemptuous [adj]	Verachtung verachtenswert geringschätzig	The music of the punk groups also expressed their contempt of adult society.	= disdain, disparagement, scorn ≠ respect, admiration
(to) contend contention contentious [adj]	behaupten kämpfen Behauptung, Streit kontrovers; streitsüchtig	The judge contended that the massive advertising campaign influenced young people. Farmers must contend with forces beyond their control – most notably the weather.	= maintain, argue, claim = fight against, combat

word family	dt. Bedeutung	English sentence	synonyms/opposites
content [adj]	zufrieden	We become content with second-hand experience.	= satisfied, pleased, happy
(to) continue continuation continuance continuing [adj]	andauern, fortfahren Fortsetzung Fortdauer ständig, andauernd, anhaltend	Is the continuing rise in juvenile delinquency a sign that the children of working mothers are more likely to "turn bad"?	= constant, stead, continuous, consistent, permanent ≠ temporary
continual [adj] continuous [adj]	andauernd fortwährend		
(to) contribute contribution	beitragen, beisteuern Beitrag	In commercials the personality of the actor contributes a great deal to the effectiveness of the advertisement.	= add
(to) convene convention	zusammentreffen (Partei-)Versammlung, Übereinkommen	The Republicans held their national party convention in August.	= assembly, meeting
conventional [adj]	herkömmlich		
(to) convert conversion	umwandeln Umwandlung	The audio signal is amplified and converted into sound in the speaker.	= transform
(to) convey conveyance conveyor belt	befördern Beförderung, Transport Montageband, Fließband	Tom Birch stands at the conveyor belt all day.	= assembly line
(to) convict convict (to) convince conviction	überführen Verurteilter, Sträfling überzeugen Überzeugung	Most convicts serve only a fraction of their prison terms before they are released. The Prime Minister must convince Parliament that the proposed law is really necessary.	= prisoner = assure, persuade

word family	dt. Bedeutung	English sentence	synonyms/opposites
costly [adj]	teuer, kostspielig	Cutting emissions from nuclear power stations is a costly ambition.	≠ cheap, inexpensive, economical, low-cost
cowardice	Feigheit	He despised them for their cowardice and ignorance.	≠ courage, boldness, bravery, valour
cowardly [adj]	feige	We blacks are too cowardly to face the fact that our leaders have been lying to us for years.	≠ courageous, brave
(to) create	(er)schaffen, produzieren	But some economists argue that alien workers may in fact create as many new jobs as they take.	≠ kill, eliminate, destroy, remove, do away with
creation	Schaffung, Bau	The building of a tunnel under the channel also stimulated the creation of new highways and railroad lines.	= construction
creature	Geschöpf		
creative [adj]	schöpferisch		
(to) criticize	kritisieren		
criticism	Kritik, Ablehnung	The more fundamental criticism of the public school elite is that it reinforces a class system.	≠ approval, support, praise, acceptance
critic	Kritiker		
critical [adj]	kritisch		
(to) cure	heilen	Although the dependence caused by marijuana is not so severe as that resulting from heroin, it is nevertheless hard to cure.	= heal, remedy
curiosity	Neugier	His curiosity to know whether George had got engaged to Susan almost killed him.	≠ indifference, disinterest, apathy
curious [adj]	seltsam, merkwürdig	These observations explain the curious British mixture.	= strange, astonishing
current [adj]	gegenwärtig, jetzig, laufend	Good pay and security are still important job aspects to the current generation.	= present; ≠ former, past, previous, future

word family	dt. Bedeutung	English sentence	synonyms/opposites
current account	Girokonto	My salary is transferred to my current account with the NatWest Bank.	= checking account
current	Lauf, Strom		
currency	Umlauf, Währung	The European Commission is currently laying the foundations for environmental regulations that set standards for air, land and water pollution.	
currently [adv]	gegenwärtig		= presently, at present
customer	Kunde	Lufthansa is an important customer of Airbus Industries, the manufacturer of the Airbus aircraft.	= client, patron
custom	Gewohnheit		
customary [adj]	gewöhnlich		
(to) cut	kürzen	Automation does not necessarily cut costs.	= reduce, lower, trim
(to) cut back on	kürzen, verringern	When companies are struggling to survive they cut back on job training.	= reduce, decrease, spend less on
debtor	Schuldner	Brazil owes millions of dollars to foreign banks: the country is a great debtor.	≠ creditor
(to) deceive	betrügen	The president confirmed that the decades of deceit and cruelty had reached an end.	= deception, fraud, trickery
deceit	Täuschung, Betrug		
deception	Täuschung		
deceitful [adj]	betrügerisch		
decency	Anstand	We must enable the poor people in the developing countries to provide a decent standard of living for their families.	= acceptable, adequate, reasonable, satisfactory
decent [adj]	anständig		
(to) decide	entscheiden		
decision	Entscheidung		
decisive [adj]	entscheidend	Decisive victories over a lot of illnesses have been won.	= definitive, final

word family	dt. Bedeutung	English sentence	synonyms/opposites
(to) decline	*ablehnen*	Will you decline to participate in the new world of work?	= refuse, be willing
decline	*Niedergang, Abnahme, Rückgang*	The decline of the economy is gathering speed.	= fall, decrease, drop
declination	*Abweichung*		≠ boom, growth
(to) deduce	*folgern*	Some observers might deduce from singular events that race-relations are deteriorating.	= deduct, infer
(to) deduct	*abziehen*		
deduction	*Schlussfolgerung, Abzug*		
defeat	*Niederlage*	The defeats at British Leyland have made some union leaders more determined.	≠ victory, success, achievement
(to) defer	*aufschieben*	What happens to a dream deferred?	= put off
deference	*Nachgiebigkeit*		
deferential [adj]	*nachgiebig*		
deficiency	*Mangel*	An apparently satisfactory calorie intake hides a widespread deficiency of essential vitamins.	= scarcity, lack, shortage, inadequacy
deficient [adj]	*mangelhaft*		
(to) defy	*sich etw. widersetzen*	The officer defied the order of the commanding general.	= resist
defiance	*Trotz*		
defiant [adj]	*aufsässig*		
delicacy	*Empfindlichkeit*	The earth's biosphere is in a state of delicate balance.	= sensitive, fragile, feeble
delicate [adj]	*empfindlich*		
(to) delude	*täuschen*	Blanche deludes herself and others that she is charming and sociable.	= betray, bluff, double-cross, mislead
delusion	*Täuschung*		
delusive [adj]	*trügerisch*		

word family	dt. Bedeutung	English sentence	synonyms/opposites
(to) demolish	abreißen, einreißen, niederreißen	The local council demolished the terraced houses and put up high-rise buildings.	= destroy, pull down
(to) deny	leugnen, verweigern	The Home Office cannot afford to treat some immigrants better than those to whom it is already denying established rights.	≠ grant, allow, permit, accept, agree to, approve of, give
denial	Leugnen, Dementi, Weigerung	Despite the denial of the defendant there is clear evidence that he committed the crime.	≠ admission, confession, revelation
(to) depart departure	verschwinden Abreise, Abschied	In many English institutions the form remains enshrined in ritual and tradition long after most of the substance has departed.	= disappear, vanish, leave
dependence dependent [adj] dependable [adj]	Abhängigkeit abhängig verlässlich	Heroin and cocaine produce physical dependence. Solar energy is not a very dependable form of energy.	= addiction = reliable
depression depressing [adj]	(wirtschaftliche) Flaute deprimierend	The US economy went through two world wars and a global depression in the first half of the 20th century. The prospects for executives are even more depressing.	≠ boom = gloomy, sad, negative, discouraging
deprived [adj]	benachteiligt	Riots broke out in one of the most deprived estates in Newcastle.	= destitute, disadvantaged, underprivileged
derived from [adj]	übernommen von	The following extracts are derived from a parliamentary debate on "The cost of monarchy".	= drawn from, taken from
(to) descend descendant	herunterführen Nachfahr(e), Nachkomme	Descendants of immigrants have come to visit Ellis Island since it was opened as a museum.	= ancestor, forebear

word family	dt. Bedeutung	English sentence	synonyms/opposites
(to) design	planen, beabsichtigen	The European court of human rights has declared unlawful a British policy designed to keep immigrants out.	= intend, plan, mean
designer drug	synthetische Droge	Designer drugs are developed in chemical laboratories.	= synthetic drug
(to) despair despair desperation desperate [adj]	verzweifeln Verzweiflung Verzweiflung verzweifelt	We should not despair if we do not yet know exactly how to make the most appropriate use of personal computers in our educational institutions.	= lose hope, lose heart
despite	trotz	Despite the restrictions of immigration acts, the number of people claiming asylum continued to increase.	= in spite of, regardless of
despised [adj]	verachtet	We, the blacks, are the most despised children of the great Western house.	≠ respected, admired, praised
(to) destine destiny destination	bestimmen (für) Schicksal Bestimmungsort, Ziel	Centuries ago the people of England established the right to control their own destiny.	= fate, fortune, lot
(to) destroy destruction destructive [adj]	zerstören Zerstörung zerstörerisch	The advertisement of the British auto industry reads: "Every seven cars which are imported into the country destroy the job of a British worker".	≠ create, secure
detergent	Reinigungs-, Waschmittel	We could do without one or the other detergent!	= cleaner, washing powder
(to) determine	bestimmen, festlegen	How well people have managed to keep up with rising prices partly depends on the way in which their income is determined.	= fix, define, regulate
detrimental [adj]	schädlich	Games and sport counteract the detrimental effects of our affluent society.	= harmful, damaging, negative, unfavourable

word family	dt. Bedeutung	English sentence	synonyms/opposites
(to) devastate	vernichten, verwüsten	Shipping was devastated by the decline in trade.	= destroy, wreck, ruin
(to) devise	ersinnen	The scientist was trying to devise a method to help	= design, contrive
device	Plan	couples who aren't able to have children in a normal way.	
(to) devote	widmen	Home schooling requires a lot of responsibility, time,	= dedication, enthusiasm
devotion	Hingabe	and devotion on the parent's part.	
devoted [adj]	begeistert		
(to) differ	unterscheiden, abweichen	Man's invisible environment is made up of – among	≠ identical, similar
difference	Unterschied	other things – many different backgrounds of culture.	
different [adj]	verschieden		
difficulty	Schwierigkeit, Problem	Even though we face the difficulties of today and	= problem, dilemma,
		tomorrow, I still have a dream.	obstacle, plight
(to) diminish (1)	vermindern	The increase in demand for some commodities is	= reduce, lower, cut back on,
		expected to diminish the Community's surplus	curb
		foodstuffs.	
(to) diminish (2)	sich verringern, abnehmen	The numbers of native Indians diminished rapidly as	= decrease, fall; ≠ increase,
diminution	Verringerung	white settlement advanced.	intensify
diminutive [adj]	klein, winzig		
directive	Anweisung	It is rare that party members disobey the party directive	= order, guideline, policy
		on how they shall vote.	
disadvantage	Nachteil	The disadvantage of speed in transport lies in the fact	= drawback, handicap
		that it is generally obtained at the expense of our	≠ advantage
		natural resources and our environment.	

word family	dt. Bedeutung	English sentence	synonyms/opposites
(to) disappear	(ver)schwinden	The construction of even faster cars is irresponsible in view of the disappearing natural resources.	= dwindle, vanish
disappearance	Verschwinden	After the official disappearance of the Soviet Union, Americans are reconsidering their view of the former enemy and of America as well.	≠ birth, emergence, creation, rise
discount	Rabatt	Many firms allow a discount of 3 % for cash payment.	= rebate, reduction
(to) discover	entdecken, herausfinden	A crack was discovered, probably caused as the sixteen white horses dragged the bell over Westminster Bridge after its first casting in 1856.	= find, detect
disease	Krankheit	We cannot refuse to cure disease in order to limit world population.	= illness, sickness, ailment
(to) dismiss	entlassen	I cannot believe that they want to dismiss more than 500 people from their jobs!	= discharge, sack, fire ≠ hire, employ
(to) dispatch	absenden, abfertigen	We shall dispatch the goods you ordered tomorrow.	= send off
(to) dispose of	beseitigen	We will not be able to dispose of an endless stream of waste.	= get rid of, throw away, dump
disposal disposable [adj]	Beseitigung, Entsorgung Wegwerf-, Einweg-	Any drink sold in a disposable bottle should cost twice as much as the same drink offered in a returnable bottle.	= non-returnable, expendable, replaceable
(to) distinguish distinction distinctive [adj] distinctly [adv]	unterscheiden Auszeichnung charakteristisch deutlich, klar	Many disadvantages of the old factories are distinctly present in modern production lines.	= clearly, obviously, markedly

word family	dt. Bedeutung	English sentence	synonyms/opposites
diversity	Vielfalt, Mannigfaltigkeit	Cultural diversity is one of the main characteristics of a multi-racial society.	= variety
diverse (1) [adj]	verschiedenartig, vielfältig	The old-fashioned adjectives "new, super, giant" etc. have been applied to diverse goods of different sort and quality.	= various, numerous
diverse (2) [adj]	verschiedenartig, gemischt	Intermarriage produced a population of diverse blood.	= mixed, varied
(to) divert	ablenken, umlenken	In order to attract as many viewers as possible TV programming is concentrated on entertainment and diversion.	= amusement, dissipation, distraction
diversion	Ablenkung, Unterhaltung; Umleitung		
domestic [adj]	heimisch, inländisch	Trade forces domestic industries to adjust to changing technology before they become hopelessly inefficient.	≠ foreign
(to) dominate	beherrschen	Margaret Thatcher feared that a reunited Germany would dominate a political European Community.	= control, domineer
domination	Vorherrschaft		
dominant [adj]	beherrschend		
(to) doubt	zweifeln	Biologists have no doubt that the ozone layer is damaged.	≠ certitude; confidence
doubt	Zweifel		
doubtful [adj]	skeptisch; unsicher		
doubtless [adj]	zweifellos		
dubious [adj]	zweifelhaft		
drug pusher	Drogenhändler	Drug pushers often approach young boys and girls to sell them the deadly stuff.	= drug dealer, drug trafficker, drug peddler
drug trafficking	Drogenhandel	Gangsters in Columbia turned drug trafficking into a multi-billion dollar business.	= drug trade

word family	dt. Bedeutung	English sentence	synonyms/opposites
dull [adj]	langweilig, stumpfsinnig	Household appliances relieve us from dull work.	= boring, repetitive
dump	Müllhalde	Dumps overflow with cans, bottles and cartons.	= rubbish-heap
earnest [adj]	ernsthaft, sorgfältig	John W. Smith is an earnest man; you can really rely on him.	= conscientious, diligent, serious, honest
earnings	Verdienst	Poor people spend a high proportion of their earnings on food.	= wages, income, pay
(to) ease	erleichtern	New developments could ease, but not end, global environment problems.	≠ worsen, complicate, aggravate
easiness	Leichtigkeit		
ease	Bequemlichkeit, Ruhe	Grandfather hopes for a life of ease when he retires.	= comfort, leisure, relaxation
easy [adj]	leicht		
(to) eat	essen		
eatable [adj]	essbar	Edible plants and berries were used as food and some-times as medicine.	
edible [adj]	essbar		≠ inedible
(to) economise	sparen	The companies do not have the technically qualified staff who could invent or work out more economical production methods.	
economy	Wirtschaft		
economic [adj]	wirtschaftlich		
economical [adj]	sparsam		≠ wasteful, extravagant
(to) edit	(einen Text) herausgeben, redigieren	We edited our articles for the school magazine.	= rewrite, revise, adapt, alter
effect	(Aus-)Wirkung	Sociologists study migration to analyze the effects it has on social structures.	= consequence, repercussion
effective [adj]	wirksam, fähig		
effectively [adv]	eigentlich, praktisch	The monarch has effectively no political power.	= virtually, practically

word family	dt. Bedeutung	English sentence	synonyms/opposites
efficiency efficient [adj]	Tüchtigkeit leistungsfähig	I've always admired the efficiency of professional musicians.	= competence, skill, proficiency
effort	Anstrengung	The government did not make any effort to keep inflation down.	= attempt, endeavour
election	Wahl	The next general election will be held in November.	= ballot, poll, vote
(to) emerge emergence	auftauchen Auftauchen	The emergence of powerful economies in Asia increased the global integration of business and finance.	
emphasis	Betonung	The emphasis in advertising today lies less on factual information and more on subtle temptation.	= priority, stress, accent
(to) employ employment employee employer	beschäftigen, anstellen Anstellung Angestellter Arbeitgeber	The biggest firm in our town employs more than 1,400 workers.	= engage, hire, recruit, give work to, pay
(to) endure endurance endurable [adj]	bestehen, aushalten, ertragen Ausdauer erträglich	There is every indication that Western European-style monarchy will endure for a long time to come.	= continue, last, persist
enemy	Feind	Many immigrants came from countries where the police was considered the natural enemies of the people.	= opponent, adversary, antagonist, foe ≠ ally, friend, supporter
(to) enforce enforcement	durchsetzen Durchsetzung	A broad coalition is now gathering to enforce the just demands of the world.	= accomplish, execute, fulfil
(to) enjoy	genießen, sich erfreuen an	We enjoy achievements such as computers.	≠ hate, lack

word family	dt. Bedeutung	English sentence	synonyms/opposites
(to) enlarge	vergrößern	The consumer price index of Los Angeles rose less than	
largeness	Größe, Weite	of the other metropolitan areas, thanks largely to illegal	
large [adj]	groß	workers.	
largely [adv]	im Wesentlichen, größtenteils		= chiefly, on the whole
enormity	Ungeheuerlichkeit	All over the world man has put enormous amounts of	
enormous [adj]	riesig, ungeheuer groß	harmful and hazardous chemicals into the air we breathe and the water we drink.	= huge, gigantic; ≠ small, minute, diminutive
(to) enquire siehe auch inquire	sich erkundigen		
(to) ensure	sichern, garantieren	The Queen ensures that the democratic process is carried out as it is supposed to be.	= make certain, see to it, guarantee, secure; ≠ prevent, endanger, destroy
entire [adj]	ganz	The entire class visited the exhibition.	= whole, complete, total
entrepreneur	Unternehmer	Entrepreneurs have their own complaints about the public-school system.	= businessman, executive, employer, industrialist
environment	Umwelt	We have been massively intervening in the environment without being aware of many of the harmful consequences of our acts.	= surroundings
(to) envy	beneiden	Because of this variety of talent his classmates looked	
envy	Neid	upon him with a mixed feeling of awe and envy.	= jealousy
envious [adj]	neidisch		
enviable [adj]	beneidenswert		

word family	dt. Bedeutung	English sentence	synonyms/opposites
(to) equal equality equal [adj]	gleichkommen, ergeben Gleichberechtigung gleich	What could the government do to ensure more equality, to avoid discrimination?	≠ inequality, discrimination
err erroneous [adj]	irren irrig	The Secret Service said they were acting on an erroneous tip.	= false, inaccurate
especially [adv]	im Besonderen	Working mothers also feel that they should carry the main responsibility, especially for the children.	= particularly, in particular
essence essential [adj] essentially [adv]	(innerstes) Wesen lebensnotwendig, wesentlich im Wesentlichen, in der Hauptsache	In the poor countries the people's diets lack proteins and essential vitamins. England's activities are essentially industrial and commercial, and only slightly agricultural.	= necessary, vital, needed = mainly, primarily, basically
(to) establish establishment established [adj]	gründen Unternehmen, Einrichtung fest	This old firm was established in 1895. We moved here years ago and are now considered established members of the community.	= found, set up = accepted, settled
(to) estimate estimation	(ab)schätzen, veranschlagen Einschätzung	Scientists estimate that the surface of the earth will warm by about another 3.5 % over the next century.	= calculate, assess
(to) evade evasion evasive [adj]	ausweichen Ausflucht ausweichend	His mother is evasive in her answers to some of his questions.	= equivocating, shifty
event eventful [adj] eventual [adj] eventually [adv]	Ereignis ereignisreich schließlich schließlich, endlich	The information could eventually be stored on a chip smaller than a baby's fingernail.	= finally, in the end, at last

word family	dt. Bedeutung	English sentence	synonyms/opposites
evidence	Beweis	There is clear evidence that Jim Clayton set fire to the	= proof
evident [adj]	augenscheinlich	house of the Miller family.	
(to) exact	(dringend) fordern, eintreiben	The judge tried to exact a confession from the criminal.	= demand
exactitude	Genauigkeit		
exactness	Genauigkeit	The clockmaker guarantees that Big Ben's time is always	
exact [adj]	genau	exact.	= precise, accurate, correct
(to) exceed	übersteigen, überschreiten	If inputs of any nutrient greatly exceed outputs, the	= surpass
excess	Übermaß	ecosystem becomes stressed or overloaded, resulting	
excessive [adj]	übermäßig	in pollution.	
(to) except	ausschließen		
exception	Ausnahme		
except	außer	Our Government has no power except that granted by	= apart from, save
exceptional [adj]	außergewöhnlich	the people.	≠ including
(to) exclude	ausschließen	Drug misuse is associated with other problems such as	
exclusion	Ausschluss	truancy and school exclusion.	
exclusive [adj]	ausschließlich		
(to) execute	(eine Bestellung) ausführen	We shall execute your order as soon as possible.	= carry out
execution	Durchführung; Hinrichtung		
executive [adj]	ausübend(e Gewalt)		
(to) exempt	verschonen	All colour additives permitted for use in foods are	
exemption	Befreiung	classified as "exempt from certification".	
exempt [adj]	befreit		= free from; ≠ subject to

word family	dt. Bedeutung	English sentence	synonyms/opposites
(to) exert exertion	*ausüben; sich anstrengen* *Anstrengung*	Although the years of the Cold War are over, George Orwell's "1984" still exerts a strong hold on our imaginations.	= exercise
(to) exhaust exhaustion exhaustive [adj] exhausted [adj]	*erschöpfen* *Erschöpfung* *erschöpfend* *erschöpft*	Why should people work longer hours if they are then too exhausted to enjoy the extra income?	= very tired, dead beat, tired out, dog-tired, worn out
(to) expand expansion expanse expansive [adj] expansionary [adj]	*ausweiten, expandieren, zunehmen* *Erweiterung* *Ausdehnung* *ausgedehnt* *expansionistisch*	In the 19th and early 20th centuries business and industry in the US were expanding.	= extend, spread, increase, augment, enlarge; ≠ reduce, decrease, shrink, decline, be in decline
(to) expend expense expensive [adj]	*ausgeben* *Kosten, Ausgabe* *teuer*	Most children in Britain are educated at the public expense.	= cost, expenditure
experiment	*Versuch*	The scientist carried out a dangerous experiment.	= test, examination, analysis
(to) exploit exploitation	*ausbeuten, ausnutzen* *Ausbeutung*	The government will exploit all their instruments of influence to achieve better conditions for the country.	= take advantage of, use
(to) expose exposure exposition	*aussetzen, bloßstellen* *Ausgesetztsein, Aussetzung* *Ausstellung, Darlegung*	One of the main aims of Greenpeace is to expose environmental criminals.	≠ cover, shelter; guard, protect

word family	dt. Bedeutung	English sentence	synonyms/opposites
(to) extend extension extent extensive [adj]	verlängern Verlängerung Ausdehnung ausgedehnt	Can't you extend your visit for a few days?	= prolong, continue
(to) exterminate extermination	ausrotten Ausrottung	The Nazi regime aimed at the systematic extermination of Jews and other minorities.	= annihilate, eradicate, extinguish, root/wipe out
(to) extinguish extinction (to) become extinct	auslöschen, erlöschen Aussterben aussterben	If species cannot adapt to the environmental changes, they become extinct.	= die out
extracts	Auszüge (Pl.)	Let us study these extracts from a debate in Parliament.	= excerpts, passages
extraordinary [adj]	außergewöhnlich, ungewöhnlich	The immigrants helped give America the extraordinary social mobility which is the essence of an open society.	= exceptional, unusual
(to) face	gegenübertreten	Together as friends and allies we can face the uncertainties of the future.	= confront
(to) facilitate facility facilities	erleichtern Erleichterung Einrichtung	In 1957 an economic union was formed to facilitate trade across national borders. A welfare state provides free treatment in hospitals, and other public health facilities.	= ease
factory	Fabrik	Helen works in a shoe factory from 9 a.m. to 4.30 p.m.	= manufacturers, plant
(to) fail (1) (to) fail (2) failure	versagen, nachlassen durchfallen (bei Prüfung) Misserfolg	Some observers call for control of the press should the media fail to stop covering terrorist actions. My first attempt at windsurfing was a complete failure.	= not be prepared, be unable = flunk = flop, disaster, catastrophe

word family	dt. Bedeutung	English sentence	synonyms/opposites
faint [adj]	schwach	She called for help in a faint voice.	= weak, feeble, powerless
fairness fair [adj] fairly [adv]	Fairness, Gerechtigkeit gerecht ziemlich	Though a fairly large black middle class has emerged, many blacks continue to exist on the economic margins.	= rather, quite
faith	Glaube, Vertrauen	Many immigrants brought with them the faith in political and economic institutions.	= trust, belief, confidence
faithful [adj]	treu	A faithful dog obeys his master.	= loyal, dependable
(to) falsify falsehood false [adj]	fälschen Unwahrheit, Falschheit falsch	What you're saying is false.	= wrong, faulty, erroneous
(to) familiarize family family planning familiarity familiar [adj]	vertraut machen Familie Familienplanung Vertrautheit vertraut	Family planning should be made freely available. A familiar person is no longer a stranger.	= birth control = well-known, acquainted
(to) fancy fancy fanciful [adj]	etwas gern tun Fantasie fantastisch	Stevenson seized the public's fancy with "Kidnapped" and "Dr. Jekyll and Mr Hyde" in 1886.	= imagination, fantasy, imaginativeness
(to) fascinate fascination fascinating [adj]	faszinieren Begeisterung faszinierend, anregend, interessant	Think of a bookstore full of people looking for fascinating stories.	≠ boring, dull, uninteresting

word family	dt. Bedeutung	English sentence	synonyms/opposites
fast [adv]	schnell	Third-world peoples – Asians, Latin Americans, and blacks are the fastest growing segment of the US immigrant population.	≠ slowly, gradually, bit by bit, step by step
fate fatal [adj]	Schicksal tödlich	It's very unlikely that anybody could tell you your fate correctly.	= destiny, lot, good fortune
fathers	Vorfahren	I sing of the "Land where my fathers died".	= ancestors, forebears
(to) fatten fatness fatty [adj]	mästen Beleibtheit fettig	Common sense should tell you that eating many fatty meals is not good for you.	= greasy
fault faulty [adj]	Fehler fehlerhaft	There is a fault in the electric system in this house.	= defect, weakness, flaw
(to) favour favour favourable [adj] favourite [adj]	befürworten Befürwortung, Bevorzugung, Gunst positiv, günstig Lieblings-	Economists, in general, favour a liberal approach to immigration. The critical response to the book was overwhelmingly favourable.	= approve, accept, approbate ≠ oppose, reject, disagree with ≠ unfavourable
(to) feed	füttern, ernähren, versorgen	There are more mouths to feed as people live longer.	= provide for, sustain
ferocity ferocious [adj]	Wildheit wild	Napoleon' surrounds himself with ferocious guard dogs.	= savage, bestial; ≠ gentle
(to) fertilize fertility fertile [adj]	düngen, befruchten Fruchtbarkeit fruchtbar	Critics of genetic engineering are worried about the commercialization of fertility technology.	≠ infertility, sterility, barrenness

word family	dt. Bedeutung	English sentence	synonyms/opposites
fervour	Glut		
fervent [adj]	inbrünstig, glühend, leidenschaftlich	Fervent supporters of total independence from London are found in Scotland in the ranks of the Scottish National Party (SNP).	= passionate
fiction	Erfindung		
fictional [adj]	erfunden		
fictitious [adj]	erdacht	Titus Oates gave the authorities details of a fictitious plot by Catholics to murder the King.	= fictional, fictive, imaginary, unreal; ≠ real, genuine
fierce [adj]	heftig, scharf, grimmig	Today in all of the developing countries a fierce struggle for survival is taking place.	= intense, violent, brutal, cruel
final [adj]	endgültig	After a six-hour debate Parliament took a final decision.	= definitive, decisive
finally [adv]	schließlich	He stared at me for a long time and finally asked whether I was Angela Davis.	= eventually, in the end, at last, ultimately
fine [adj]	schön	Young people get so lazy, they choose to spend a fine day in semi-darkness, glued to their computers.	= bright, nice, pleasant
firm	Firma	He doesn't work for this firm any more.	= company, business
(to) fit	genügen, passen	The schools must ensure that the workers are able to fit the requirements of industry.	= meet, come up to, suit
(to) flee	fliehen		
flight	Flucht	Millions left their home countries in Europe to flee from poverty and hunger.	= escape, break away, fly, run away
(to) flourish	blühen, gedeihen	The economies in the industrialized countries flourished.	= grow, thrive, prosper, bloom, do well, expand

word family	dt. Bedeutung	English sentence	synonyms/opposites
fluid fluid [adj]	Flüssigkeit flüssig	Water, coffee, beer and milk are fluids.	= liquid
for good	endgültig	The golden times were over for good.	= forever
(to) forbid	verbieten	In all public places smoking is forbidden.	= prohibit, ban
(to) force force forcible [adj]	zwingen Gewalt gewaltsam	If you want to bring about a change, you shouldn't do it by force.	= violence, brutality
foreign [adj] foreign trade	ausländisch Außenhandel	Foreign visitors come to England to see Buckingham Palace and all the other sights of London.	= overseas, non-domestic = overseas trade
(to) foretell	vorhersagen	I don't believe that anybody can foretell your future.	= predict, forecast, foresee
(to) forge	formen, schaffen, schmieden	The Commonwealth bond was forged by once being part of an empire.	= build, establish, form, mould
fortune fortunate [adj]	Glück, Vermögen glücklich, Glück haben	Bob was fortunate. A neighbour walking by the apartment smelt gas and pulled Bob out into the fresh air.	= lucky
fragile [adj]	schwach, zerbrechlich	Despite the striking advances of the middle class, the gains remain fragile and partial.	≠ solid, sound
fragrance fragrant [adj]	Duft duftend	In his wonderful garden he could smell sweet fragrances filling the air.	= aroma, balm, perfume, scent; ≠ stench, stink
frailty frail [adj]	Gebrechlichkeit zerbrechlich	Holden is attracted to the weak and the frail, and he feels sorry for "losers of all kinds".	= decrepit, feeble, fragile, infirm; ≠ robust, strong

word family	dt. Bedeutung	English sentence	synonyms/opposites
frequency frequent [adj]	Häufigkeit häufig	People, when they hear the name "Big Ben", think of the high tower or of the huge clock which towers some 316 feet above the River Thames at Westminster, no doubt	= daily, everyday, constant, continual, regular
frequently [adv]	oft	because of the clock's frequent appearance on TV.	= often, repeatedly
(to) frighten fright frightful [adj]	erschrecken Schrecken, Schreck entsetzlich	Amy cried out in fright.	= terror, panic, horror, alarm, shock
(to) frustrate frustrated [adj]	entmutigen, enttäuschen enttäuscht	Many people feel frustrated in the face of increasing violence.	≠ encourage, motivate = discontented, dissatisfied, disappointed
funds	Geldmittel (Pl.)	The local council has no funds to finance a new recreation centre.	= resources, cash, money
fury furious [adj]	Raserei, Wut wütend, zornig	If you say to a Scotsman that he's English, you will arouse him to fury.	= rage, outrage, frenzy, indignation
(to) gain gain	gewinnen, profitieren Nettogewinn, Reingewinn	What does a country gain being a member of the EU?	= profit, benefit ≠ damage, harm, loss
garbage	Müll, Abfall	We have thrown into the seas of the world millions of tons of garbage.	= litter, refuse, trash
(to) gather	sich versammeln	When people gather somewhere, they come together in a group.	= congregate, assemble, convene
(to) gaze	starren auf, anstarren	From abroad tourists come to gaze in awe upon the Houses of Parliament.	= stare

word family	dt. Bedeutung	English sentence	synonyms/opposites
general [adj]	allgemein	The general standard of education is very high.	= overall, common, regular
generally [adv]	im Allgemeinen	Wool and cotton blankets are generally cheapest.	= normally, usually; ≠ in parti-
in general	im Allgemeinen	Civil rights legislation in general has been enforced.	cular, particularly, especially
(to) generate	hervorbringen, erzeugen	Over the next two decades, cities like Mexico City, Sao Paolo and Shanghai are expected to double in size,	= cause, bring about, create, produce
generosity	Großzügigkeit	generating economic and social problems that will far	= liberal, benevolent,
generous [adj]	großzügig	outstrip all previous experience.	unselfish
gentleness	Sanftheit		
gentle [adj]	sanft, leicht	She sat on the terrace and felt a gentle breeze.	= light, faint, pleasant
genuineness	Echtheit		
genuine [adj]	echt, ehrlich	Quite often magazine articles on shopping are written with the genuine intention of benefiting the reader.	= real, honest, sincere, true, authentic; ≠ counterfeit, fake
giant	Riese, Hüne		
giant [adj]	riesig	When the first astronaut landed on the moon people	= enormous, huge, gigantic,
gigantic [adj]	riesig	thought that was a giant step forward.	immense, tremendous
gift	Gabe, Begabung	Sarah has a real gift for story-telling.	= talent, faculty, genius
gloom	Düsterkeit		
gloomy [adj]	dunkel, düster, schwermütig, traurig	The scenario paints the gloomiest picture of rising carbon dioxide levels.	= dark, bad, pessimistic
(to) glorify	verherrlichen		
glory	Ruhm	I did it for the theatre, not for my own personal glory.	= fame, honour, prestige
glorious [adj]	prächtig	These are the most glorious flowers I've ever seen.	= splendid, delightful, won- derful, superb, magnificent

word family	dt. Bedeutung	English sentence	synonyms/opposites
goal	Ziel	Can Americans and Europeans be united by common goals?	= aim, target, objective
goods	Waren	We sell our goods to almost all countries of the world.	= commodities, articles, products, merchandise
(to) grade grade gradual [adj] gradually [adv]	einteilen Rang stufenweise allmählich	Tolerance, education and integration could gradually lead to an improvement in the status of disabled people in our society.	= continually, bit by bit
grains	Korn, Getreide(arten)(Pl.)	The rotation of corn with other grains keeps the soil fertile.	= cereals
(to) grant	geben, gewähren	It is not likely that permission will be granted for the building of a new factory.	= give, concede, allow
gratitude grateful [adj]	Dankbarkeit dankbar	Queen Victoria regarded Lewis Carroll's "Alice" a masterpiece and sent word that she would be grateful to get a copy of his next book.	= obliged, thankful ≠ ungrateful
greed greediness greedy [adj]	Gier Gier gierig	Moral degeneration is seen as inevitable in the absence of social controls against greed and competition.	= avarice, gluttony
(to) grieve grief grievance grievous [adj]	sich grämen Gram, Kummer Missstand kränkend	First the King died, and then the Queen died of grief.	= sorrow, distress, sadness, woe

word family	dt. Bedeutung	English sentence	synonyms/opposites
(to) grow growth growing [adj]	wachsen Wachstum wachsend	The fitness market has been growing rapidly. Computing is still a growth industry. A growing number of school children have been tempted to try cannabis.	= expand, rise, increase = expansion, development ≠ falling, decreasing, diminishing, dwindling
(to) hang on to	festhalten an	Male managers are determined to hold on to their jobs.	≠ give up, quit, resign from
(to) harm harm harmful [adj]	schaden, schädigen Schaden schädlich	The ozone layer shields life from the sun's harmful ultraviolet rays.	= damaging, hazardous
harsh [adj]	herb, grell, streng, schroff, barsch	Prominent authors expressed harsh criticisms of America.	= severe, strong
(to) hazard hazard hazardous [adj]	wagen, riskieren Gefahr, Wagnis gefährlich, schädlich	In many cases scientists disagree about the medical hazards of chemical substances.	= danger, risk, peril = harmful, perilous, unsafe
(to) head for	sich aufmachen nach, lossteuern auf	British emigrants head for countries like Australia and Canada.	= go to, migrate to
(to) heighten height high [adj]	erhöhen, verstärken Höhe hoch	The implications of heightened environmental concern are far-reaching for commerce and trade.	= increase, intensify ≠ lower, reduce, decrease
(to) hire	einstellen	The best training is done by employers who need to hire workers.	≠ dismiss, sack, fire
(to) honour honour honourable [adj]	erfüllen, erlösen Ehre ehrenhaft	Participants observed that the country continued to honour its commitments.	= fulfil

word family	dt. Bedeutung	English sentence	synonyms/opposites
horror horrible [adj] horrid [adj]	Entsetzen, Abscheu, Gräuel schrecklich abscheulich	Having detonated an atomic bomb, the physicists looked back in horror at what they had wrought.	= repugnance, disgust
hostility hostile [adj]	Feindseligkeit feindlich	The charge is that he and his policies are hostile to the nation's poor.	≠ in favour of
House of Commons	(brit.) Unterhaus	The House of Commons is more important than the House of Lords.	= Lower House
House of Lords	(brit.) Oberhaus	The British Parliament consists of the House of Commons and the House of Lords.	= Upper House
household	Haushalt	A lot of energy is needed for the many household appliances we use.	= domestic
humanity human [adj] humanitarian [adj] humane [adj]	Menschheit, Menschlichkeit menschlich humanitär menschlich, human	I dream of a day when humanity expands beyond Earth. Those who commit crimes against humanity cannot forever be safe from justice.	= mankind, human race
(to) humble humbleness humble [adj]	demütigen Demut demütig	The old fisherman is humble and unpretentious; it doesn't bother him at all that his shirt has been patched and re-patched.	= modest; ≠ arrogant, haughty
(to) humiliate humility humiliation	erniedrigen, demütigen Demut Demütigung	The media can bring down a president or a king, elevate the lowly and humiliate the proud.	= degrade, demean, lower, sink

word family	dt. Bedeutung	English sentence	synonyms/opposites
(to) hunger hunger hungry [adj]	*hungern* *Hunger* *hungrig*	The Department of Agriculture (USDA) attempts to curb poverty, hunger and malnutrition by issuing food stamps to the poor.	= starvation, famine
hurdle	*Hürde, Hindernis*	The first hurdle in any presidential election are the primary elections.	= obstacle
hypocrisy hypocritical [adj]	*Heuchelei* *heuchlerisch*	Thoughtful whites criticised the American hypocrisy, pointing to the contradiction between what the US required from others and what it practised at home.	≠ sincerity
(to) ignore ignorance ignorant [adj]	*nicht beachten* *Unwissenheit* *unwissend*	People are afraid that their local interests will be ignored.	= neglect, disregard, overlook ≠ consider, see, recognize
ill	*Übel, Missstand*	Many people blamed a lot of the country's ills on the EU.	= difficulty, problem, trouble
(to) imagine imagination imaginative [adj] imaginable [adj] imaginary [adj]	*sich vorstellen* *Fantasie* *einfallsreich* *denkbar* *ausgedacht, fiktiv, eingebildet*	The idea about possible life on Mars was the subject of several imaginary stories.	= fancied; ≠ real, concrete
(to) imitate imitation imitable [adj]	*nachahmen* *Nachahmung* *nachahmbar*	Many experts contend that some youngsters will imitate the brutality of video games in real life.	= copy
immediate [adj] immediately [adv]	*unmittelbar, sofortig* *sofort*	Man must think about the harmful consequences of his acts for coming generations and not only for his immediate future.	= imminent = at once, instantly, promptly

word family	dt. Bedeutung	English sentence	synonyms/opposites
immensity immense [adj]	Unermesslichkeit riesig, enorm	Jack London's "Call of the Wild" was published in 1903 and had an immediate and an immense success.	= enormous, huge, gigantic ≠ tiny, small, minute
(to) immigrate immigration	einwandern Einwanderung	The second force behind immigration has been political oppression.	≠ emigration
immunity immune [adj]	Unempfindlichkeit unempfindlich, immun	During the early contact with Indians, millions died from such European diseases as measles and smallpox, for which the natives had no immunity.	≠ susceptibility
impact	Auswirkung, Einfluss	This new industrial revolution will equal in its impact the first Industrial Revolution.	= influence, effect(s), consequence(s), result(s)
impartiality impartial [adj]	Unparteilichkeit, Objektivität unvoreingenommen	Prime Ministers of both major parties have praised the Queen's wit and impartiality.	≠ bias
(to) imply implication implicit [adj]	etw. andeuten Verwicklung, Folge unausgesprochen, indirekt	Low incomes imply small markets and therefore a low degree of specialization.	= indicate, suggest
importance important [adj]	Bedeutung wichtig	Through these meetings they can work together on important world issues, such as fighting poverty, and advancing world peace.	= significant, substantial, vital, weighty
(to) impose	auferlegen, aufbürden	On Thursday the Home Secretary imposed a new requirement that all immigrants from Sri Lanka get a visa before travelling to Britain.	= levy, demand, introduce
(to) imprison imprisonment	einsperren Einkerkerung, Haft	Amnesty's central function was to campaign against unjust imprisonment on the grounds of individual belief.	≠ release, freeing

word family	dt. Bedeutung	English sentence	synonyms/opposites
improbability improbable [adj]	Unwahrscheinlichkeit unwahrscheinlich	Some incidents in the first act of the play could be regarded as highly improbable.	= doubtful, dubious, unlikely
(to) improve improvement	verbessern Verbesserung	The only good news for smokers is that their health begins to improve immediately after they stop.	≠ deteriorate, weaken
in fact	genau genommen	In fact, the trend to flexible working hours appears to be inevitable.	= really, actually, indeed
in terms of	hinsichtlich	Realities inside Northern Ireland, in terms of Protestant-Catholic relations, did not change very much.	= as far as … are concerned, concerning
in view of	angesichts	In view of the high unemployment level in France and England, the prospect of new jobs through the channel project was very attractive.	= with regard to
incapability incapable [adj]	Unfähigkeit, Unvermögen unfähig, ungeeignet	The incapability of King George III soon became evident.	= incapacity, incompetence, ineffectiveness
(to) include inclusion inclusive [adj]	umfassen, einschließen, beinhalten Einschluss einschließlich	Development policies should include national population programmes.	= contain, embrace, comprise
income	Einnahme, Einkommen	Amnesty's income comes from membership and donations.	≠ expense, outgoings
incompetent [adj]	unfähig	The opposition tries to convince the public that the present government is incompetent.	= useless, incapable

word family	dt. Bedeutung	English sentence	synonyms/opposites
incomprehensible [adj]	unverständlich, unbegreiflich	The messages which the agent passed on to head-quarters were incomprehensible to outsiders.	≠ understandable, logical, clear
inconvenience	Unannehmlichkeiten, Unbequemlichkeit	The chairman apologized for the inconvenience and delays experienced by visitors.	= bother, trouble ≠ convenience
inconvenient [adj]	ungelegen		
increase	Wachstum, Zunahme	In many Third World countries rates of natural popula-tion increase exceed 3 percent annually.	= growth ≠ decrease
indestructible [adj]	unzerstörbar, unverwüstlich	The bicycle is an almost indestructible means of transport.	= unbreakable, everlasting
(to) indicate indication indicative [adj]	andeuten, zeigen Andeutung aufschlussreich	If you lack experience in a particular computer pro-gramme, indicate your willingness to take a course.	= show, hint at, suggest
indignation indignant [adj]	Entrüstung empört	Biff and Harry expressed their indignation at their father's behaviour.	= anger, fury, rage, wrath
(to) induce	herbeiführen	Drugs induce strong euphoric feelings.	= cause
(to) indulge indulgence indulgent [adj]	einer Laune nachgeben Nachsicht, Schwäche nachgiebig	The world's problems seem all too serious for two nations to indulge in quarrelling.	= wallow, revel
(to) industrialise industry industrial [adj] industrious [adj]	zum Industriestaat werden Industrie; Fleiß industriell fleißig	When other countries began to industrialise, they had to compete with Britain. The people who worked for Sutter were industrious and faithful labourers.	= diligent, persevering ≠ idle, inactive; lethargic

word family	dt. Bedeutung	English sentence	synonyms/opposites
ineligible [adj]	ungeeignet	Subversives were declared ineligible.	= unsuitable, unfit
inevitability inevitable [adj]	Unvermeidlichkeit unvermeidlich, unvermeidbar	The introduction of flexible working hours was inevitable.	= unavoidable; ≠ preventable
(to) infect infection infectious [adj]	anstecken Ansteckung ansteckend	Anthrax ("Milzbrand") is an infectious, often fatal disease of sheep and cattle that can also kill humans.	= contagious
inferiority inferior [adj]	Minderwertigkeit minderwertig	During the period of British colonial domination, non-whites were looked down upon as an inferior race.	≠ superior, outstanding, best
inflow	Zustrom	The ending of the postwar boom led to a decline of the inflow of immigrants.	= influx
influx	Zustrom	The influx of West Indians to the USA was restricted.	= flood, flowing in, stream
(to) inherit inheritance heredity hereditary [adj]	erben Erbe Erblichkeit erblich	Gandhi advocated heavy taxes and limited rights of inheritance as a way of creating a just and equal society.	= heritage, legacy
inmate	(Gefängnis-)Insasse, Häftling	Last year, the number of inmates in state and federal prisons grew by 26,000.	= prisoner
innocence innocent [adj]	Unschuld unschuldig	The investigation proved that H. M. Swindon is innocent, so the police will release him immediately.	= not guilty
(to) inquire/enquire inquiry/enquiry inquisition inquisitive [adj]	sich erkundigen Erkundigung, Anfrage Untersuchung, Verhör neugierig	He called the sales manager to inquire/enquire about the latest prices.	= ask, question

word family	dt. Bedeutung	English sentence	synonyms/opposites
insanity **insane** [adj]	Geisteskrankheit verrückt	When the ghost reappears Macbeth seems totally insane to his guests.	= mad, crazy; ≠ sane, rational
(to) insist **insistence** **insistent** [adj]	bestehen Beharren beharrlich	Insistent demands for social reforms finally led to the creation of the Welfare State.	= perseverant, persisting
(to) instruct **instruction** **instructive** [adj]	anweisen Anweisung, Unterricht lehrreich	They'll have to instruct all polling-stations to close the doors at 10 p.m.	= direct, order
insular [adj]	Insel-	England is, in effect, insular and maritime.	≠ continental
(to) intend **intention** **intent** [adj]	beabsichtigen Absicht gespannt	The member countries intended to agree on a common defence policy.	= to plan, aim at
(to) intensify **intensity** **intense** [adj] **intensive** [adj]	(sich) verstärken Stärke intensiv, stark gründlich, stark	The economic problems will intensify until the population problem can be mastered. If crime figures are decreasing, it may be the result of intense surveillance by video cameras in public places.	≠ decrease, become smaller, disappear ≠ lax, loose
(to) interfere **interference**	stören, beeinträchtigen Einmischung, Störung	In a system of free enterprise government should interfere in commerce as little as possible.	= disturb, interrupt
(to) intimidate **timidity** **timid** [adj]	einschüchtern, bange machen Ängstlichkeit ängstlich	Sweatshop employers intimidated their illegal workers.	= scare, frighten

word family	dt. Bedeutung	English sentence	synonyms/opposites
intolerance	Intoleranz, Unduldsamkeit		
intolerable [adj]	unerträglich	The situation for the animals on Mr Jones' farm became	= unbearable; ≠ tolerable
intolerant [adj]	unduldsam	intolerable.	≠ tolerant
(to) intrude	stören	In answer to the public concern about media intrusion	= interfere, intervene; bother,
intrusion	Aufdringlichkeit,	the publishers of Britain's papers have committed	disturb, pester
	Eingriff ins Privatleben	themselves to a minimum ethical standard.	
intrusive [adj]	aufdringlich		
(to) invent	erfinden	The immigration authorities should be more inventive	
invention	Erfindung	and take legal measures against uncontrolled	
inventive [adj]	erfinderisch	immigration.	= resourceful, innovative
(to) invest	investieren, anlegen	Massive investments were needed to build the new	
investment	Investition, Anlage	Olympic stadium.	= sums of money, capital
(to) invigorate	stärken	These immigrants spread over the land and their	= strengthen, reinforce,
		contributions invigorated the nation's life.	intensify
invoice	Rechnung	Please find enclosed our invoice.	= bill
involvement	Beteiligung, Verstrickung	For those involved in equal rights for men and women	= concerned with,
involved in	mit etw. zu tun haben	the economic necessity provided the breakthrough.	having to do with
		The electoral system in the USA is more involved than	
involved [adj]	kompliziert, verworren	in Britain.	= complex, complicated
irrelevant [adj]	unwichtig, nebensächlich	We only become aware how totally irrelevant television	= unimportant, insignificant,
		is when we spend a holiday far away from civilisation.	non-essential

word family	dt. Bedeutung	English sentence	synonyms/opposites
(to) irritate **irritation** **irritable** [adj]	(ver)ärgern Gereiztheit, Ärger reizbar	The cliché of Britain as the "sick man of Europe" irritated modern Britons.	= annoy, aggravate ≠ delight, please
issue	Streitfrage, Kernfrage	The main issue in the election was the financial situation.	= matter, problem
jealousy **jealous (of)** [adj]	Eifersucht eifersüchtig (auf)	Beauty competitions are often bound up with jealousy.	≠ unselfishness, generosity
job centre **jobless** [adj]	Arbeitsamt arbeitslos	Every morning there is a long queue of job hunters outside the job centre.	= labour office (AE) = unemployed, out of work
(to) join	beitreten	In 1973 Britain joined the European Community.	= become a member, enter, sign up for; ≠ leave
joint-stock company	Aktiengesellschaft	Andrew Lloyd Webber, the composer of "Jesus Christ Superstar", founded a joint-stock company.	= corporation
judiciary **judicial** [adj] **judicious** [adj]	Richter, Richterstand gerichtlich klug, weise	In a democracy power is separated into three branches – the executive, the legislative and the judiciary.	= judges of a country
just about	fast, beinahe	In future, just about everything will be done differently.	= almost, more or less, nearly, practically, virtually
(to) justify **justice** **justification** **just** [adj] **justifiable** [adj]	rechtfertigen Gerechtigkeit Rechtfertigung gerecht zu rechtfertigen	To justify the killing of the native population the concept of "Manifest Destiny" was propagated.	= approve, authorize, sanction

word family	dt. Bedeutung	English sentence	synonyms/opposites
keen [adj]	begeistert, leidenschaftlich	In my younger days I was a keen supporter of our local football team.	= enthusiastic, eager, ardent, excited
(to) labour labour (1) labour (2) laborious [adj]	arbeiten, sich abmühen Arbeitskräfte (Pl.) Arbeit, Mühe mühsam, schwerfällig	Those societies in Western Europe with the most flexible supplies of labour have achieved the highest growth rates since 1945.	= workers
(to) lament lamentation lamentable [adj]	über etw. klagen Wehklage bedauerlich	A series of reports lamented the state of public education.	= deplore; ≠ rejoice
(to) launch	einführen, einleiten	The agricultural revolution launched a slow wave of change.	= start ≠ stop, end, finish
law	Recht, Gesetz	Congress passed stricter immigration laws.	= regulation, legislation, statute
lawbreaker	Gesetzesbrecher	Many people maintain that sometimes lawbreakers do not receive the same punishment for the same crime.	= offender
(to) lead leader leadership leading [adj]	führen Führer Führung führend	According to leading international agencies the United States is still spending too much on agricultural support.	= most important, principal ≠ unimportant, irrelevant
(to) legalise legality legal [adj]	legal machen, legalisieren Rechtmäßigkeit gesetzlich erlaubt	Women's rights movements increased efforts to legalise abortion.	= make legal, sanction

word family	dt. Bedeutung	English sentence	synonyms/opposites
legislation legislative legislative [adj]	Gesetzgebung gesetzgebende Gewalt gesetzgebend	Martin Luther King's actions led to the famous civil rights legislation in the 60s.	= laws
lethal [adj]	tödlich	Many addicts took a lethal overdose to end their misery.	= deadly
level	Höhe, Niveau, Stand	In view of the high unemployment level, the prospect of new jobs through a international project was attractive.	= rate, quota
likelihood	Wahrscheinlichkeit	There is a great likelihood that people will resort to force if their basic needs are neglected.	= probability, possibility, chance
likely [adj]	wahrscheinlich	It is quite likely that the US proposal will meet with scepticism abroad.	= possible, probable, potential
(to) limit	einschränken	The founders of America's political institutions sought to limit governmental powers.	= confine, restrict
(to) link to	in Verbindung stehen mit	The long-term exposure to pesticides is linked to cancer.	= associate with, connect with, relate to
link linkage	Verbindung, Bindeglied Verbindung	There is a significant link between the child and the emotional security of both its parents.	= connection, relationship
little by little	allmählich, nach und nach	Little by little, television cuts us off from the real world.	= gradually, continually
(to) look to (to) look after	erwarten sich kümmern um	These students are looking to the colleges to prepare them directly for a career. The good companies make every effort to look after their staff.	= expect = take care of, care about, be concerned about
loyalty loyal [adj]	Treue treu	People emphasized their loyalty to the Crown and the Union Jack.	= allegiance, faithfulness

word family	dt. Bedeutung	English sentence	synonyms/opposites
magnitude	Größe, Ausmaß	Change of this magnitude makes people nervous.	= size, scope, extent, dimension
mainly [adv]	hauptsächlich	Britain became an alternative for East Africans, mainly Kenyans.	= chiefly, above all, mostly, principally, to a large extent,
(to) maintain maintenance	aufrechterhalten Erhaltung, Unterhalt	In Britain, the Queen and the Prime Minister play an important role to maintain democracy.	= keep up, sustain
majority major [adj]	Mehrheit wichtig, Haupt-, größer, bedeutender	One of the major issues of science lies in the prediction and control of human intervention into nature.	= chief, primary, principal, main, leading, important, outstanding; ≠ minor
(to) make a speech	eine Rede halten	After more than six months in Parliament the M. P. for Fulham managed to make a speech for the first time.	= deliver a speech
malice malicious [adj]	Bosheit boshaft	The malice that exists between the two characters is due to their rivalry.	= malevolence, spite, maliciousness; ≠ kindness
(to) manage management managerial [adj]	führen, leiten Verwaltung, Leitung leitend	Some colonies were allowed to manage their own affairs under governors appointed by the mother country.	= conduct, run
(to) manifest manifestation manifest [adj]	offenbaren Kundgebung offenbar	Smaller countries just serve the larger countries to manifest their power and reputation.	= display, show, exhibit
manpower	Arbeitskräfte (Pl.)	As the new product sold rather well, the firm decided to increase manpower in the production plant.	= workers, labour force

word family	dt. Bedeutung	English sentence	synonyms/opposites
manufactured goods	Fertigwaren	More money is earned with the sale of manufactured goods than with the sale of primary products.	= finished products
marked [adj]	deutlich, klar	Class has always been a part of British life – even though today the barriers are less high and less marked.	= obvious, prominent, clear, distinct
mass	Masse	The country's prosperity is based on the sale of airplanes, cars, TV sets and mass-produced clothing.	≠ handmade, made to order, made to measure
mass-produced [adj]	serienmäßig hergestellt		
massive [adj]	massig, dicht	The supply of money in the economy has increased massively in recent years.	= enormously, immensely
massively [adv]	gewaltig		
(to) mature	erwachsen werden	Females mature sexually earlier than males.	= develop, grow up
maturity	Reife		
mature [adj]	reif, erwachsen		≠ immature
means	Mittel, Geld	Overdrafts and generous hire purchase terms make it possible for us to buy things in advance of earning and saving the means to pay for them.	= money, funds, resources
(to) meditate	nachdenken, meditieren	Simon goes off to the jungle to meditate.	= ponder, deliberate
meditation	Nachdenken		
meditative [adj]	nachdenklich		
(to) meet	erfüllen	The country's requests for small quantities of drugs, rice, etc, are difficult to meet.	= fulfil
merchandise	Ware	A great part of our merchandise is on display in our show-rooms in Regent Street.	= goods, articles, products

word family	dt. Bedeutung	English sentence	synonyms/opposites
mercy merciful [adj] merciless [adj]	Gnade gnädig ungnädig	In the end Ralph crashes through the jungle and tumbles onto the beach, "trying to cry for mercy".	= clemency; ≠ revenge
merely [adv]	bloß, nur, lediglich	Some of the immigrants from Sri Lanka may merely be seeking work and welfare in European countries.	= just, only, simply
metropolis	Metropole, Hauptstadt	A great number of migrants simply follow the attraction of greater economic opportunity in a metropolis.	= city, town, capital
minority minor minor [adj]	Minderheit Minderjährige(r) geringer	The United Kingdom has a large black minority. Agriculture is the most dangerous occupation to minors in the United States.	≠ majority = child
misery miserable [adj]	Elend, Not ärmlich, elend	Demonstrators protested against the misery of the disadvantaged Indians.	= suffering
moderate [adj]	maßvoll	Drugs cannot be taken in a moderate way.	= reasonable
modesty modest [adj]	Bescheidenheit bescheiden	That modest sum is a small sign of recognition.	≠ huge, enormous, incredible
moist [adj]	feucht	A moist climate keeps pastures green.	= damp, humid
more than	über	From 1882 to 1902 more than two million immigrants sailed to New York from Bremen alone.	= over
mortality rate	Sterberate	The rate of mortality among children is very low.	= death rate; ≠ birth rate
(to) move movement motion	bewegen, rühren, ergreifen Bewegung Bewegung, Gang	Poisoned fish and lakes, especially other people's, did not much move polluters.	= affect, touch, influence, alarm

word family	dt. Bedeutung	English sentence	synonyms/opposites
murder	Mord	The murder of a two-year-old boy shocked Britain.	= homicide, killing
mystery	Geheimnis	The scientists tried to solve the mystery of what	= secret
mysterious [adj]	geheimnisvoll	happened to the space shuttle as it re-entered the Earth's atmosphere.	
(to) nationalize	einbürgern, verstaatlichen		
nation	Volk, Staat		
nationality	Staatsangehörigkeit		
national [adj]	national, Landes-	There is no national service in countries which have a	
national service	Wehrdienst	professional army.	= military service
nearly [adv]	beinahe	Nearly all the sports practised nowadays are competitive.	= almost, virtually
(to) necessitate	etw. erfordern	The civil rights leader explained the miserable social	
necessity	Notwendigkeit	conditions of the African-Americans and the necessity	= need, urgency
necessary [adj]	nötig	for a change.	
need	Bedarf, Notwendigkeit	The need for independent advice is more urgent than ever, because the housewife today is confronted with a bewildering variety of goods.	= demand, necessity, urgency
(to) neglect	vernachlässigen, nicht beachten	Man has neglected the unemployed masses in the developing countries too long.	= ignore, disregard
negligence	Nachlässigkeit		
neglectful [adj]	nachlässig		
negligent [adj]	nachlässig		
negligible [adj]	nebensächlich		

word family	dt. Bedeutung	English sentence	synonyms/opposites
negotiations (to) negotiate	Verhandlungen (Pl.) verhandeln	If negotiations fail the printers will go on strike and there won't be any newspapers tomorrow.	= talks
(to) nominate	nominieren, aufstellen	In July and August the Republicans and the Democrats nominate their candidates for the presidency.	= appoint, assign
(to) note note notation notion noted [adj] notable [adj]	bemerken, notieren Zeichen, Notiz Bezeichnung Begriff, Vorstellung bekannt, berühmt (wegen) bemerkenswert	As soon as strong feelings of rivalry are aroused, the notion of playing the game according to the rules always vanishes. American youths were noted for the acceptance of the traditional American way of life.	= idea, concept = known, famous
(to) notice notice noticeable [adj]	bemerken Kenntnis, Kündigung merklich	When two of the most respected education specialists criticise our education system, we should take notice.	≠ disinterest, disregard, indifference
(to) nourish nourishment nourishing [adj]	nähren, ernähren Nahrung nahrhaft	Breadfruit trees were imported as a source of nourishment fort he slaves.	= food, sustenance
nuisance	Ärgernis	The public regard football hooligans as a nuisance.	= annoyance, plague; ≠ joy
(to) number number numerous [adj]	zählen Zahl, Anzahl zahlreich	The 1924 Johnson Act established quotas for immigration based on the number of former nationals of each country in the United States.	= amount
nutrition nutritious [adj]	Ernährung, Ernährungs- wissenschaft nahrhaft, nährstoffreich	Nutrition experts warn that confectionery and snacks should not replace balanced meals.	= nourishing, wholesome

word family	dt. Bedeutung	English sentence	synonyms/opposites
(to) obey **obedience** **obedient** [adj]	befolgen, gehorchen Gehorsam gehorsam	There are general rules to obey in business conversations.	= adhere to, comply with, observe ≠ break, disregard, transgress
(to) object to **objection** **object** **objectionable** [adj]	etw. einwenden gegen, Einspruch erheben Einwand Gegenstand, Ziel nicht einwandfrei	Three in four women consumers object to exploitation of sex in advertising.	≠ agree to, approve of, consent to, accept
(to) oblige **obligation** **obligatory** [adj] **obliging** [adj]	verpflichten, zwingen Verpflichtung verpflichtend gefällig	The newcomers were obliged to take low-status jobs.	= force, compel
(to) obscure **obscurity** **obscure** [adj]	verdunkeln, verschleiern Dunkelheit unbekannt, unverständlich	The origins of the Inuit living in the territories, largely in the coastal areas, are obscure.	= unclear, inscrutable, mysterious ≠ clear, obvious
(to) observe **observation** **observance** **observant** [adj]	einhalten, beachten; beobachten, befolgen Beobachtung Befolgung, Brauch aufmerksam	The president asked the nation to observe a moment of silence for victims of the attack.	= keep; see; discern
obsolete [adj]	veraltet	The American electoral system is complicated and to a large extent obsolete.	= outmoded, out of date ≠ up-to-date, modern

word family	dt. Bedeutung	English sentence	synonyms/opposites
obstinacy **obstinate** [adj]	*Hartnäckigkeit, Eigensinn* *eigensinnig*	Dudley, who seems to be very obstinate, is spoilt by his excessively caring mother.	= hard-headed, self-willed, unruly; ≠ compliant
obvious [adj]	*offensichtlich, klar, deutlich*	In Britain, solar energy is not a very dependable form of energy for obvious reasons.	= evident, clear
(to) occupy **occupation**	*sich beschäftigen; besetzen Beruf, Beschäftigung; Besetzung, Besitz*	You have to fill in your occupation in this form.	= job, profession
(to) occur **occurrence**	*sich ereignen, passieren Vorkommen, Vorfall*	Massive migration from Europe did not occur until the late 1840s.	= happen, take place
(to) offend **offence** **offensive** [adj]	*beleidigen; eine Straftat begehen Beleidigung; Vergehen beleidigend*	I'm very sorry, but I certainly did not intend to offend you personally.	= insult
opportunity	*(günstige) Gelegenheit*	America was a country that presented opportunities to become rich.	= chance
(to) oppose **opposition** **opposite** [adj]	*sich widersetzen Widerstand entgegengesetzt*	Itzhak Rabin was assassinated by a fanatic Israeli who opposed the plans for peace with Israel's Arab neighbours.	= resist, fight against ≠ agree to, accept
(to) oppress	*unterdrücken*	"We must fight for the liberation of oppressed people."	= suppress, persecute
Orange and Green		Realities inside Ulster, in terms of the relations between Orange and Green, did not change very much.	= Protestants and Catholics

word family	dt. Bedeutung	English sentence	synonyms/opposites
(to) organize organ organism organization organic [adj]	organisieren Organ Organismus Organisation organisch, biologisch	George Washington had to organize an army out of about 16,000 men, who knew little of fighting and less of military discipline. Organic food stores ("Bioläden") can now be found in most major US cities.	= set up, start, put together, muster
(to) originate origin original [adj]	entstehen, seinen Ursprung haben Ursprung ursprünglich	The physicists picked up signals which seemed to originate from a very distant planet.	= come from, derive, stem from
outcome	Ergebnis	We learnt to respect the rights of others to govern themselves in their own ways: This was the outcome of experience learnt the hard way in 1776.	= result, consequence, effect
(to) outlaw outlaw	für ungesetzlich erklären Geächteter, Vogelfreier, Bandit	We demand to implement existing laws, pass new ones and outlaw all those who threaten the right to life of any human being.	= ban, prohibit, forbid = bandit, criminal
overt [adj]	offen, offenkundig	Economic racism is more often found than the overt racism of the past.	≠ hidden, secret, concealed
(to) overthrow	absetzen, stürzen	A group of generals managed to overthrow the dictator.	= topple
pace	Tempo, Schritt	It seems likely that the evolution of the organization of work will continue along established lines, probably at an accelerated pace.	= speed, rate, tempo
paramount [adj]	übergeordnet, höchst	Of paramount importance is the need to build up more confidence.	≠ secondary, minor, subordinate

word family	dt. Bedeutung	English sentence	synonyms/opposites
(to) part part; partition partial [adj]	teilen Teil, Anteil; Teilung teilweise	Diabetes may cause partial or total blindness.	≠ whole, complete, total
particularly [adv]	vor allem, besonders	In large comprehensive schools violence and truancy are increasing, particularly in large cities.	= especially, chiefly, primarily
passion passionate [adj]	Leidenschaft leidenschaftlich	The minister pursued his aim with passion and defend it with care.	= enthusiasm, fervour, zeal ≠ apathy, disinterest
pastime	Zeitvertreib, Freizeit- beschäftigung	Watching TV all day is not the ideal pastime.	= recreation, hobby, distraction, diversion
peasant	(Klein-)Bauer	In the nineteenth century dozens of millions, mostly peasants, moved across Europe from East to West.	= farmer, countryman
peculiarly [adv]	besonders	It is peculiarly difficult to analyse the methods used by advertisers on the television screen.	= especially, particularly
penalty	Strafe	The judge announces the penalty.	= punishment
(to) perceive	bemerken, wahrnehmen, empfinden	The opinion polls show that the President and his wife are perceived as "people who like elegance and parties".	= see, regard, look upon
perhaps	vielleicht	Before lunch the Queen holds audiences, perhaps with a lord or a foreign diplomat.	= maybe, possibly, conceivably
(to) permit permission permissible [adj] permissive [adj]	gestatten Erlaubnis zulässig zulässig, tolerant	The American colonists felt the need for internal stability to permit the new nation to grow and prosper.	= allow ≠ forbid

word family	dt. Bedeutung	English sentence	synonyms/opposites
(to) persecute persecution	verfolgen Verfolgung	Racists persecute a minority out of prejudice, hatred or envy.	= harass, torment
(to) persist persistence persistent [adj]	andauern, beharren Anhalten, Beharrlichkeit beharrlich	While a deep recession persists, and the gulf between rich and poor widens, the net of social services grows thinner.	= continue, endure, last, go on
personnel	Personal, Belegschaft	There are rumours about a slight reduction of the personnel in the Hendon branch office.	= staff, workforce
(to) persuade persuasion persuasive [adj]	überzeugen, überreden Überredung überzeugend	The trade union official tried to persuade the management to grant shorter working hours and introduce more democracy on the shop floor.	= convince ≠ dissuade
piety pious [adj]	Frömmigkeit fromm	The town of Limerick gained a reputation for piety.	= holiness, sanctity
pitch	Spielfeld, Platz	Many politicians think that national prestige can be won on the football pitch.	= field, ground
plant	Werk, Fabrik	Newspapers published photos of the chairman of the board and several hundred workers cycling near the plant.	= factory, works
platform	(Wahl-)Programm	The platform of a political party is what they say they will do if they are elected.	= programme, manifesto
(to) play down	herunterspielen	Writers favourable of Northern Ireland have had reasons to play down the tensions between the communities.	≠ exaggerate, blow up

word family	dt. Bedeutung	English sentence	synonyms/opposites
(to) please	jdm. gefallen		
pleasure	Vergnügen		
pleasurable [adj]	angenehm	Dinner for two is a pleasurable occasion.	≠ disagreeable, disgusting, unpleasant
pleasant [adj]	angenehm		
(to) poison	vergiften	We have ignored the warnings of poisonous air too long.	
poison	Gift		
poisonous [adj]	giftig		= toxic, noxious
poor [adj]	armselig, schlecht	Much of the blame for the poor image of the EU rests with British politicians. Consider how poorly American society is dealing with the elderly.	≠ excellent, splendid, positive
poorly [adv]	schlecht		= badly, low
(to) populate	bevölkern	Brixton, a district in South London, is populated by black people, mostly from the West Indies.	= inhabit, occupy
population	Bevölkerung		
populous [adj]	dicht besiedelt		
(to) possess	besitzen, verfügen über	Saudi Arabia and Pakistan possess about 25% of all proven oil reserves.	= hold, own, retain
possession	Besitz		≠ dispossess (enteignen)
possessive [adj]	besitzanzeigend		
possible [adj]	möglich	Since the Chernobyl disaster everyone has become more aware of the possible dangers of atomic power plants.	= potential
(to) precede	vorhergehen	The Unionists in Northern Ireland demanded that decommissioning must precede Sinn Fein's entry into government.	≠ follow
precedence	Vorrang		
precedent	Präzedenzfall		
precedent [adj]	vorhergehend		

word family	dt. Bedeutung	English sentence	synonyms/opposites
precision	Genauigkeit, Präzision	The laser was invented in 1960, and used for precision cutting and optical surgery.	= accuracy, exactitude, exactness, preciseness
precise [adj]	genau, präzise		≠ imprecise
(to) predict	vorhersagen	Experts predict that there will soon be millions of people with lots of time on their hands.	= foretell, forecast, foresee
prediction	Vorhersage		
predictable [adj]	vorhersehbar, voraussagbar		
predominantly [adv]	überwiegend	In the poor countries diets are predominantly starchy.	= chiefly, largely, mainly, primarily
(to) prefer	etw. vorziehen	Most people prefer living in a suburb to living in the noisy city centre.	= opt for, tend to choose
preference	Vorzug, Vorliebe		
preferable [adj]	besser, vorzuziehen		
preferential [adj]	bevorzugt		
(to) prepare	vorbereiten	British statesman have not been prepared to devote to Ireland the amount and time of attention its good government required.	= able and willing, ready
preparation	Vorbereitung		
prepared [adj]	bereit		
preparatory [adj]	vorbereitend		
(to) press for	bestehen auf, drängen auf	The union officials press for a strike.	= insist on, want, ask for
pressing [adj]	dringend	Each nation is naturally concerned with its own pressing problems.	= urgent, vital, serious, acute
(to) presume	vermuten, annehmen	It would be wrong, however, to presume that all initiatives to save energy are in vain.	= suppose, think, assume
presumption	Vermutung		
presumptive [adj]	mutmaßlich		
presumptuous [adj]	überheblich		

word family	dt. Bedeutung	English sentence	synonyms/opposites
(to) pretend pretence pretended [adj]	so tun also ob, vortäuschen Vorwand angeblich	I don't pretend to have any definitive answers but one thing is clear: We must reduce the CFC emissions.	= make believe
pretty [adv]	ziemlich	Most of us are pretty contradictory when it comes to protecting the environment.	= fairly, rather, to some extent, quite, more or less
(to) prevail prevalence prevailing [adj] prevalent [adj]	vorherrschen Vorherrschen (vor)herrschend, bestehend vorherrschend	It is our duty to abolish the prevailing misery among the poorest people in the world.	= current, existing
(to) prevent prevention preventive [adj]	etw. verhindern Verhinderung vorbeugend	In order to prevent Western Europe becoming Communist, the US government adopted a new strategy towards Russia.	= permit
previous [adj]	vorhergehend, vorausgehend	Young people are demanding more satisfaction from a job than did previous generations.	= former, earlier
primary [adj]	Haupt-, vorrangig	Economic growth and employment are the primary goals of many countries.	≠ main, chief, principal
primary products	Rohstoffe (Pl.)	Peru sells primary products like minerals, zinc and silver.	= raw materials
principally [adv]	hauptsächlich, Haupt-	Like ordinary beach sand, micro-chips are made principally of silicon.	= basically, mainly, chiefly
(to) proceed procedure process procession	voranschreiten Verfahren Verfahren, Prozess Umzug	I have always believed that agriculture should proceed in harmony with nature, recognising that there are natural limits to our ambitions.	= advance, progress ≠ recede

word family	dt. Bedeutung	English sentence	synonyms/opposites
(to) proclaim **proclamation**	*erklären, ausrufen* *Ausrufung, Kundgabe*	The Prime Minister proclaimed, "We must try to find ways to starve the terrorist and hijacker of the publicity on which they depend."	= declare, announce, state
(to) produce **production** **product** **produce** **productive** [adj]	*herstellen* *Herstellung* *Fabrikerzeugnis* *Naturerzeugnis* *produktiv, ertragreich*	During World War II (1939–45), many efforts were made to produce atomic weapons.	= make, construct, manufacture
(to) profess **profession** **professional** [adj]	*bekennen; ausüben* *Bekenntnis; Beruf* *Berufs-*	Some 85 percent of Britain's population professes to be Christian.	= assert, affirm, declare,
(to) profit **profit** **profitable** [adj]	*Gewinn machen* *Gewinn* *Gewinn bringend, rentabel*	The multinational corporations have a clear goal: maximum trade and maximum profit.	= earnings, proceeds, return ≠ loss
(to) progress **progress** **progressive** [adj]	*Fortschritte machen* *Fortschritt* *fortschrittlich*	Science and technology cannot make progress without taking some risks.	= advance
(to) prohibit **prohibition** **prohibitive** [adj]	*verbieten* *Verbot* *Schutz-*	Discrimination on the basis of race, sex, handicap, religion, and national origin is prohibited.	= forbid, ban, outlaw ≠ permit
prominence **prominent** [adj]	*Hervorragen* *weithin bekannt, berühmt*	A prominent economist argues that drinking habits in Ireland often scare away potential foreign investors.	= well-known, famous, important

word family	dt. Bedeutung	English sentence	synonyms/opposites
(to) promote promotion promotional [adj]	fördern Beförderung, Werbung Werbe-	Rapid growth helped to promote a remarkable mobility in the American population.	= further, encourage, bring about
propaganda	Werbung, Reklame	Solar energy has not been given enough propaganda.	= publicity
proportion proportional [adj] proportionate [adj]	Anteil, Verhältnis proportional angemessen	The proportion of female managers has doubled in recent years.	= rate, ratio, scale
(to) propose proposal	vorschlagen, beabsichtigen Vorschlag, Antrag	The changes we're proposing come from a belief that a thriving economy is the best program for low-income people.	= suggest, offer, put forward = suggestion, plan, idea
proprietor	Eigentümer, Besitzer	Richard Branson, the proprietor of the Virgin company, is a multi-millionaire.	= owner
prospect	Aussicht	The immigrant had the prospect of earning a living.	= chance, expectation, hope
(to) prosper prosperity prosperous [adj]	gedeihen, florieren Wohlstand wohlhabend	While many of our citizens prosper, others doubt the promise – even the justice – of our own country.	= succeed, flourish, thrive
(to) protect protection protective [adj]	schützen Schutz Schutz-	It seems almost impossible to protect youngsters from the dangers of smoking and drinking.	≠ destroy, harm, damage, contaminate, ruin
(to) prove proof proven [adj]	beweisen Beweis bewiesen	Do you need more proof that we don't need the Royal Family?	= evidence

word family	dt. Bedeutung	English sentence	synonyms/opposites
(to) provide	zur Verfügung stellen, sorgen für	The scientists provided a solution to the health problem.	= supply, offer, furnish
provision	Bereitstellung, Versorgung		
provisional [adj]	provisorisch, vorläufig		
publicity	Werbung, Reklame	The Boeing company have launched a publicity campaign to improve the company's image.	= advertising, propaganda
(to) publish	veröffentlichen	The first continuously published newspaper in England was the Weekly News (1622–41).	= issue, produce; distribute
publication	Veröffentlichung		
public [adj]	öffentlich		
purchase	Kauf, Erwerb	The purchase of a house is one of the biggest decisions.	= buy, buying
(to) purify	reinigen	Oxygen helps purify our water.	= clean, cleanse
(to) pursue	verfolgen	If a woman does pursue a career, she must be able to maintain that career along with a family.	= seek to accomplish, proceed
pursuit	Streben		
pursuant [adj]	entsprechend		
(to) put up	errichten, erbauen	Industrial development, however, brings with it many other changes: new housing estates have to be put up; new power stations must be installed.	= build, establish, erect
quality	Eigenschaft	The humour of the advertising slogan is more important than the quality of the actual product.	= characteristic, nature, feature
(to) quicken	beschleunigen	The already mad pace of working life is quickening.	= speed up; ≠ slow down
quickness	Schnelligkeit		
quick [adj]	schnell		

word family	dt. Bedeutung	English sentence	synonyms/opposites
(to) quote quotation	zitieren; berechnen Angebot, Kostenvoranschlag; Zitat	This quotation remains open for acceptance by you for 30 days.	= offer, estimated costs
(to) radiate radiation radiance radiant [adj]	ausstrahlen Strahlung Glanz, Strahlen strahlend, leuchtend	Believers in the paranormal claimed the crop circles radiated mysterious energy forces.	= disperse, spread
(to) raise	heben, aufheben, hochheben	Would those in favour of the motion raise their hands?	= lift, put up
(to) rank	ordnen, einreihen, klassifizieren	We often rank countries according to their GNP per head of population.	= classify, rate, order
rate of exchange	Wechselkurs	The rate of exchange of the US dollar is fixed every day.	= trading rate/position
(to) ravage	verwüsten	Algae bloom will ravage fishing grounds and swimming areas.	= spoil, devastate
readiness ready [adj]	Bereitschaft bereit, willens	Even managers are ready to accept less well-paid jobs.	= willing, disposed, inclined, prone; ≠ reluctant
(to) rebel rebellion rebellious [adj]	sich auflehnen Auflehnung, Empörung	A rebellion is a violent, organized action by people who are trying to change their country's political system.	= revolt, revolution
(to) receive reception receptive [adj]	erhalten, bekommen Aufnahme, Empfang empfänglich	Participants can receive a discount if they register early for the convention.	= get, obtain, be given, be granted

word family	dt. Bedeutung	English sentence	synonyms/opposites
recent [adj]	*jüngst*	A recent UN report describes the stress of technological change on the educational system.	≠ out of date, antiquated, obsolete
recession	*Konjunkturrückgang*	At the height of the recession the companies cut back on job training.	= depression, stagnation, slump; ≠ boom, recovery
(to) reconcile **reconciliation** **reconcilable** [adj]	*versöhnen, unter einen Hut bringen* *Versöhnung* *vereinbar*	For the time being, nobody can see how the opposing parties can be reconciled.	≠ estrange
redundant [adj]	*überflüssig, unnötig*	The Electors, who are directly elected by the population, are not really needed, they are redundant.	= superfluous, unnecessary
(to) refuse **refusal**	*ablehnen* *Ablehnung*	We cannot refuse to cure disease in order to limit world population. The refusal of the Senate to ratify the treaty was not received very well abroad.	= decline, reject = denial, disallowance, rejection; ≠ acceptance, agreement, approval
(to) regret **regrettable** [adj]	*bedauern, beklagen* *bedauerlich*	One day you'll regret talking about the European Parliament with such disrespect.	= feel sorry for, be sorry for ≠ reasonable, acceptable
(to) reject	*ablehnen, abweisen, zurückweisen*	In some areas planning departments reject proposals for buildings reaching above the tree-line.	= refuse, turn down
(to) relate **relation** **relative** [adj]	*sich beziehen auf Bezug; Verwandte(r)* *vergleichbar; relevant*	The findings of the survey relate to the performance of girls in A-level examinations.	= apply to

word family	dt. Bedeutung	English sentence	synonyms/opposites
(to) release (1)	freilassen	The investigation proved that H. M. Swindon is innocent, so the police will release him immediately.	= set free, let go
(to) release (2)	freigeben, freisetzen	Games and sport enable people to release their natural aggressions.	= get rid of
(to) relieve relief	erleichtern Erleichterung	Sedative drugs are used to relieve fear, tension and to forget problems.	= ease, get rid of
reluctance reluctant [adj]	Widerwillen zögernd, widerwillig	Amnesty has never been reluctant to criticize governments that otherwise enjoy popular support.	≠ willingness, inclination ≠ eager, zealous, keen
(to) rely on reliance reliable [adj]	sich verlassen auf Vertrauen, Verlass verlässlich	People in the Third World countries rely on our contribution to improve their situation.	= trust, count on
(to) remain remainder	bleiben Rest, Überbleibsel	The airline regrets the delays and trusts that the remainder of your journey will be pleasant.	= rest
(to) remember remembrance	sich erinnern Andenken, Erinnerung	Congress met for a special ceremony at Federal Hall in New York City in remembrance of September 11.	= reminiscence, reminder
(to) remind reminder	jmdn. erinnern Mahnung	The shooting of a Catholic in Belfast late last week is a reminder that not everyone is ready to talk peace.	= admonition, warning
renowned [adj]	berühmt	British soldiers are renowned for their discipline.	= famous, well-known, famed
(to) repeat repetition repetitive [adj]	wiederholen Wiederholung monoton, stumpfsinnig	Many disadvantages of the old factories are distinctly present in modern production lines: the noise and the boredom induced by repetitive work.	= boring, monotonous,

word family	dt. Bedeutung	English sentence	synonyms/opposites
(to) repent repentance repentant [adj]	bereuen Reue reuig	The only way to deal with pain and resentment is not to forgive and forget, but to remember and repent.	= regret, deplore
reply	Antwort, Reaktion	Henry VIII wrote a book on the Sacraments in reply to Luther.	= answer, response
(to) require requirement requisite [adj]	brauchen, erfordern Erfordernis, Forderung erforderlich	To make the UN machinery work requires the rebuilding of confidence that was shattered by two world wars.	= demand, ask for, call for
research	Forschung, Untersuchung	According to the latest research there is no higher delinquency among children of working mothers.	= study, investigation
(to) resemble resemblance	ähneln Ähnlichkeit	The earliest existing organisms were cells, resembling modern bacteria.	≠ differ, vary
(to) resent resentment resentful [adj]	übel nehmen Groll verbittert	The Scots particularly resent constant English interference and unjust treatment.	= feel bitter
(to) reside resident residence	wohnen Bewohner, Anwohner Wohnsitz	Naturally, most of these changes are unwelcome to local residents.	= inhabitant, tenant, dweller, citizen
(to) resist resistance resistant [adj]	widerstehen, Widerstand leisten Widerstand ablehnend gegenüberstehen, resistent	For many people it is extremely difficult to resist the attraction of "the box". M. L. King, who had always fought with means of non-violent resistance, was assassinated in 1968.	= withstand, oppose, dispute, fight, repel; ≠ accept, support, welcome, approve of = opposition

word family	dt. Bedeutung	English sentence	synonyms/opposites
(to) resolve resolve, resolution resolute [adj]	beschließen Entschluss entschlossen	"These acts shattered steel, but they cannot dent the steel of American resolve," the president exclaimed.	= determination, firmness
resources resourceful [adj]	Mittel erfinderisch	The terrorists who committed the attacks were flexible and resourceful.	= inventive, clever
(to) resort (to)	Zuflucht nehmen zu	When victory or defeat can make a difference of thousands of pounds, sportsmen sometimes resort to stimulants.	= use, employ, avail oneself of
respect	Achtung	America has held out to the world the promise of respect for the rights of man.	≠ disrespect, disregard
(to) respond response in response to responsibility responsive [adj] responsible [adj]	antworten Antwort aufgrund, infolge Verantwortung gut reagierend verantwortlich	Most immigrants came in response to employment opportunities.	= reply, answer
(to) restrain restraint	zurückhalten, unterdrücken Zurückhaltung, Zwang	Many people find the laws insufficient to restrain the violence in our society.	= suppress
(to) retain retention	beibehalten, zurückbehalten Bewahrung	Britain managed to retain garrisons in her former colonies for a long time.	= preserve, keep, hold
(to) retreat	sich zurückziehen	After losing the first battle, the army had to retreat.	= withdraw
(to) reveal revelation	zeigen, offenbaren Enthüllung, Offenbarung	Only the future will reveal how the new immigrants will build their American Dream.	≠ conceal

word family	dt. Bedeutung	English sentence	synonyms/opposites
(to) reverse reversal reverse [adj]	umkehren Wende umgekehrt	The Administration's cuts in social spending reversed the gains of Lyndon Johnson's War on Poverty.	≠ maintain, forward
riches rich [adj]	Reichtümer wohlhabend, reich	People have always come to America in search of riches or in flight from poverty and persecution.	= wealth, prosperity = wealthy, well-to-do
right to vote	Stimmrecht	Blacks have been denied the right to vote for too long.	= suffrage, franchise
root	Wurzel	Most problems of the developing countries arise from two roots: too little food and unemployment.	= source, cause
rough [adj] roughly [adv]	hart, anstrengend ungefähr, grob	The immigrants work long hours in rough jobs. The most visible candidates for retraining are the roughly two million so-called displaced workers.	≠ easy, pleasant, nice = approximately, about, just about; ≠ exactly, precisely
rude [adj]	unverschämt, grob	At times Higgins can be quite bad-tempered and rude.	= impolite, impertinent
(to) sack	entlassen	The talk is forgotten the day after the unlucky ones have been sacked.	≠ employ, hire
(to) sacrifice	opfern	The flexibility of the English language allows for the "catchiness" of advertising slogans without sacrificing the literal meaning.	= give up, lose, drop
sample	Probe, Muster	We are sorry to tell you that the goods you sent us do not correspond to the sample.	= specimen
(to) sanction	billigen	Some go so far as to sanction government control – censorship, in fact – should the media fail to respond this call of voluntary restraint.	≠ reject, turn down, object to

word family	dt. Bedeutung	English sentence	synonyms/opposites
sanity sane [adj]	geistige Gesundheit	The lawyer called twelve witnesses to testify to the defendant's sanity.	≠ insanity ≠ insane
savagery savage [adj]	Wildheit, Rohheit wild, roh, grausam	As soon as you feel that you will be disgraced if you lose in a sports game, the most savage instincts are aroused.	= uncivilized, wild; ≠ civilized
scarcity scarce [adj]	Knappheit, Mangel knapp	The scarcity of petrol forced cars off the roads.	≠ abundance, affluence
schedule	Plan, Zeitplan, Fahrplan	Plans to cut sulphur dioxide emitted from power stations are slipping behind schedule.	= time, timetable, programme, plan
scheme	Plan, Konzept, Projekt, Programm	The estate was built as part of the town's slum clearance scheme.	= plan, project
scorn	Verachtung	Higgins reserves for the flower girl Eliza a brand of scorn he would not dream of showing to a young woman of his own class.	= disrespect, disdain, contempt
seas	Meere, Gewässer	We have thrown into the seas of the world millions of tons of garbage.	= waters, oceans
(to) seek (1)	suchen	Most immigrants have come to America seeking a better life for themselves and, above all, for their children.	= look for, search for
(to) seek (2)	trachten nach	Foreigners seek to escape from poverty and persecution in their homelands.	= try, attempt
segregation	Rassentrennung	But black Americans say segregation's legacy persists and that such privileges are not universally available.	≠ integration, desegregation

word family	dt. Bedeutung	English sentence	synonyms/opposites
(to) seize seizure	*ergreifen* *Ergreifung*	Orange radicals were all too eager to seize a chance to generate a crisis.	= grasp, capture
seldom [adv]	*selten*	Mechanisation at work means that workers are seldom physically exhausted when they get home.	= rarely, hardly, ever
(to) select selection selective [adj]	*auswählen* *Auswahl* *auswählend, selektiv*	Natural selection favours or suppresses a particular gene.	≠ rejection
(to) sell sale saleable [adj]	*verkaufen* *Verkauf, Absatz* *verkäuflich*	The new taxes could affect the production, sale and use of fertilizers and anything else that contributes to pollution.	≠ purchase, buy, buying
(to) sense sense **(common) sense** sensation sensitive [adj] sensible [adj]	*wahrnehmen* *Empfindung, Gefühl;* *Verstand* *gesunder Menschenverstand* *Gefühl* *empfindlich* *vernünftig*	The showing of commercials during news programmes leaves the viewer with the sensation that the commercials and for example the war are one and the same. There are a lot of sensible people who are sincerely worried about the way industry and housing are eating up the countryside.	= feeling, emotion = reasonable, rational, intelligent
(to) separate separation separate (it) [adj] separable [adj]	*trennen* *Trennung* *getrennt* *trennbar*	The law said that blacks and whites could be forced to go to separate schools.	= segregated ≠ desegregated
severity severe [adj]	*Härte, Strenge* *schwer wiegend, hart*	The dependence caused by marijuana is not so severe as that resulting from heroin.	= grave, serious

word family	dt. Bedeutung	English sentence	synonyms/opposites
sewage	Abwasser	Many rivers and lakes have long been polluted by untreated sewage.	= waster water
share	Aktie	Young Jonathan Winter has just bought his very first share.	= stock certificate
(to) shatter	zerschmettern, zertrümmern	Then came the Vietnam War – with the result that the golden image of America was shattered.	= destroy, break to pieces, smash
(to) ship	versenden	Manufacturers do not have to worry about tariff barriers when they ship goods to other countries.	= transport, move, take, carry, send
(to) shorten shortness shortage short [adj]	kürzen Kürze Knappheit kurz	The debate is clouded by emotion and confused by the shortage of reliable statistics.	≠ abundance, mass
(to) show	zeigen, beweisen	The opinion polls show that the president and his wife are seen as "people who like elegance and parties".	= prove, indicate, demonstrate, illustrate
(to) shrink	abnehmen	Without immigration, New York would be a declining city with a population shrinking towards 6 million.	≠ increase, grow, rise, swell
(to) side (with)	Partei ergreifen für	The Prime Minister has sided with the Europeans.	= cooperate with, join, agree with, support
(to) sign sign signature	unterschreiben (An-)Zeichen, Hinweis Unterschrift	Is the continuing rise in juvenile delinquency a sign that the children of working mothers are more likely to "turn bad"?	= indication, proof, signal

word family	dt. Bedeutung	English sentence	synonyms/opposites
(to) signify **significance** **significant (of)** [adj]	*bedeuten* *Bedeutung* *bedeutsam (für)*	There is a significant link between the emotional security of the child and both its parents, not merely the mother.	= important, considerable
similarity **similar** [adj]	*Ähnlichkeit* *ähnlich*	The majority of people in Third World countries live in similar circumstances of poverty and hunger.	≠ different
(to) simplify **simplicity** **simplification** **simple** [adj] **simplified** [adj] **simply** [adv]	*vereinfachen* *Einfachheit* *Vereinfachung* *einfach* *vereinfacht* *einfach, bloß*	Steam is simply a carrier of heat.	= just, only, merely
since	*da, weil*	There is a lot of discrimination, since most farm-workers come from racial minorities.	= because, as
sincerity **sincere** [adj]	*Aufrichtigkeit* *ehrlich, aufrichtig*	The Queen expressed her sincere gratitude to the founding fathers of the great republic for having taught Britain a very valuable lesson.	= honest, genuine, frank
skill **skilful** [adj]	*Geschicklichkeit, Fertigkeit* *geschickt*	In games people test their own skill against that of others.	= ability, dexterity, talent
slight [adj]	*gering, unbedeutend*	Some modifications of a "new" product are of very slight benefit to the consumer.	≠ considerable, great
(to) slow down **slowness** **slow** [adj]	*verlangsamen* *Langsamkeit* *langsam*	British ministers have been trying to slow down the march to European integration.	≠ accelerate, speed up, quicken

word family	dt. Bedeutung	English sentence	synonyms/opposites
sobriety	Nüchternheit	In a sobering annual report the institute warned about the rising number of people who are infected with HIV/AIDS in Africa.	
sober [adj]	nüchtern		
sobering [adj]	ernüchternd		= matter-of-fact, pragmatic
soil	Boden	In the Great Lakes area the soil is less suited to arable farming.	= ground, earth, land
solely [adv]	nur, allein	The language of an advertising slogan is designed to stick in the mind solely.	= only, merely, simply
(to) solve	lösen	NASA specialist examined the wreckage to solve the mystery of the space shuttle catastrophe.	= find an explanation
solution	Lösung		
solvency	Zahlungsfähigkeit		
soluble [adj]	lösbar, löslich		
solvent [adj]	zahlungsfähig		
sophisticated [adj]	hoch entwickelt, kompliziert	Steam power is often used inefficiently, despite highly sophisticated boilers and computer equipment.	≠ simple, primitive
(to) sort out	in Ordnung bringen	First we must sort out our attitude to work.	= define, find out about
source	Quelle	Some have traced this entrepreneurial drive to religious sources.	= origin, root, motive
spare time	Freizeit, Mußestunden	A pure amateur earns his living during the day and trains in his spare time.	= free time, leisure (time)
(to) specify	einzeln angeben	Many of the specific effects of increasing automation are far from clear.	
specification	Angabe, Beschreibung		
specific [adj]	bestimmt, besonders		≠ general, overall

word family	dt. Bedeutung	English sentence	synonyms/opposites
spectacle **spectacular** [adj]	*Schauspiel, Anblick* *Aufsehen erregend, sensationell*	The introduction of this new procedure has been accompanied by spectacular increases in productivity.	= astonishing, striking
(to) spend	*(Geld) ausgeben*	Nowadays people have more money to spend than ever before.	≠ save
(to) spoil	*ruinieren*	High-rise buildings change the skyline of a town completely and spoil its character.	= damage, destroy
(to) squander	*vergeuden, verschwenden*	Resources are squandered without consideration of their renewal.	≠ conserve, save
(to) squeeze out	*herausdrücken, beseitigen*	Free trade forces both individual firms and entire economies to squeeze out less productive activities.	= force out, eliminate, remove
(to) starve **starvation**	*hungern* *Hunger*	Every day thousands die of starvation.	= famine, hunger
(to) state **statement**	*erklären, angeben* *Aussage, Erklärung, Äußerung*	The biggest question facing the 21st century can be stated in a few words.	= express, say, affirm, articulate, voice
stature	*Format, Kaliber, Größe*	The changing and diminishing stature of Britain in the world has been a most painful experience.	= importance, influence, position, role
steadily [adv]	*ständig, stetig*	Energy consumption in the industrialized countries is steadily increasing.	= constantly, permanently
(to) stem from	*herrühren, abstammen von*	The US electoral system stems from a period when communications were not fully developed.	= date from, originate from

word family	dt. Bedeutung	English sentence	synonyms/opposites
(to) stick to	festhalten an	The EU Commission sticks to its plans for a radical reform of agriculture.	= keep to, hold on to, not give up, continue, insist on
still	(immer) noch	"Scientists are still narrowly educated", he maintained.	≠ no longer, not any longer, not any more, not yet
stock exchange stocks and shares	Börse Wertpapiere	London is an important exchange for commodities from tropical countries.	= stock market = securities, bonds
(to) stop	aufhören	Authorities in Britain have stopped considering solar energy a commercial possibility for the production of electricity.	= give up, cease (to)
(to) strengthen strength strong [adj]	stärken, kräftigen Stärke stark	The members are anxious to strengthen the unity of their economies and to ensure their harmonious development.	≠ weaken
strike striking [adj]	Streik auffallend, eindrucksvoll	If the employers don't pay us more, there will be a strike soon.	= walkout, industrial action = astonishing, remarkable
(to) study student studious [adj]	studieren, erforschen Schüler, Student fleißig, lernbegierig	In order to succeed in his final exams, he was studious and well-behaved.	= hard-working
(to) submit	vorlegen, unterbreiten	Every time a plan for a new road is submitted to the local council, there is a public outcry and many objections are put forward.	= present, give

word family	dt. Bedeutung	English sentence	synonyms/opposites
(to) succeed (1)	Erfolg haben	The move was typical of the manager's success at blending capitalism and environmentalism.	≠ failure
success	Erfolg		
successful [adj]	erfolgreich		
(to) succeed (2)	nachfolgen		
succession	Nachfolge		
successor	Nachfolger	Margaret Thatcher's successor, John Major, agreed with the European political union.	≠ predecessor
successive [adj]	aufeinander folgend		
(to) suffer	leiden	The advantages of open trade apply to the economy generally: specific sectors can suffer greatly.	≠ profit, benefit, gain, capitalize
suitable [adj]	passend, geeignet	The members of the House of Commons searched for a suitable name for the bell in the clock-tower.	= appropriate, fitting, proper
superficial [adj]	oberflächlich	Even a superficial look at history reveals that no social advance rolls in automatically.	≠ thorough
superiority	Überlegenheit	Among Northern whites there was a sense of superiority in discussions of race.	≠ inferiority
(to) suppose	annehmen, vermuten	It is a mistake to suppose that we cannot reverse the damaging trend.	= assume, believe, reckon, suspect, think
supposition	Annahme, Voraussetzung		
supremacy	Vorherrschaft	California's agricultural supremacy dates from 1947, when its farms produced more than any other state.	= dominance
supreme [adj]	höchste(r, s)		
sureness	Sicherheit	The attitude which I feel sure is no longer valid is the arrogance of power.	= certain, convinced
surety	Bürge		
sure [adj]	sicher		≠ unsure, insecure, uncertain

word family	dt. Bedeutung	English sentence	synonyms/opposites
surplus	Überschuss	The Commission accepts that there may be temporary surpluses of some products, such as milk and cereals.	≠ shortage, lack of
surprising [adj]	überraschend	It is hardly surprising that the best universities recruit largely from the best schools.	= astonishing, amazing, astounding
(to) suspect suspicion suspect [adj] suspicious [adj]	vermuten, mutmaßen Verdacht verdächtig verdächtig	Some scientists suspect that mobile phone radiation may have a damaging biological effect on human brain cells.	= assume, believe, gather, be inclined to think
(to) sustain sustenance	aushalten; ernähren Lebensunterhalt	Can the Earth sustain the growing population?	= nourish, support
(to) tackle	fertig werden mit, (ein Problem) anpacken	How will the mayor tackle the problem of the homeless and poor?	= cope with, take on
temporary [adj] temporarily [adv]	zeitweilig, vorübergehend zeitweilig, vorübergehend	The public are warned that there may be temporary shortages of oil and petrol.	= for the time being, fleetingly, momentarily
(to) tempt temptation tempting [adj]	verleiten Versuchung verführerisch	From time to time, we have been tempted to believe that society has become too complex to be managed by self-rule.	= entice, seduce
(to) tend tendency	zu etw. neigen Richtung, Neigung	Managers tend to promote others with whom they feel at ease.	= be inclined, be disposed

word family	dt. Bedeutung	English sentence	synonyms/opposites
(to) terrify	jdn. erschrecken, jdm. Angst und Schrecken einjagen	In the 1960's the militant Black Power movement terrified the American nation.	≠ calm down, appease, pacify
(to) terrorize	terrorisieren		
terror	Terror		
terrorism	Terrorismus		
terrible [adj]	schrecklich		
(to) think	denken, glauben	People think of waste as whatever is useless.	= see, regard, consider
(to) think of	halten für		
thought	Gedanke		
thoughtful [adj]	nachdenklich		
(to) threaten	bedrohen	Another threat to the seas of the world is beginning to get more attention: algae bloom.	= menace, danger, hazard, peril, risk
threat	Bedrohung		
threatening [adj]	bedrohlich		
throughout	überall in	The Royal Family enjoys support throughout the world.	= all over, everywhere in
tide	Flut, Zustrom	In the 19th century a tide of immigration began bringing more than 40,000,000 persons into the USA.	= inflow, influx, stream, rush
(to) tighten	festziehen, anziehen	If immigration does not increase efficiency, tighter controls might be justified.	
tightness	Festigkeit		
tight [adj]	streng, dicht, straff		= strict, tough, close
(to) tolerate	dulden	The residents must learn to tolerate strange customs and additional competition.	≠ reject, disapprove of, object to
tolerance	Toleranz, Nachsicht		
toleration	Duldung		
tolerant [adj]	duldsam		

word family	dt. Bedeutung	English sentence	synonyms/opposites
(to) transform	umwandeln, verwandeln	We will be able to transform the jangling discords of our nation into a beautiful symphony of brotherhood.	= change, alter, convert
tremendous [adj]	ungeheuer, gewaltig, enorm	The hurricane was accompanied by tremendous tidal waves.	= enormous, huge, overwhelming, immense
trend	Richtung	We can observe a new trend in advertising today.	= tendency, strategy
trial	Gerichtsverfahren, Prozess	The defendant in a trial is the person who has been accused of a crime.	= law-suit
(to) trigger	etw. auslösen	The industrial revolution triggered a faster wave of change.	= cause, prompt, produce, bring about, start off
trouble	Unannehmlichkeit, Schererei, Ärger	The manager told him he had better stay unless he wanted to get into serious trouble.	= difficulty
turn-over	Umsatz	The company's turn-over has increased by 18 %.	= sales, sales volume
(to) tyrannize tyranny tyrant tyrannical [adj] tyrannous [adj]	tyrannisieren Tyrannei Tyrann tyrannisch tyrannisch	A tyrant is a cruel, unjust or oppressive ruler.	= despot, dictator
Ulster		Realities inside Ulster, in terms of Protestant-Catholic relations, did not change very much.	= Northern Ireland
ultimately [adv]	letztlich, schließlich	Those who are responsible for government in Ireland ultimately depend on Irish initiatives to solve Ireland's problems.	= finally, in the end, eventually, at last

word family	dt. Bedeutung	English sentence	synonyms/opposites
uncommon [adj]	selten	In an earlier era, highly toxic forms of waste were uncommon.	= unusual, rare
underfed [adj]	unterernährt	We must not become accustomed to our own prosperity and forget about the underfed millions in the Third World.	= undernourished
undocumented [adj]	illegal, ohne (Arbeits-, Einreise-)Papiere	Undocumented Mexicans hold one-third of Houston's commercial-construction jobs.	= non-registered, illegal
unemployed [adj]	arbeitslos	Coloured immigrants were often unemployed.	= jobless, out of work, without a job, without jobs
unhappy [adj]	unglücklich	Girl offenders are unhappy.	= sad, depressed
unjust [adj]	ungerecht	He thought it very unjust when authorities wanted to confiscate his property.	= unfair
(to) urge urgency urgent [adj]	dringen auf, (jdn.) drängen Dringlichkeit dringend	A growing number of voices urge us to accept unemployment.	= impel, drive, press
(to) use (to) be used to use usage useful [adj] usual [adj] usually [adv]	gebrauchen, benutzen gewohnt sein Gebrauch, Nutzen Verwendung nützlich gewöhnlich gewöhnlich, normalerweise	One of the principles that we had been used to is no longer valid. British Standards for consumer goods are usually easily discernible by a number or a mark stamped on them.	= accustomed to = generally, as a rule

word family	dt. Bedeutung	English sentence	synonyms/opposites
(to) vacate vacancy vacation vacant [adj]	räumen, aufgeben freie Stelle Ferien frei	In his letter the owner told the tenant to vacate the house.	= move out of, leave, quit
valour valiant [adj]	Tapferkeit tapfer	Iago admits the dependence of the Venetians on his valour.	= bravery, courage
(to) value value valuable [adj]	schätzen Wert wertvoll	Our aims are to contribute to the growth of the company in order to increase its value.	= quality, worth, stature
(to) vandalize	mutwillig zerstören, verwüsten	The trouble is that recreation facilities are often vandalized by those very hooligans for whom they are intended.	= destroy, damage, break
(to) vary variety various [adj]	sich verändern Vielfalt verschieden(artig)	The Prime Minister presented a variety of ideas to his Cabinet to solve the Irish problem.	= collection, lot, assortment
vast [adj] vastly [adv]	riesig wesentlich, erheblich	Every day, television consumes vast quantities of creative work. The reality is vastly different.	= huge, enormous, immense = considerably, greatly, rather; ≠ somewhat, slightly
vessel	Schiff	An aircraft carrier is an important vessel for any navy.	= ship, boat
(to) view	sehen, betrachten	Women view their return to work after maternity leave not as a right but as a choice.	= see, regard, consider
view	Meinung, Ansicht	I cannot support the view that man is killing nature.	= opinion

word family	dt. Bedeutung	English sentence	synonyms/opposites
violation	Verletzung, Nichtbeachtung	Amnesty has always fought against the violation of human rights.	≠ respect for, keeping to
violence violent [adj]	Gewalt gewalttätig	Many spectators draw pleasure from watching violence.	≠ non-violence
virtually [adv] VR = virtual reality	praktisch, eigentlich virtuelle Realität	The police found virtually no traces of the drug in his blood.	= practically, nearly, effectively, almost
vital [adj]	lebenswichtig	The friendship between our nations has grown over the years and has played a vital part in world affairs.	= important, essential, crucial
(to) voice	Ausdruck geben, äußern	Mass organisations like the trade unions voice the feelings and demand of their members.	= express, utter, verbalize
(to) volunteer volunteer voluntary [adj]	freiwillig dienen Freiwilliger freiwillig	Many observers call for voluntary restraint by the media in covering terrorist actions.	≠ compulsory, (en)forced
warehouse	Lagerhaus, Speicher	We shall store your goods at our Ealing warehouse.	= storehouse
warrior	Krieger	This book is about the noble king, his bravest warrior and the greatest battles.	= fighter, combatant
wealth wealthy [adj]	Reichtum wohlhabend, reich	An old and very wealthy friend of mine told me he had had an extremely unpleasant experience.	≠ poor
(to) welcome	willkommen heißen	The firm's mostly young, concerned workers welcomed the bicycles for environmental reasons.	≠ refuse, reject, object to, turn down
well [adv]	gut	A recent UN report describes well the stress of technological change on the educational system.	≠ badly, poorly, inadequately, inappropriately

word family	dt. Bedeutung	English sentence	synonyms/opposites
whole [adj]	ganz, vollständig	Whole communities developed in which crime was an accepted activity.	= complete, entire
(to) widen width wide [adj]	verbreitern Breite breit	Will the gulf between the haves and have-nots widen?	≠ decrease, narrow, become smaller, be bridged
willing [adj]	bereit, gewillt	Fanatics are willing to kill to impose their views.	= prepared, ready, inclined
wisdom wise [adj]	Weisheit weise, klug	The conventional wisdom is that the Internet, television and the telephone will blend.	= knowledge, insight ≠ unwise, foolish
(to) withdraw withdrawal	sich zurückziehen Rückzug, Zurücknahme	After losing the first battle, the soldiers had to withdraw.	= retreat
(to) wonder	sich fragen, sich wundern	Many Europeans wondered how a country that brought forth such senseless violence could ever have served as their ideal.	= ask oneself, be surprised to see
(to) work	arbeiten, schuften	Blacks were transported from Africa to work on the plantations in the South.	= labour, toil, slave
(to) work together	zusammenarbeiten	With this faith we will be able to work together.	= cooperate
(to) worsen worse [adj]	(sich) verschlimmern, verschlechtern schlimmer, schlechter	In Britain, industrial performance has been steadily worsening. The situation for underprivileged has become worse.	≠ improve, prosper, flourish, do well, thrive, better ≠ better
zeal zealous [adj]	Eifer eifrig bedacht	With almost missionary zeal, he criticised the decline of the inner cities.	= passion, enthusiasm ≠ apathy, indifference

Ihre Meinung ist uns wichtig!

Ihre Anregungen sind uns immer willkommen. Bitte informieren
Sie uns mit diesem Schein über Ihre Verbesserungsvorschläge!

Titel-Nr.	Seite	Vorschlag

Bitte hier abtrennen

Die echten Hilfen zum Lernen ... **STARK**

15-V1T

Bitte ausfüllen und im frankierten Umschlag an uns einsenden. Für Fensterkuverts geeignet.

STARK Verlag
Postfach 1852
85318 Freising

Zutreffendes bitte ankreuzen!

Die Absenderin/der Absender ist:
- Lehrer/in in den Klassenstufen:
- Fachbetreuer/in
- Fächer:
- Seminarlehrer/in
- Fächer:
- Regierungsfachberater/in
- Fächer:
- Oberstufenbetreuer/in
- Schulleiter/in
- Referendar/in, Termin 2. Staatsexamen:
- Leiter/in Lehrerbibliothek
- Leiter/in Schülerbibliothek
- Sekretariat
- Eltern
- Schüler/in, Klasse:
- Sonstiges:

Unterrichtsfächer: (Bei Lehrkräften!)

Kennen Sie Ihre Kundennummer?
Bitte hier eintragen.

Absender (Bitte in Druckbuchstaben!)

Name/Vorname

Straße/Nr.

PLZ/Ort

Telefon privat   Geburtsjahr

E-Mail-Adresse

Schule/Schulstempel (Bitte immer angeben!)

Bitte hier abtrennen

Sicher durch das Abitur!

Effektive Abitur-Vorbereitung für Schülerinnen und Schüler:
Klare Fakten, systematische Methoden, prägnante Beispiele sowie Übungs-
aufgaben auf Abiturniveau <u>mit erklärenden Lösungen zur Selbstkontrolle</u>.

Mathematik

Analysis Pflichtteil Baden-Württemberg	Best.-Nr. 84001
Analysis Wahlteil Baden-Württemberg	Best.-Nr. 84002
Analysis – LK	Best.-Nr. 94002
Analysis – gk	Best.-Nr. 94001
Analytische Geometrie Baden-Württemberg	Best.-Nr. 84003
Analytische Geometrie und lineare Algebra 1	Best.-Nr. 94005
Analytische Geometrie und lineare Algebra 2	Best.-Nr. 54008
Stochastik – LK	Best.-Nr. 94003
Stochastik – gk	Best.-Nr. 94007
Kompakt-Wissen Abitur Analysis	Best.-Nr. 900151
Kompakt-Wissen Abitur Analytische Geometrie	Best.-Nr. 900251
Kompakt-Wissen Abitur Wahrscheinlichkeitsrechnung und Statistik	Best.-Nr. 900351
Kompakt-Wissen Algebra	Best.-Nr. 90016
Kompakt-Wissen Geometrie	Best.-Nr. 90026

Physik

Elektrisches und magnetisches Feld (LK)	Best.-Nr. 94308
Elektromagnetische Schwingungen und Wellen (LK)	Best.-Nr. 94309
Atom- und Quantenphysik (LK)	Best.-Nr. 943010
Kernphysik (LK)	Best.-Nr. 94305
Physik 1 (gk)	Best.-Nr. 94321
Physik 2 (gk)	Best.-Nr. 94322
Kompakt-Wissen Abitur Physik 2 Elektrizität, Magnetismus und Wellenoptik	Best.-Nr. 943013
Kompakt-Wissen Abitur Physik 3 Quanten, Kerne und Atome	Best.-Nr. 943011

Chemie

Training Methoden Chemie	Best.-Nr. 947308
Chemie 1 – Baden-Württemberg	Best.-Nr. 84731
Chemie 2 – Baden-Württemberg	Best.-Nr. 84732
Chemie 1 – Bayern LK K 12	Best.-Nr. 94731
Chemie 2 – Bayern LK K 13	Best.-Nr. 94732
Chemie 1 – Bayern gk K 12	Best.-Nr. 94741
Chemie 2 – Bayern gk K 13	Best.-Nr. 94742
Rechnen in der Chemie	Best.-Nr. 84735
Abitur-Wissen Protonen und Elektronen	Best.-Nr. 947301
Abitur-Wissen Struktur der Materie und Kernchemie	Best.-Nr. 947303
Abitur-Wissen Stoffklassen organischer Verbindungen	Best.-Nr. 947304
Abitur-Wissen Biomoleküle	Best.-Nr. 947305
Abitur-Wissen Biokatalyse u. Stoffwechselwege	Best.-Nr. 947306
Abitur-Wissen Chemie am Menschen – Chemie im Menschen	Best.-Nr. 947307
Kompakt-Wissen Abitur Chemie Organische Stoffklassen · Natur-, Kunst- und Farbstoffe	Best.-Nr. 947309

Biologie

Training Methoden Biologie	Best.-Nr. 94710
Biologie 1 – Baden-Württemberg	Best.-Nr. 84701
Biologie 2 – Baden-Württemberg	Best.-Nr. 84702
Biologie 1 – Bayern LK K 12	Best.-Nr. 94701
Biologie 2 – Bayern LK K 13	Best.-Nr. 94702
Biologie 1 – Bayern gk K 12	Best.-Nr. 94715
Biologie 2 – Bayern gk K 13	Best.-Nr. 94716
Chemie für Biologen	Best.-Nr. 54705
Abitur-Wissen Genetik	Best.-Nr. 94703
Abitur-Wissen Neurobiologie	Best.-Nr. 94705
Abitur-Wissen Verhaltensbiologie	Best.-Nr. 94706
Abitur-Wissen Evolution	Best.-Nr. 94707
Abitur-Wissen Ökologie	Best.-Nr. 94708
Abitur-Wissen Zell- und Entwicklungsbiologie	Best.-Nr. 94709
Kompakt-Wissen Abitur Biologie Zellen und Stoffwechsel · Nerven, Sinne und Hormone · Ökologie	Best.-Nr. 94712
Kompakt-Wissen Abitur Biologie Genetik und Entwicklung · Immunbiologie · Evolution · Verhalten	Best.-Nr. 94713
Lexikon Biologie	Best.-Nr. 94711

Geschichte

Training Methoden Geschichte	Best.-Nr. 94789
Geschichte 1 – Baden-Württemberg	Best.-Nr. 84761
Geschichte 2 – Baden-Württemberg	Best.-Nr. 84762
Geschichte – Bayern gk K 12	Best.-Nr. 94781
Geschichte – Bayern gk K 13	Best.-Nr. 94782
Abitur-Wissen Die Antike	Best.-Nr. 94783
Abitur-Wissen Das Mittelalter	Best.-Nr. 94788
Abitur-Wissen Die Französische Revolution	Best.-Nr. 947810
Abitur-Wissen Die Ära Bismarck: Entstehung und Entwicklung des deutschen Nationalstaats	Best.-Nr. 94784
Abitur-Wissen Imperialismus und Erster Weltkrieg	Best.-Nr. 94785
Abitur-Wissen Die Weimarer Republik	Best.-Nr. 47815
Abitur-Wissen Nationalsozialismus und Zweiter Weltkrieg	Best.-Nr. 94786
Abitur-Wissen Deutschland von 1945 bis zur Gegenwart	Best.-Nr. 947811
Kompakt-Wissen Abitur Geschichte Oberstufe	Best.-Nr. 947601
Lexikon Geschichte	Best.-Nr. 94787

Politik

Abitur-Wissen Internationale Beziehungen	Best.-Nr. 94802
Abitur-Wissen Demokratie	Best.-Nr. 94803
Abitur-Wissen Sozialpolitik	Best.-Nr. 94804
Abitur-Wissen Die Europäische Einigung	Best.-Nr. 94805
Abitur-Wissen Politische Theorie	Best.-Nr. 94806
Kompakt-Wissen Abitur Politik/Sozialkunde	Best.-Nr. 948001
Lexikon Politik/Sozialkunde	Best.-Nr. 94801

(Bitte blättern Sie um)

Wirtschaft/Recht

Betriebswirtschaft	Best.-Nr. 94851
Abitur-Wissen Volkswirtschaft	Best.-Nr. 94881
Abitur-Wissen Rechtslehre	Best.-Nr. 94882
Kompakt-Wissen Abitur Volkswirtschaft	Best.-Nr. 948501

Erdkunde

Training Methoden Erdkunde	Best.-Nr. 94901
Erdkunde Relief- und Hydrosphäre · Wirtschaftsprozesse und -strukturen · Verstädterung	Best.-Nr. 84901
Abitur-Wissen GUS-Staaten/Russland	Best.-Nr. 94908
Abitur-Wissen Entwicklungsländer	Best.-Nr. 94902
Abitur-Wissen USA	Best.-Nr. 94903
Abitur-Wissen Europa	Best.-Nr. 94905
Abitur-Wissen Asiatisch-pazifischer Raum	Best.-Nr. 94906
Kompakt-Wissen Abitur Erdkunde	Best.-Nr. 949010
Lexikon Erdkunde	Best.-Nr. 94904

Deutsch

Training Methoden Deutsch	Best.-Nr. 944062
Analyse von Sachtexten und Erörterung	Best.-Nr. 944094
Abitur-Wissen Erörtern und Sachtexte analysieren	Best.-Nr. 944064
Abitur-Wissen Textinterpretation Lyrik, Drama, Epik	Best.-Nr. 944061
Abitur-Wissen Deutsche Literaturgeschichte	Best.-Nr. 94405
Abitur-Wissen Prüfungswissen Oberstufe	Best.-Nr. 94400
Kompakt-Wissen Rechtschreibung	Best.-Nr. 944065
Lexikon Autoren und Werke	Best.-Nr. 944081

Französisch

Landeskunde Frankreich	Best.-Nr. 94501
Themenwortschatz	Best.-Nr. 94503
Literatur	Best.-Nr. 94502
Abitur-Wissen Literaturgeschichte	Best.-Nr. 94506
Kompakt-Wissen Abitur Themenwortschatz	Best.-Nr. 945010

Englisch

Übersetzungsübung	Best.-Nr. 82454
Grammatikübung	Best.-Nr. 82452
Themenwortschatz	Best.-Nr. 82451
Grundlagen der Textarbeit	Best.-Nr. 94464
Textaufgaben Literarische Texte und Sachtexte	Best.-Nr. 94468
Grundfertigkeiten des Schreibens	Best.-Nr. 94466
Sprechfertigkeit mit CD	Best.-Nr. 94467
Englisch – Übertritt in die Oberstufe	Best.-Nr. 82453
Abitur-Wissen Landeskunde Großbritannien	Best.-Nr. 94461
Abitur-Wissen Landeskunde USA	Best.-Nr. 94463
Abitur-Wissen Literaturgeschichte	Best.-Nr. 94465
Kompakt-Wissen Abitur Themenwortschatz	Best.-Nr. 90462
Kompakt-Wissen Kurzgrammatik	Best.-Nr. 90461

Latein

Abitur-Wissen Lateinische Literaturgeschichte	Best.-Nr. 94602
Kurzgrammatik	Best.-Nr. 94601
Wortkunde	Best.-Nr. 94603
Kompakt-Wissen Kurzgrammatik	Best.-Nr. 906011

Religion

Katholische Religion 1 (gk)	Best.-Nr. 84991
Katholische Religion 2 – (gk)	Best.-Nr. 84992
Abitur-Wissen gk ev. Religion Der Mensch zwischen Gott und Welt	Best.-Nr. 94973
Abitur-Wissen gk ev. Religion Die Verantwortung des Christen in der Welt	Best.-Nr. 94974
Abitur-Wissen Glaube und Naturwissenschaft	Best.-Nr. 94977
Abitur-Wissen Jesus Christus	Best.-Nr. 94978
Abitur-Wissen Die Frage nach dem Menschen	Best.-Nr. 94990
Abitur-Wissen Die Bibel	Best.-Nr. 94992
Abitur-Wissen Christliche Ethik	Best.-Nr. 94993
Lexikon Ethik und Religion	Best.-Nr. 94959

Ethik

Ethische Positionen in historischer Entwicklung – gk	Best.-Nr. 94951
Abitur-Wissen Philosophische Ethik	Best.-Nr. 94952
Abitur-Wissen Glück und Sinnerfüllung	Best.-Nr. 94953
Abitur-Wissen Freiheit und Determination	Best.-Nr. 94954
Abitur-Wissen Recht und Gerechtigkeit	Best.-Nr. 94955
Abitur-Wissen Religion und Weltanschauungen	Best.-Nr. 94956
Abitur-Wissen Wissenschaft – Technik – Verantwortung	Best.-Nr. 94957
Abitur-Wissen Politische Ethik	Best.-Nr. 94958
Lexikon Ethik und Religion	Best.-Nr. 94959

Sport

Bewegungslehre (LK)	Best.-Nr. 94981
Trainingslehre (LK)	Best.-Nr. 94982

Kunst

Kunst 1 Grundwissen Malerei (LK)	Best.-Nr. 94961
Kunst 2 Analyse und Interpretation (LK)	Best.-Nr. 94962

Fachübergreifend

Richtig Lernen Tipps und Lernstrategien – Oberstufe	Best.-Nr. 10483
Referate und Facharbeiten – Oberstufe	Best.-Nr. 10484
Training Methoden Meinungen äußern, Ergebnisse präsentieren	Best.-Nr. 10486

Bestellungen bitte direkt an: STARK Verlagsgesellschaft mbH & Co. KG
Postfach 1852 · 85318 Freising · Tel: 08161 / 179-0 · FAX: 08161 / 179-51
Internet: www.stark-verlag.de · E-Mail: info@stark-verlag.de